China's New Role in Africa and the South

A search for a new perspective

Fahamu Books

Dorothy-Grace Guerrero and Firoze Manji (eds) (2008) *China's New Role in Africa and the South: A Search for a New Perspective*. Nairobi, Oxford and Bangkok: Fahamu and Focus on the Global South. ISBN: 978-1-906387-26-6

Hakima Abbas (ed) (2007) *Africa's Long Road to Rights: Reflections on the 20th Anniversary of the African Commission on Human and Peoples' Rights / Long trajet de l'Afrique vers les droits: réflexions lors du 20ème anniversaire de la Commission Africaine des Droits de l'Homme et des Peuples*. Nairobi and Oxford: Fahamu. ISBN: 978-1-906387-25-9

Patrick Burnett and Firoze Manji (eds) (2007) *From the Slave Trade to 'Free' Trade: How Trade Undermines Democracy and Justice in Africa*. Oxford: Fahamu. ISBN: 978-0-9545637-1-4

Issa Shivji (2007) *Silences in NGO Discourse: The Role and Future of NGOs in Africa*. Oxford: Fahamu. ISBN: 978-0-9545637-5-2

Firoze Manji and Stephen Marks (eds) (2007) *African Perspectives on China in Africa*. Nairobi and Oxford: Fahamu. ISBN: 978-0-9545637-3-8

Patrick Burnett, Shereen Karmali and Firoze Manji (eds) (2007) *Grace, Tenacity and Eloquence: The Struggle for Women's Rights in Africa*. Nairobi and Oxford: Fahamu and Solidarity for African Women's Rights coalition (SOAWR). ISBN: 978-0-9545637-2-1

Roselynn Musa, Faiza Jama Mohammed and Firoze Manji (eds) (2006) *Breathing Life into the African Union Protocol on Women's Rights in Africa*. Oxford, Nairobi and Addis Ababa: Fahamu, SOAWR and the African Union Commission Directorate of Women, Gender and Development. ISBN: 978-1-9-4855-66-8

Roselynn Musa, Faiza Jama Mohammed and Firoze Manji (eds) (2006) *Vulgarisation du protocole de l'union africaine sur les droits des femmes en Afrique*. Oxford, Nairobi and Addis Ababa: Fahamu, SOAWR and the African Union Commission Directorate of Women, Gender and Development. ISBN: 978-1-904855-68-2

Firoze Manji and Patrick Burnett (eds) (2005) *African Voices on Development and Social Justice: Editorials from Pambazuka News 2004*. Dar es Salaam: Mkuki na Nyota Publishers. ISBN: 978-9-987417-35-3

China's New Role in Africa and the South

A search for a new perspective

EDITED BY DOROTHY-GRACE GUERRERO AND FIROZE MANJI

PAMBAZUKA

FOCUS on the Global South

CHINA BRIEF

中国发展简报

Published 2008 by Fahamu – Networks for Social Justice
Cape Town, Nairobi and Oxford
www.fahamu.org   www.pambazuka.org

and

Focus on the Global South
Bangkok
www.focusweb.org

Fahamu, 2nd floor, 51 Cornmarket Street, Oxford OX1 3HA, UK

Fahamu Kenya, PO Box 47158, 00100 GPO, Nairobi, Kenya

Focus on the Global South, Wisit Prachuabmoh Building, Social Research Institute,
Chulalongkorn University, Phyathai Road, 10330 Bangkok, Thailand

British Library Cataloguing in Publication Data

A catalogue record for this book is available from the British Library

ISBN: 978-1-906387-26-6

Cover illustration and design: Judith Charlton, Fahamu

Project manager: Shereen Karmali

Manufactured on demand by Lightning Source

CONTENTS

ACKNOWLEDGEMENTS

The publishers are grateful for the support provided by China Development Brief, Christian Aid, Euro Burma, Misereor, Oxfam Hong Kong's China Unit, OxfamNovib, Open Society Initiative and the Transnational Institute, both for the conference at which these papers were first presented and for the publication of this book.

The articles by Yu Xiaogang and Ding Pin, Xu Weizhong and Fu Tao were translated from Chinese by Lewis Husain.

ABOUT THE CONTRIBUTORS

Ali Askouri is the director of the London-based Piankhi Research Group working in the field of development and human rights.

Alexandre de Freitas Barbosa is a consultant at Instituto Observatório Social. He holds a PhD in applied economics from Universidade de Campinas (UNICAMP) and a masters in economic history from Universidade de São Paulo (USP).

Walden Bello is executive director of Focus on the Global South.

Peter Bosshard is the policy director of International Rivers, an environmental and human rights organisation based in Berkeley, USA. He coordinates a programme to monitor China's role in global dam building and to strengthen the environmental policies of Chinese financiers.

Lucy Corkin is projects director at the Centre for Chinese Studies (CCS) at Stellenbosch University and lectures on China's political economy. Lucy coordinated and formed part of the CCS research team that investigated China's investment in the infrastructure and construction sectors in Africa, a research undertaking completed in November 2006 for DFID-China as well as a Rockefeller Foundation-sponsored scoping study of China–Africa relations.

Ding Pin is a journalist with *China Environment News*.

Fu Tao is the editor and researcher of *China Development Brief* (Chinese version).

Dorothy-Grace Guerrero is a senior research associate with Focus on the Global South and heads its China programme.

Shalmali Guttal is a senior research associate with Focus on the Global

South. Over the past 15 years, she has worked in India, the United States, the Lao PDR, Thailand, Cambodia and other countries in Southeast Asia. At Focus, she does research, advocacy and campaign work on globalisation, privatisation, trade, natural resources, and alternatives. She is the coordinator of the Reclaiming and Defending the Commons programme at Focus.

Dot Keet is originally from Zimbabwe and has worked as a researcher and lecturer in African political economy. She is currently a research associate of the Alternative Information and Development Centre (AIDC) in Cape Town, South Africa and is also a Transnational Institute fellow on the Africa and Alternative Regionalisms programme.

Khin Zaw Win has been a human rights activist and development practitioner. He is now advocating for much-needed economic reform in Myanmar as part of the larger effort of facilitating the country's multiple and difficult transitions.

Luk Tak Chuen is currently head of the Research and Development Centre of the China Unit, Oxfam Hong Kong.

Firoze Manji is founder and executive director of Fahamu and co-editor of Pambazuka News.

Barry Sautman is a political scientist and lawyer in the Division of Social Science, Hong Kong University of Science and Technology whose research concerns nationalism and ethnic politics in China, as well as China–Africa relations. His most recent monograph, co-authored with Yan Hairong, is *East Mountain Tiger, West Mountain Tiger: China, the West, and 'Colonialism' in Africa* (Baltimore: University of Maryland Series on Contemporary Asian Studies, 2007).

Xu Weizhong has worked in African studies for more than 20 years and is currently director of the Department of African Studies in the Institute of Asian and African Studies, China Institute of Contemporary International Relations. His major publications include *Developing World: Active Response to Economic Globalization* and *African Ethnic Problems, Research on National Problems in the World.*

Yan Hairong teaches in the Department of Applied Social Sciences, Hong Kong Polytechnic University. Her research interests include rural-to-urban labour migration in China, domestic service, gender, and development, as well as China–Africa links. Her book, *Belaboring Development: Migration, Subjectivity and Domestic Service in Post-Mao China*, will be published by Duke University Press.

Yu Xiaogang is founding director of the Greenwatershed Project in Yunnan Province. He is also the winner of the 2006 Goldman Environmental Prize for Asia, which honours grassroots environmental heroes.

Yuza Maw Htoon did a masters in international public policy at the School of Advanced International Studies, Johns Hopkins University, and is now an executive of the Mingalar Foundation based in Yangon. She is currently working on coastal conservation and related advocacy and education issues.

INTRODUCTION: CHINA'S NEW ROLE IN AFRICA AND THE SOUTH

DOROTHY-GRACE GUERRERO AND FIROZE MANJI

What I find a bit reprehensible is the tendency of certain Western voices to … rais[e] concerns about China's attempt to get into the African market because it is a bit hypocritical for Western states to be concerned about how China is approaching Africa when they have had centuries of relations with Africa, starting with slavery and continuing to the present day with exploitation and cheating.[1]

Open any newspaper and you would get the impression that the African continent, and much of the rest of the world, is in the process of being 'devoured' by China. Phrases such as the 'new scramble for Africa', 'voracious', 'ravenous' or 'insatiable appetite for natural resources' are typical descriptors used to characterise China's engagement with Africa. In contrast, the operations of Western capital with the same ends are described with anodyne phrases such as 'development', 'investment', 'employment generation'.[2] Is China indeed the voracious tiger it is so often portrayed as?

China's involvement in Africa has three main dimensions: foreign direct investment, aid and trade. In each of these dimensions China's engagement is dwarfed by those of US and European countries, and is often smaller than those of other Asian economies.

Foreign direct investment (FDI) by Asian economies across the world has been growing. The total flow of FDI from Asia to Africa is estimated to have averaged $1.2 billion a year during 2002–04.[3] Chinese FDI in Africa, however, has been small in comparison to investment from Singapore, India and Malaysia. These countries are the principal Asian sources of FDI in Africa, according to UNDP,[4] and had investment stocks of $3.5 billion, $1.9 billion

1

and $1.9 billion respectively by 2004. Such investments are greater than those of China. The same report goes on to say, however, that Asian investments in Africa are dwarfed by those of the United Kingdom (with a total FDI stock of $30 billion in 2003), the United States ($19 billion in 2003), France ($11.5 billion in 2003) and Germany ($5.5 billion in 2003). And if China sits in fourth place amongst the Asian 'tigers', the scale of its investments in Africa are miniscule in comparison to the more traditional imperial powers.

Asian FDI flows to Africa have certainly grown tenfold since the 1980s, but at a lesser rate than the 14-fold growth in FDIs globally in the same period. Compared with India, for example, China's FDI is small. India has a larger investment in oil in Sudan and Nigeria than does China. Of 126 greenfield FDI projects in Africa, Indian companies accounted for the largest number. Indeed, amongst the Asian economies, Malaysian companies dominate in the mineral extraction sector in Africa. Africa's share of total outward flow of Chinese FDI is marginal – only 3 per cent goes to Africa, while Asia receives 53 per cent and Latin America 37 per cent. It should also be borne in mind that China is a net recipient of FDI, and receives a flow of FDI from Africa: SAB Miller breweries and SASOL from South Africa, Chandaria Holdings of Kenya, among many others.

Africa is certainly an important trade partner for China, the volume increasing from $11 billion in 2000 to some $40 billion in 2005. China has a growing trade surplus with Africa. According to UNDP,[5] China has become Africa's third largest trading partner, after the United States and France. China has focused primarily on the import of a limited number of products – oil and 'hard commodities' from a few selected African countries. China's trade with Africa represents only a small proportion of Africa's trade with the rest of the world, and is comparable to India's trade with Africa, although both have been growing rapidly. China imports from Africa five main commodities: oil, iron ore, cotton, diamonds and logs. The export of these commodities, and in particular oil, has grown significantly in the last ten years. A few African countries (Sudan, Ghana, Tanzania, Nigeria, Ethiopia, Uganda and Kenya) source a significant share of their imports of manufactured products, mainly clothing and textiles, from China.[6] China has been vigorously castigated for its support of repressive regimes but, in almost all cases, China's involvement has been in support of its need for strategic natural resources, especially oil. And it is perhaps here that one finds the reason for the fears expressed in the West about China's role in Africa. USA is the world's largest consumer of oil products, with

25 per cent of its requirements destined to come from Africa. While China sources some 40 per cent of its oil from the Middle East, it currently sources 23 per cent from Africa.

Much attention has been drawn to the negative impact of the cheap Chinese commodities on African economies. Certainly this has contributed to the decline of industrial production and the growing retrenchment of workers. But China has essentially taken advantage of the 'opening up' of Africa's market that has resulted from the neoliberal economic policies that the international financial institutions, backed by the majority of the international aid agencies, have forced Africa's governments to adopt. Given that the relative size of Chinese imports is small in comparison to imports from industrialised countries, the blame for the decline in industrial production and growing unemployment in Africa can hardly be placed entirely at China's door.

Just like Western powers, China has used aid strategically to support its commercial and investment interventions in Africa. Aid has taken the form of financial investments in key infrastructural development projects, training programmes, debt relief, technical assistance and a programme of tariff exemptions for selected products from Africa, not dissimilar to the agreements that Africa has had with Europe, US and other Western economies.

The evidence available suggests that the needs of China's rapidly developing capitalism are similar to those of its Western counterparts. It is the scale of its intervention in Africa that remains as yet small in comparison to those of Europe and US. The advantage that China has over Western capital is that it has no history of enslavement, colonisation, financing or support for coups against unfriendly regimes, or the presence of military forces in support of its foreign policies. As has been commented, 'Perhaps the material distinction is not between Chinese capital and Western, but rather between the merely rapacious, and the more sophisticated. Each of these are not two separate categories, but at least as much two different faces, each of which may be presented as convenient.'[7]

This book arises from a conference held at the margins of the African Development Bank meeting in Shanghai, China in May 2007. The conference was an initiative by several organisations to nurture the development of dialogue between civil society and academic institutions from within and beyond China. The resulting book reflects the general concerns for a fuller and more nuanced understanding of China's geopolitical positioning in Africa and within the South. Such understanding also touches on the increasing competition between China and other industrialised countries. The papers in this volume identify possible arenas and strategies for intervention and influence from which to build future cooperative and solidarity endeavours between Chinese civil society and international groups. The authors came from specialist academic institutions and NGOs that are focused on themes around development, the environment, social justice, the operations of international financial institutions and their impacts on local communities.

In the first chapter **Walden Bello** argues that global overcapacity has significantly dampened global economic growth, but China and the United States appear to be bucking the trend. Whether this growth is a reflection of economic health or an indicator of a crisis in which the two countries are bound together, with China's growth dependent on American consumers and America's high consumption rate relying on loans from Beijing, remains to be seen.

Luk Tak Chuen argues that China's strategy for natural resources in not unique to China, but should be viewed as part of neoliberal gobalisation, which has shaped capitalist countries' exploitative relations towards Africa. Within the World Bank and the Asian Development Bank, critical institutions for globalisation, China has positioned itself as both client and competitor. **Shalmali Guttal** looks at how China has strategically used its membership of these two international financial institutions to skilfully develop its own physical, social and financial infrastructure, institutions and services with the money it borrows from them while using its massive trade surplus and foreign exchange reserves to compete with them in securing influence in the economies of less developed countries. **Yu Xiaogang** and **Ding Pin** discuss how the Equator Principles have been used to try and ensure that financial assistance from Chinese banks goes to projects in China that minimise damage to the environment. They point out the crucial yet still developing role of Chinese NGOs in helping this happen. China's relationship with Africa has changed over the last 50 years from the period when China was viewed as a supporter of Africa's independence movement. **Xu Weizhong** considers the challenges to implementing the shift to its current role, and argues that careful management of that changing relationship will be crucial for a continued healthy development of Sino-African relationships. But how will China's economic operations differ from those of the imperialist West? Looking past the formal declarations and South–South rhetoric, **Dot Keet** suggests that the overriding question is whether the rapidly growing role of China in Africa is one of partnership and cooperation, or more akin to colonial or neocolonial patterns, or reflective of a new imperialism.

China's expanded links to Africa have clearly created a discourse of how to characterise those ties. Western political forces and media have criticised every aspect of China's activities in Africa, while the Chinese, with significant support from Africans, have mounted a spirited defence. **Barry Sautman** and **Yan Hairong** look at the Chinese model, the Beijing consensus and aid and migration, and argue that China might be less of a threat than the West. **Lucy Corkin** looks at how Chinese multinationals have begun to claim their share of the African market in a number of sectors. Africa could benefit from the operations of these companies provided that there are robust institutional regulatory frameworks and the capacity to monitor and direct investment. **Ali Askouri** is more sceptical about the benefits of Chinese engagement in Africa, arguing that this has led to forced displacement of populations, social tension and conflict.

The entry of the Chinese construction industries into Angola, albeit controversial, has marked a period of rapid infrastructural regeneration, argues **Lucy Corkin** in an extensive review of China's economic ventures. The case study emphasises her concern about the challenges posed by a lack of institutional frameworks and the government's capacity to monitor and encourage direct investment in terms of local skills development and technology transfer.

Looking beyond Africa, **Dorothy-Grace Guerrero** examines China's increasing economic power and political influence in Asia. It is now an important economic partner of all ASEAN member countries and the free trade agreements that it is negotiating will further strengthen that position. It implies too that China's increasing significance in the security sphere is challenging the traditional leadership of both the United States and Japan in the region. As to be expected with neighbours, relations between China and Myanmar have had their ups and downs. What marks the present age, say **Yuza Maw Htoon** and **Khin Zaw Win**, is that economic and population growth, the return of peace to Myanmar's border areas, its difficult political transition and globalisation itself have all intensified relations between the two countries to a degree not seen before. Whether this results in good or ill depends on the governments and citizens of both countries. **Alexandre de Freitas Barbosa** discusses the main features of the economic and geopolitical relations that have grown up in recent times between China and the countries of Latin America, examining the macroeconomic impact, effect on the domestic industries and impact on foreign investment. As for many African countries, many of the negative consequences of China's engagement in Latin America may be aggravated by the lack of clarity over industrial policy and governments' capacity to have a coherent vision of what is expected of China.

Fu Tao argues that the circumstances of civil society in China today are very different from what they were ten years ago. The similar interests of African and Chinese civil society in ensuring the equitable distribution of the benefits and opportunities arising from economic development are a strong foundation for future cooperation.

China's growing cooperation with Africa, Asia and Latin America has boosted infrastructure investment and economic growth in many developing countries. However, as within China itself, the concerns of economic growth, social equity and environmental protection all need to be integrated within this cooperation. **Peter Bosshard** argues that civil society groups can play a critical role in promoting a balanced development approach.

Notes

1 Kwesi Kwaa Prah (2007) 'Africa and China: Then and Now', in F. Manji and Stephen Marks (eds) *African Perspectives on China in Africa*. Oxford/Nairobi: Fahamu, pp. 57–61.

2 E. Mawdsely (2008) 'Fu Manchu versus Dr Livingstone in the Dark Continent? How British broadsheet newspapers represent China, Africa and the West', *Pambazuka News* <http://www.pambazuka.org/en/category/comment/45593>.

3 UNCTAD (2006) *World Investment Report 2006: FDI from Developing and Transition Economies: Implications for Development*. New York/Geneva: United Nations, sales no. E.06.II.D.11.

4 UNDP (2007) *Asian Foreign Investment In Africa: Towards a New Era of Cooperation Among Developing Countries*. New York/Geneva: United Nations Publications, UNCTAD/ITE/IIA/2007/1.

5 UNDP (2007).

6 R. Kaplinsky, D. McCormick and M. Morris (2007) *The Impact of China on Sub-Saharan Africa*, IDS Working Paper, no. 291.

7 S. Marks (2006) 'The summit in Beijing', *Pambazuka News*, no. 282, 14 December <http://www.pambazuka.org/en/category/features/38845>.

CHAIN-GANG ECONOMICS: CHINA, THE US, AND THE GLOBAL ECONOMY

WALDEN BELLO

Global overcapacity has significantly dampened global economic growth, but China and the United States appear to be bucking the trend. But is this growth an accurate sign of economic health or is it an indicator of a crisis in which the two countries are bound together, with China's growth dependent on American consumers and America's high consumption rate relying on loans from Beijing?

'The world [is] investing too little,' according to one prominent economist. 'The current situation has its roots in a series of crises over the last decade that were caused by excessive investment, such as the Japanese asset bubble, the crises in Emerging Asia and Latin America, and most recently, the IT bubble. Investment has fallen off sharply since, with only very cautious recovery.'

These are not the words of a Marxist economist describing the crisis of overproduction but those of Raghuram Rajan, the new chief economist of the International Monetary Fund (IMF). His analysis, though a year old, continues to be on the mark.[1]

Overproduction: the key trend in the global economy

Overcapacity has been the key link between the global economy in the Clinton era and the Bush period. The crisis has been particularly severe in the so-called core industries. At the beginning of the 21st century, the US computer industry's computer capacity was rising at 40 per cent annually, far above projected increases in demand. The world auto industry was selling just 74 per cent of the 70.1 million cars it sold each year, creating a profitability crunch for the weakest players, like former giant General Motors, which lost $10.6 billion in 2005, and Ford, which lost $7.24 billion in the first nine months of 2006. In steel, global excess capacity neared 20 per cent. It was estimated, in volume terms, to be an astounding 200 million tons, so that plans by steel producing countries to reduce capacity by 100 million tons by 2005 would still leave 'a sizeable amount of capacity which...would not be viable'. In telecommunications, according to Robert Brenner, overcapitalisation has resulted in a 'mountainous glut: the utilization rate of telecom networks

---

The centrality of the United States to both global growth and global crisis is well known. What is new is China's critical role

---

hovers today at a disastrously low 2.5–3 per cent, that of undersea cable at just 13 per cent.' As former General Electric Chairman Jack Welch put it, there has been 'excess capacity in almost every industry.'

Global overcapacity has made further investment simply unprofitable, which significantly dampens global economic growth. In Europe, for instance, GDP growth has averaged only 1.45 per cent in the last few years. And if countries are not investing in their economic futures, then growth will continue to stagnate and possibly lead to a global recession.

China and the United States, however, appear to be bucking the trend, though GDP growth in the US has flattened very recently. But rather than signs of health, growth in these two economies – and their evermore symbiotic relationship with each other – may actually be an indicator of crisis. The centrality of the United States to both global growth and global crisis is well known. What is new is China's critical role. Once regarded as the greatest achievement of this era of globalisation, China's integration into the global economy is, according to an excellent analysis by political economist Ho-Fung Hung, emerging as a central cause of global capitalism's crisis of overproduction.[2]

China and the crisis of overproduction

China's 8–10 per cent annual growth rate has probably been the principal stimulus of growth in the world economy in the last decade. Chinese imports, for instance, helped to end Japan's decade-long stagnation in 2003. To satisfy China's thirst for capital and technology-intensive goods, Japanese exports shot up by a record 44 per cent, or $60 billion. Indeed, China became the main destination for Asia's exports, accounting for 31 per cent while Japan's share dropped from 20 to 10 per cent. As Singapore's *The Straits Times* pointed out, 'In country-by-country profiles, China is now the overwhelming driver of export growth in Taiwan and the Philippines, and the majority buyer of products from Japan, South Korea, Malaysia, and Australia.'

At the same time, China became a central contributor to the crisis of global overcapacity. Even as investment declined sharply in many economies in response to the surfeit of productive capacity, particularly in Japan and other East Asian economies, it increased at a breakneck pace in China. Investment in China was not just the obverse of disinvestment elsewhere, although the shutting down of facilities and sloughing off of labour was significant not only in Japan and the United States but in the countries on China's periphery like the Philippines, Thailand, and Malaysia. China was significantly beefing up its industrial capacity and not simply absorbing capacity eliminated elsewhere. At the same time, the ability of the Chinese market to absorb its own industrial output was limited.

Agents of overinvestment

A major actor in overinvestment was transnational capital. In the late 1980s and 1990s, transnational corporations (TNCs) saw China as the last frontier, the unlimited market that could endlessly absorb investment and endlessly throw off profitable returns. However, China's restrictive rules on trade and investment forced TNCs to locate most of their production processes in the country instead of outsourcing only a selected number of them. Analysts termed such TNC production activities 'excessive internalisation'. By playing according to China's rules, TNCs ended up overinvesting in the country and building up a manufacturing base that produced more than China or even the rest of the world could consume.

By the turn of the millennium, the dream of exploiting a limitless market had vanished. Foreign companies headed for China not so much to sell to millions of newly prosperous Chinese customers but rather to make China a manufacturing base for global markets and take advantage of its inexhaustible supply of cheap labour. Typical of companies that found themselves in this quandary was Philips, the Dutch electronics manufacturer. Philips operates 23 factories in China and produces about $5 billion worth of goods, but two-thirds of their production is exported to other countries.

The other set of actors promoting overcapacity were local governments, which invested in and built up key industries. While these efforts are often

China's 8–10 per cent annual growth rate has probably been the principal stimulus of growth in the world economy in the last decade

'well planned and executed at the local level,' notes Ho-Fung Hung, 'the totality of these efforts combined ... entail anarchic competition among localities, resulting in uncoordinated construction of redundant production capacity and infrastructure.'

As a result, idle capacity in such key sectors as steel, cars, cement, aluminium and real estate has been soaring since the mid-1990s, with estimates that over 75 per cent of China's industries are currently plagued by overcapacity and that fixed asset investments in industries already experiencing overinvestment account for 40–50 per cent of China's GDP growth in 2005. China's State Development and Reform Commission projects that the motor vehicle industry will produce double what the market can absorb by 2010. The impact on profitability is not to be underestimated if we are to believe government statistics: at the end of 2005, Hung points out, the average annual profit growth rate of all major enterprises had plunged by half and the total deficit of losing enterprises had increased sharply by 57.6 per cent.

The low-wage strategy

The Chinese government can mitigate excess capacity by expanding people's purchasing power via a policy of income and asset redistribution. Doing so would probably mean slower growth but more domestic and global stability. This is what China's so-called 'New Left' intellectuals and policy analysts have been advising. China's authorities, however, have apparently chosen to continue the old strategy of dominating world markets by exploiting the country's cheap labour. Although China's population is 1.3 billion, 700 million people – or over half – live in the countryside and earn an average of just $285 a year, according to some estimates. This reserve army of rural poor has enabled manufacturers, both foreign and local, to keep wages down.

Aside from the potentially destabilising political effects of regressive income distribution, the low-wage strategy, as Hung points out, 'impedes the growth of consumption relative to the phenomenal economic expansion and great leap of investment'. In other words, the global crisis of overproduction will worsen as China continues to dump its industrial production on global markets constrained by slow growth.

Chain-gang economics

Chinese production and American consumption are like prisoners who seek to break free from one another but cannot because they are chained together. This relationship is progressively taking the form of a vicious cycle. On the one hand, China's breakneck growth has increasingly depended on the ability of American consumers to continue their consumption of much of the output of China's production brought about by excessive investment. On the other hand, America's high consumption rate depends on Beijing's lending the US private and public sectors a significant portion of the trillion-plus dollars it has accumulated from its yawning trade surplus with Washington.

This chain-gang relationship, says the IMF's Rajan, is 'unsustainable'. Both the United States and the IMF have decried what they call 'global macroeconomic imbalances' and called on China to revalue the renminbi to reduce its trade surplus with the United States. Yet China cannot really abandon its cheap currency policy. Along with cheap labour, cheap currency is part of China's successful formula of export-oriented production. And the United States really cannot afford to be too tough on China since it depends on that open line of credit to Beijing to continue feeding the middle-class spending that sustains its own economic growth.

The IMF ascribes this state of affairs to 'macroeconomic imbalances'. But it is really a crisis of overproduction. Thanks to Chinese factories and American consumers, the crisis is likely to get worse.

Notes

1 Raghuram Rajan (2005) *Global Imbalances: An Assessment*, International Monetary Fund, Washington DC, October <http://www.imf.org/external/np/speeches/2005/102505>.
2 Ho-Fung Hung (2005) 'The rise of China and the global overaccumulation crisis', paper presented at the Global Division of the Annual Meeting of the Society for the Study of Social Problems, 10–12 August, Montreal, Canada.

REGULATING CHINA?
REGULATING GLOBALISATION?

LUK TAK CHUEN

Looking at African perspectives on China's role in Africa, the author argues that China's aggressive resource extraction strategy has to be seen not as a strategy specific to China but as part of the neoliberal globalisation system that is shaping many countries' exploitative relations towards Africa.

This roundtable discussion is a good opportunity for the NGOs and academics of China and Africa to come together and exchange views and contribute to the hot debate on China's rise and its impact on the development of Africa. It is particularly appropriate given the high profile engagement of the top Chinese leadership in the Forum of China–Africa Cooperation (*zhongfei luntan*) in Beijing in 2006, and the subsequent sponsorship of the annual meeting of the African Development Bank in Shanghai recently. My article will not respond to the dominant North-centric discourses in the global media and policy community, where the North primarily regards China as being from the South and a key rival for the North's economic and political hegemony in Africa. I want to primarily engage with the variety of African perspectives on the challenges raised by China's road in Africa.

Many African perspectives primarily concern themselves with the economic and political consequences of China's strategies to secure a supply of energy and raw material, develop markets, and create economic partnerships and political alliances with individual African countries. In particular, an emerging debate focuses on the China factor in shaping the economic and political development of post-colonial African states, particularly on the development of the Africa Union as a regional body regulating the development of the Africa continent.

Many of the debates, however, fail to address China in the context of a changing global political economy. Without contextualising China in the neoliberal global order, it is too easy to single out the country without addressing the structural and institutional forces that are driving not only China, but also other more recently emerging powers, to look with covetous eyes at Africa's natural resources and markets. We therefore have to identify the forces driving the Chinese government and transnational enterprises to

Some still regard China as a Stalinist planned economy in which the Africa strategy is well planned and coordinated by the political will and machinery of the Chinese government

pursue their aggressive resource extraction strategy. We have to consider whether this strategy is specific to China or whether it is developmentalism and the neoliberal globalisation system that are actually shaping exploitative relations towards Africa. It is not only China that is eyeing the natural resources of the Africa continent; it is also other emerging powers in the South and even within Africa. If the problem is more about the institutional and structural forces of globalisation that are being inflicted on the ecology and people in the Africa continent, the issue should be about regulating globalisation rather than China.

Moreover, many African perspectives share a common bias: they regard China as a homogeneous entity. Indeed, some still regard China as a Stalinist planned economy in which the Africa strategy is well planned and coordinated by the political will and machinery of the Chinese government. However, after two decades of reform in China, of decentralisation and privatisation, Chinese strategies and presence in Africa are more of a mix of government initiatives and the endeavours of private enterprises and individuals. The ability of the Chinese government to regulate its enterprises and citizens abroad is limited, especially in this era of neoliberal globalisation. Therefore, it is important to appreciate that China is a heterogeneous grouping of various collective actors, i.e. the government, state enterprises, private enterprises and the public in general, and that the interests among the various actors within each sector might well differ. For example, the foreign ministry may be keen to develop better political alliances with African states, while the ministry of commerce is trying its best to secure raw materials and develop markets in Africa. These issues are crucial for African academics and activists to consider in their analysis of the Chinese government and Chinese transnational corporations.

The fate of governance reform is another hot spot for African academics and activists assessing the impact of China's bilateral diplomacy and non-conditional aid. There is a strong tendency for the African perspectives to converge around the expectation that China should conform to the governance reform pursued by the bilateral or multilateral aid offered by Northern donors, or the various corporate-led ethical initiatives. These discussions, however, failed to address the controversies embedded in various governance reform projects and, therefore, the complicated dynamics which the China factor would introduce. Some governance reform projects are dominated by Northern interests which are strongly tied to the neoliberal agenda. Some suspect that the self-regulatory practices of the private sector are greenwashing[1] and cosmetic. The fragmentation of the Africa continent makes regional governance weak and vulnerable; it is a fact and reality that we have to deal with. As a result, the simple debate over requiring China to conform to these governance

Some governance reform projects are dominated by Northern interests which are strongly tied to the neoliberal agenda

reform initiatives could easily slip into co-opting China into the bigger game of 'humanising neoliberal globalisation in Africa' instead of making use of the positive dynamics of the China factor to address the issues of a genuine governance reform that would be favourable to Africa communities.

Many African perspectives still hinge on the broken hopes of state-building projects in post-colonial Africa. Most of them, therefore, primarily address the challenges China poses to the national economic and political development of African states. It is understandable that many African activists and academics still see the nation state as their guardian after years of colonialism, internal conflicts and governance failures. Making the national interest supreme, however, overshadows the voices and interests of the local communities who bear the impact of China's road in Africa. The voices and perspectives of grassroots communities should be developed and strengthened to address the impacts of China – one of the agents of globalisation, albeit a latecomer in Africa.

The problems inflicted on African communities by the rise of China are not unique; they are a recurrence with greater intensity of the economic and political problems driven by neoliberal globalisation. If it was the imperialist West in the past, the neocolonial North and China in the present, then it may be Brazil, India or other rising regional powers inflicting similar problems on Africa communities in the future. If there are more fundamental issues about the quest for developmentalism, unregulated and irresponsible investment and the trade practices of global capitalism, the targets and agents of change favourable to the development of African communities would offer a completely different agenda from what we have discussed today.

This article reflects the author's ideas and arguments, not the analysis or position of Oxfam Hong Kong.

Notes
1 'Greenwashing' refers to the practice where an organisation spends more resources advertising it is green than on environmentally sound practices.

CLIENT AND COMPETITOR: CHINA AND INTERNATIONAL FINANCIAL INSTITUTIONS

SHALMALI GUTTAL

Within the World Bank and the Asian Development Bank, China has positioned itself as both client and competitor. Shalmali Guttal looks at how China has strategically used its membership of the two international financial institutions to skilfully develop its own infrastructure and institutions with the money it borrows from them while using its massive trade surplus and foreign exchange reserves to secure influence in the economies of less developed countries.

Introduction

The growing economic, financial and diplomatic ties between numerous African nations and the People's Republic of China are attracting considerable attention from national and international policy makers, press and media, financiers, development agencies, non-governmental organisations (NGOs) and private corporations. Although China has been economically active in Africa for several decades, the China–Africa relationship came into the spotlight in November 2006 at the summit meeting of the Forum on China–Africa Cooperation (FOCAC) in Beijing, and again in May 2007 during the Annual Meetings of the African Development Bank (AfDB) in Shanghai.

The FOCAC summit was telling of how China is positioning itself in Africa. Attended by 48 African delegations (many led by heads of state), it was dominated by Beijing's plan for cementing China's 'strategic partnership' with Africa, which included raising the volume of trade to US$100 billion by 2010; doubling official assistance by 2009; the provision of US$3 billion worth of preferential loans and US$2 billion worth of export credits; establishing a

China–Africa Development Fund to support Chinese companies investing in Africa with an initial capitalisation of US$5 billion; and unilateral cancellation of interest-free government loans owed to China by the heavily indebted and poorest African countries that matured at the end of 2005.[1]

While Chinese money, equipment and technical expertise are welcomed by many African governments, contemporary Chinese forays into the heartlands of Africa are motivated more by the single-minded pursuit of economic interests than by the solidarity rationale of the past. In Africa, China seeks oil, mineral, agricultural and forestry resources to feed its rapidly growing economy, markets for its abundant mass produced goods, contracts for its nascent but expanding private sector, and employment for an increasing work force of workers and farmers displaced in China by its embrace of capitalism as an engine of economic growth. China imports oil from Sudan and Angola, and timber and other forest products from Cameroon, Gabon and Equatorial

---

While Chinese money, equipment and technical expertise are welcomed by many African governments, contemporary Chinese forays into the heartlands of Africa are motivated more by the single-minded pursuit of economic interests than by the solidarity rationale of the past

---

Guinea. Chinese firms mine copper in Zambia and Congo-Brazzaville, cobalt in the Congo, gold in South Africa, and uranium in Zimbabwe. China is planning to invest at least US$5 billion in rehabilitating physical infrastructure and mines in the Democratic Republic of Congo (DRC) for which it would be repaid in copper and cobalt in the initial phase and, further down the line, through concessions in nickel and gold and tolls from railroads and roads to be built as part of the investment package.[2]

China's economic largesse is also raising eyebrows and alarm closer to home in Southeast Asia and the Pacific, where it is promoting ambitious trade, aid and investment projects in aid dependent countries such as the Lao PDR (Laos), Cambodia, Burma and East Timor. Here, as in Africa, the driving forces behind China's economic plans are the extraction of key natural resources for energy and raw materials to feed its growth and the capture of markets and employment for its goods, private- and state-owned enterprises and labour. Over 30,000 Chinese families have been relocated to Laos to work in plantations and infrastructure projects and run shops, markets, restaurants and hotels. In Laos and Cambodia, China has secured massive concessions for mining (gold, copper, iron, potassium and bauxite), rubber plantations, commercial agriculture and tourism. It is the largest investor in hydropower and energy projects in Burma, Laos and Cambodia and wields significant political influence over these countries by dint of its huge economic footprint. In East Timor, Chinese investors are negotiating an investment package that includes the creation of a retail bank, shopping centre and port development area, as well as the construction of a road network and aircraft runways.

At the same time, China is one of the largest borrowers from international financial institutions (IFIs) such as the World Bank and the Asian Development Bank (ADB) for developing its own physical, social and financial infrastructure, institutions and services. Because of a massive trade surplus and foreign exchange reserves, it has plenty of money to spend in less fortunate countries and yet it continues to borrow from IFIs at near market terms. This seeming paradox is in actuality an effective strategy that combines development, investment and diplomacy to strengthen China's economic and political muscle in the global arena. Often times, the World Bank and ADB find themselves competing with China – one of their largest and most efficient clients – to secure influence over the economies of other smaller clients. And while China is not eligible to borrow from the African Development Bank (AfDB), it can certainly compete with the institution in the African development and investment arenas.

China and IFIs

Membership in IFIs – including the International Monetary Fund (IMF) – are opportunities for countries to wield influence over regional and global finance, economies, development and politics. How much influence a country can actually exert within these institutions is of course based on its economic strength and potential. China is member of several IFIs and is using its membership strategically to build itself up as an economic powerhouse as well as to position itself as a political entity to be reckoned with.

There is a big difference between IFI members such as Laos, Cambodia and Nepal on the one hand, and the United States, Japan and Britain on the other. Laos and Cambodia are low-income developing countries, heavily indebted to IFIs and almost completely dependent on foreign aid for meeting social and economic development goals. They do not have enough votes to be able to influence decision making within IFIs about institutional policies and directions. The US and Japan, on the other hand, are wealthy donor countries and along with other similar members (for example Britain, Canada, Australia and France), are able to shape the policies and programmes of these institutions.

China is different in that it straddles both ends of this spectrum. China is a developing country, but with an economy larger and more dynamic than many developed countries. China has a high domestic savings rate – in 2006, it saved approximately half its GDP, about US$1.1 trillion[3] – and a

---

China's economic largesse is also raising eyebrows and alarm closer to home in Southeast Asia and the Pacific, where it is promoting ambitious trade, aid and investment projects in aid dependent countries

---

relentlessly increasing trade surplus that has the US and other trade majors scrambling to find just about any means to curb China's exports.[4]

China has 45,049 votes in the World Bank, which is 2.78 per cent of the total. In the ADB, China has the largest percentage of votes (5.442 per cent) among what are called developing member countries (DMCs), followed closely by India (5.352 per cent). DMCs are ADB members who contribute subscription capital and borrow from the institution, as opposed to members such as Japan, the US, Australia, Britain and Turkey who contribute subscription capital but do not borrow.

In the IMF, China's quota is US$8,090.10 million of special drawing rights (SDRs).[5] China's percentage of votes in the IMF is 3.67 – the highest among developing countries, and sixth highest among all IMF members (countries with more votes than China are the US, Britain, Germany, France and Japan). China is not a current borrower of the IMF and has no outstanding payments or loans to the IMF. At about US$900 billion, China's foreign exchange reserves are much larger than the IMF's lending capabilities. If China were to experience a financial crisis similar to the 1997 East Asian crisis, the IMF would not have the reserves required to bail it out.

China as borrower

China is both a borrower from the World Bank and the ADB, as well as one of the largest contributors of subscription capital to these institutions. The size of its economy, its geography, internal diversity, and its embrace of capitalism make it one of the most important clients of the World Bank and ADB.

Total World Bank lending to China from 1981 to 2007 amounts to US$41,911.51 million (i.e. almost US$42 billion) for 281 projects. Of this, International Bank for Reconstruction and Development (IBRD)[6] loans amounted to US$31,964.809 million (almost US$32 billion) and International Development Agency (IDA)[7] assistance to US$9,946.71 million (almost US$10 billion). In the fiscal year 2005–06 alone, the World Bank lent China about US$1.45 billion for 11 projects.

China is the fifth largest country portfolio of the International Finance Corporation (IFC) and one of the IFC's fastest growing client countries. The IFC is a specialised agency of the World Bank Group that provides finance, investment advice and technical support to private companies investing in developing countries. From its first investment in 1985 up till 30 June 2006, the IFC has invested in 115 projects in China for which it has mobilised US$2.86–2.24 billion from its own account, and US$930 million from other participating banks. In the financial year 2006, the IFC committed US$639 million to 24 projects in China.

China has received US$17.95 billion loans in total assistance since joining the ADB in 1986. In cumulative terms, it is the ADB's second largest borrower and the second largest client for private sector financing.[8] In 2006, China was the ADB's largest loan recipient and received US$1.6 billion, or 21 per cent, of the US$7.4 billion in loans that the ADB extended in 2006. China also received the largest share of ADB's non-sovereign loans and technical assistance in 2006 – 21 per cent of US$2.6 billion. China gets 'sovereign,' 'sub-sovereign' and 'non-sovereign' loans and technical assistance from the ADB. Non-sovereign loans and technical assistance go to private sector actors and public sector enterprises without government guarantees.

China as donor and investor

China is a large contributor to projects sponsored by the ADB. In 2005, it contributed US$30 million to the Asian Development Fund, and established the US$20 million PRC Regional Cooperation and Poverty Reduction Fund – the first developing country to set up such a fund with an international development agency. By virtue of its size and geographic spread, China is part of the ADB's subregional programmes – the Greater Mekong Subregional

---

China ... straddles both ends of this spectrum.
China is a developing country, but with an
economy larger and more dynamic than
many developed countries

Economic Strategy (GMS) and Central Asia Regional Economic Cooperation (CAREC) – in which it is viewed as a formidable investor. It is also getting involved in the South Asia Subregional Economic Cooperation (SASEC) by pledging investment towards transportation and energy infrastructure.

China is also a bilateral donor to numerous developing countries in Africa and Asia. As Chinese aid and investment become hot news items in Africa, China is also establishing itself as an economic powerhouse in its more immediate neighbourhood – Southeast Asia. China is one of the most influential donors and investors in the Mekong region and Chinese capital, technology and labour are increasingly visible in transportation, energy, mining, agribusiness, plantations, telecommunication, tourism and recreation projects, especially in Burma, Lao PDR and Cambodia. Chinese aid has moved further afield as well, to better-off countries such as the Philippines and newly formed nations such as Timor-Leste. China has also spurred bilateral and regional trade with numerous Asian countries – including members of the Association of Southeast Asian Nations (ASEAN) – by offered preferential tariff schemes (including zero tariffs) under 'Early Harvest Programmes'.

Over the past 15 odd years, China has started to play a leading role in speeding up investments in the Southeast Asia region through the GMS and ASEAN+3 frameworks. China is arguably becoming the most dominant driver of trade and investment in the region, as well as one of the most sought after markets for exports of the region's raw materials and processed products. China has signed numerous agreements with other GMS member countries in areas such as transportation, animal epidemics prevention, information technology, superhighway construction, power trade, tourism and environmental protection. According to an official Chinese daily newspaper, 'Ever since the inception of the GMS Programme, China has been both a beneficiary of, and a contributor to it and has made large investments in infrastructure construction within the region.'[9]

Chinese aid comes in the form of cash and equipment grants, extremely low interest loans (on which payment can be rescheduled without difficulties) and unilateral debt relief. Much of China's aid goes towards complicated physical infrastructure projects in difficult terrains such as remote rural roads, bridges over deep and fast flowing rivers, and deep-sea ports. What makes Chinese aid particularly attractive to recipient countries is the fact that it comes unencumbered by the kinds of policy conditions demanded by the IFIs and Northern donors for policy and governance reforms. Equally important, Chinese aid does not come with packages of expensive consultants that are commonplace in most Northern-donor financed aid and IFI loan projects. Chinese 'experts' and consultants are not associated with the lavish lifestyles of their counterparts from Northern aid agencies. They live in relatively sparse conditions, a picture of frugality, hard work and adaptability.

In early 2006, China offered Cambodia US$600 million in loans with no strings attached for bridges, a hydropower plant and a fibre optics network to connect Cambodia's telecommunications with that of Vietnam and Thailand. In contrast, later in the year Cambodia's traditional donors and creditors collectively pledged US$700 that was laden with policy conditions, several related to checking corruption. Also in 2006, the World Bank temporarily suspended payments on two loans because of allegations of corruption. While corruption is certainly a serious problem in Cambodia and IFIs and Northern donors attempt to bring it up in every major donors' meeting, few have taken a consistent stand against it by cancelling projects altogether or conducting independent investigations. The World Bank's temporary suspension of payments on the two loans was viewed by many as a stop-gap ploy to give the illusion the World Bank was taking action against corruption rather than a demonstration of serious intent. Also in 2006, China offered the Philippines a package of US$2 billion in loans from its Export-Import Bank over the next three years, over-shadowing the US$200 million offered by the World Bank and ADB and the US$1 billion loan that was being negotiated with Japan.

China is criticised by Northern donors and creditors for being secretive about its aid intentions and for its apparent unwillingness to coordinate aid activities through forums managed by the World Bank. It is true that Chinese announcements of aid, trade and investment packages often surprise even the governments to whom they are offered. And it would indeed be naive to assume that China's donor ambitions are fuelled purely by altruism or that there are really 'no strings' attached to its generous offers. But for recipient countries, China presents both, an alternative source of development finance as well as a possible escape route from the never-ending cycle of policy

---

If China were to experience a financial crisis similar to the 1997 East Asian crisis, the IMF would not have the reserves required to bail it out

---

conditions attached to more traditional bilateral and multilateral aid and credits. Equally important, China's aid and investment behaviour is forcing IFIs and Northern donors to be less high-handed with their poorer clients.

China's official development assistance (ODA) aid to Africa dates back to 1956. While accurate updated annual figures are difficult to compute, it is estimated that by May 2006, China had contributed a total of US$5.7 billion for more than 800 aid projects. Other estimates put the number higher at US$1–1.5 billion a year, but more important are the terms of ODA. China's aid still follows the principles established by late Premier Zhou Enlai in the early 1960s: no conditions or demand for privileges can be attached to ODA; China provides ODA in the form of grants, interest-free or low-interest loans; and repayment on loans will be rescheduled if necessary. China's aid programme also includes technical assistance, with an emphasis on agricultural technology and training in Chinese institutions. While Chinese ODA has largely focused on social projects such as hospitals, schools, low-cost housing, sport venues and library and government buildings, it also includes infrastructure construction and agricultural development.[10] China has also fulfilled its pledges to cancel debts of the heavily indebted and least developed countries in Africa without insisting on the kinds of economic and political conditions demanded by the World Bank, IMF and G7/G8 countries.

An African Policy Paper issued in January 2006 articulates Chinese policy objectives toward Africa, in order to build a new type of strategic partnership, and how these objectives are to be achieved. The paper emphasises: '"mutual benefit", "common development", and "win–win" results in economic relations'.[11] The paper outlines government actions to promote trade, investment, financial services, agriculture, infrastructure and resource development, and tourism, complemented by financial and technical assistance in key social sectors such as health and education. China's current engagements in Africa reflect these policies. The US$5 billion newly committed to Congo includes a US$3 billion infrastructure component and plans to build 31 hospitals, 145 health centres and two universities.[12]

This is not to say that China extracts no returns or concessions for the vast amounts of money it pours into African and Southeast Asian countries. Just as Chinese ODA comes without the policy prescriptions demanded by IFIs and traditional Northern donors, Chinese investments in revenue generating sectors such as mining, energy, hydropower, agriculture and forestry are not tempered by commonly accepted environmental, labour and social standards. Information about the size and scope of projects, their impacts and financing

Much of China's aid goes towards complicated physical infrastructure projects in difficult terrains such as remote rural roads, bridges over deep and fast flowing rivers and deep-sea ports

are extremely hard to come by and Chinese government agencies, financiers and private companies generally refuse to divulge information to the public about their operations. The Chinese Exim Bank, for example, whose financing far exceeds Chinese ODA, has drawn the fire of numerous civil society organisations and social movements for financing large hydropower, mining and agriculture projects without adequate impact assessments and dialogue with the communities affected by a project. Chinese enterprises in Africa and elsewhere – including inside China – are heavily criticised for poor safety and working conditions, exploitative wage practices and pollution. China is particularly criticised for doing business with dictatorial or extreme authoritarian regimes such as Burma, Cambodia, Sudan and Nigeria, and for

25

ignoring the human rights dimensions of infrastructure, extractive industry and energy projects.

At the same time, however, Chinese aid and investment packages include, through the provision of grants or concessional loans, commitments to provide public goods and social services such as hospitals, schools, public buildings and technical assistance and building human resources such as training civil servants, doctors, etc. Also important is China's willingness to invest in and build and upgrade physical infrastructure such as roads, ports, highways, etc. Infrastructure projects, of course, also serve Chinese economic

---

China has also fulfilled its pledges to cancel debts of the heavily indebted and least developed countries in Africa without insisting on the kinds of economic and political conditions demanded by the World Bank, IMF and G7/G8 countries

---

interests well since they provide contracts for Chinese firms, employment for Chinese labour and procurement for Chinese equipment and materials.

A fact unpalatable to traditional donors and lenders in Africa and Asia is that it is their own unbending insistence on destructive neoliberal policy reforms and dismal track records in alleviating poverty that have rendered China a welcome alternative source of development capital among many developing countries. The IFIs have yet to come up with a way out of the debt traps that least and less developed countries find themselves mired in, which are often results of faulty policy advice and irresponsible lending from the IFIs themselves. Northern donors demand free trade and investment in exchange for aid and credits, but close their own markets and societies against Southern goods and labour. In Africa, where the wounds of colonialism are deep, raw and still fresh, the structural adjustment programmes imposed by the World Bank–IMF and development aid characterised by strict economic policy conditions are viewed by many as a perpetuation of colonial power relations.[13] The World Bank is one of the largest financiers of large-scale hydropower, energy and extractive industry projects, many of which are rife with corruption and tainted by human rights violations.

In contrast, China's 'win–win' strategy is attractive for many developing country governments that are simply fed-up with jumping through endless hoops for aid and credits from traditional donors that are slow to arrive and conditioned on the adoption of a failed development model. For sure, China is no saint; it wants raw materials, energy resources, minerals and markets from other developing countries. But in return, it is willing to woo them by offering attractive terms for finance, trade and investment.

Selective about borrowings and technical assistance

China can afford to be and is selective about what it borrows money for and the nature of technical assistance and 'policy advice' it takes from IFIs. China goes to IFIs for loans and technical assistances to enhance value addition to its agricultural, industrial, technological and finance sector capacities. It would not be far fetched to argue China uses IFI financing and technical assistance to shore up its position as a global donor, financier and investor.

Since 1999, China has not received concessional loans from IDA and is only eligible for loans at near market terms from the IBRD. China's portfolio is one of the largest in the World Bank and the bank considers China to be one of its best-performing members in terms of project implementation. Sectors for which China currently accepts IBRD financing include transportation (inner provinces to coast), urban development (urban transport, water and sanitation), rural development, energy, and human development.

Sectors for which China has taken ADB loans include: agriculture and natural resources, energy, finance, industry and trade, transport and communications, water supply, sanitation, and waste management.

China is strategic about how it uses IFI financing. China is an extremely large country with tremendous geographic, cultural and demographic diversity, and economic and social disparities among its regions. While some of its regions are wealthy, it also has pockets of intense poverty. As China transforms itself into a global economic powerhouse, it needs to fill infrastructure, human, social and institutional development gaps at home, for which it uses financing and technical assistance from IFIs. Also important to China is building a strong domestic financial sector and financial institutions that are able to keep up and comply with international practices and global trends. China is building capacity in both its private and public enterprises through financing and technical assistance from IFIs.

At the same time, China has built up an impressive manufacturing base over the past two decades by compelling transnational corporations

(TNCs), who came to China seeking cheap labour costs, to locate most of their production processes in the country rather than simply outsourcing a selected few processes. Local governments within the country have also invested heavily to build up capacity in local industries which, combined with continuing foreign investments, have helped China to beef up its export-oriented growth strategy.[14]

The paradoxical result is that even as China borrows from the IFIs to build new physical infrastructure in sectors such as transportation, water and urban development, and step up quality in sectors such as agriculture, energy and human development, it has a surplus of capital which it uses for bilateral aid and investment in poorer countries. Much of China's foreign investment is in natural resources, oil and minerals (for example copper, cobalt, gold, and uranium) to feed its own rapidly growing economy. China's growth figures and potential make it a more, rather than less, attractive client for IFIs. IFIs are more than willing to bend their lending policies to suit China's development model, unlike their less well off clients who are compelled to accept the economic strategies demanded by IFIs and Northern donors.

A preferred client

IFIs need their large developing country clients such as China, India, Indonesia and Brazil because this is where their own bread and butter comes from. China repays its loans on time and although selective about the projects it borrows for, it borrows in large quantities and ensures that projects are generally implemented on schedule without messy delays caused by popular protests, parliamentary or congressional inquiries, or compliance with domestic social and environmental safeguard measures.

World Bank and ADB documents reveal that they definitely consider China to be an extremely important client. The ADB's 2007–08 lending pipeline to China totals about US$3 billion; 85 per cent of the loan projects are likely to be located in the poorer central and western provinces. Technical assistance for the same two-year period will focus more sharply on high-priority, policy-related and knowledge-based products.

China is also a favoured client for carbon trade and associated projects. The ADB has given China a grant of US$600,000 to set up a fund to help the country benefit from the potential multi-billion dollar revenues from the Clean Development Mechanism (CDM). The ADB estimate that China can generate 'certified emission reductions' (CERs)[15] credits of between 150 to 225 million tons of carbon dioxide equivalent per year, which translate to a potential annual revenue stream of up to US$2.25 billion. The Chinese government is expected to use this grant to establish a specialised facility – the CDM Fund – which will collect levies on the revenues generated by

Just as Chinese overseas development assistance comes without the policy prescriptions demanded by IFIs and traditional Northern donors, Chinese investments in revenue generating sectors such as mining, energy, hydropower, agriculture and forestry are not tempered by commonly accepted environmental, labour and social standards

various CDM projects through CER credits. The CDM Fund will be used to support domestic climate change related activities.[16]

The ADB is clearly willing to make adjustments to its own strategy and policies to accommodate China: 'The country's rapid economic development and its growing importance in the global and regional economy require ADB to keep its operations relevant to PRC's needs at the strategic level and add value to the country's future development.' And further, 'ADB needs to establish a niche for itself in the PRC's rapid development process over the next 5–10 years.'[17] The ADB plans to establish this niche by:

- Increasing its sectoral coverage in agriculture and rural development, energy conservation, environmental protection, urbanisation, social development, financial reforms, and regional cooperation. In other words, in whichever direction China expands, the ADB is willing to follow
- Reducing 'transaction costs' to the client and introducing innovative assistance products – which means that China will be allowed to bend whatever rules needed to keep it borrowing from the ADB; even the minimal social and environmental safeguards proposed by the ADB will not be applicable to China

- Expanding private sector operations, particularly in the infrastructure sector, through private–public partnerships – China's geographic size and diversity, natural resources, population and increasing incomes offer huge revenue opportunities for the private sector, which the ADB hopes to attract by getting the Chinese government to sponsor projects through private–public partnerships.

On its part, the World Bank has lined up three of its agencies to continue to respond to China's needs. The IBRD is oriented towards supporting priority projects in China's Five Year Plan – especially for infrastructure, rural development and natural resource management – by providing loans for physical infrastructure investments, administering loans and grants provided by bilateral donors, and technical assistance in the form of 'policy advice', capacity building and analytical services. The bank considers 'knowledge sharing and transfer' particularly important in its relationship with China,

A fact unpalatable to traditional donors and lenders in Africa and Asia is that it is their own unbending insistence on destructive neoliberal policy reforms and dismal track records in alleviating poverty that have rendered China a welcome alternative source of development capital among many developing countries

both in terms of advising the Chinese government on constraints to private investment, social and financial service delivery and economic growth, and in advocating China's so called 'success stories' in poverty reduction through increased economic growth.

The IFC recognises that the private sector has become a critical component of China's economy, boosting its economic power domestically as well as abroad. One of the conditions attached to IBRD loans to China is that state-owned enterprises be privatised in order to boost efficiency and generate sufficient revenues so as to not be a drain on government expenditure. While a lot of IFC support actually goes to large, often foreign-owned companies, the IFC claims that its support for local small and medium enterprises – which have limited national institutional support – will help to alleviate the negative effects of the so called 'transformation' of state-owned enterprises.

For the IFC, China presents a wealth of opportunities for enhancing its own institutional profile and increasing its profits. The IFC is particularly interested in China's efforts to liberalise its financial sector since it offers the bank new opportunities to support the development of private institutions in the banking and insurance sectors. Its China operations are focused on:

- Encouraging the development of China's local private sector, including small and medium sized enterprises
- Investing in the financial sector to develop competitive institutions that will meet international corporate governance and operating standards
- Supporting the development of China's western and interior provinces
- Promoting private investment in the infrastructure, social services and environmental industries.

Also poised for greater expansion is the Multilateral Investment Guarantee Association (MIGA), which already provides private investors guarantees against 'sub-sovereign' (i.e., at provincial, city, county, or district levels) risks, especially in infrastructure and water projects.[18] MIGA is particularly eager to facilitate foreign direct investment in China by providing guarantees and technical assistance to support China's western and northeast regional development strategy and Chinese outward investment.

Positioning itself and calling the shots

In regional and global IFI platforms, China presents a strong 'southern' position, argues for greater South–South cooperation, challenges the hegemony of the industrialised North in providing aid, investment capital and technology, and defends the rights of developing countries to self-determination. Recently, China formally opposed the IMF's new surveillance framework that was adopted at the IMF's executive board meeting and criticised the process by which it was adopted in spite of objections and reservations from developing countries.[19]

Although China certainly benefits greatly from the infrastructure it finances (such as roads, ports, bridges, factories and hydropower plants) by gaining access to raw materials, energy, capital and trade markets, Chinese policy makers argue that China is using its growing wealth to create development opportunities for less well off developing countries and in the long term, is fostering peace, harmony and solidarity among developing countries.

This is not to say that China supports information disclosure and public accountability in the IFIs or dialogue between IFIs, host governments and civil society. On the contrary: Chinese representatives in IFIs and other regional/global platforms are notorious for being aloof and unapproachable to civil society and other 'non-official' representatives. What China argues for is the sovereign rights of governments to shape their own development strategies and to make decisions about projects and policies regardless of social, environmental and governance implications. It matters little to China

---

IFIs are more than willing to bend their lending policies to suit China's development model, unlike their less well off clients who are compelled to accept the economic strategies demanded by IFIs and Northern donors

---

that building eight dams on the Lancang river (the upper Mekong), in what it considers its own sovereign territory, will have negative impacts on critical ecologies and livelihoods in countries located downstream. It will purchase the compliance and cooperation of disgruntled governments by offers of roads, energy projects, and trade and investment preferences.

Along with other large borrowers such as India, Brazil, Indonesia and South Africa, China is shaping the lending and operational policies of many IFIs. Many middle-income clients have expressed unwillingness to borrow from the World Bank and ADB for large infrastructure projects if they are required to adhere to the environmental and social safeguard policies that come as part of the financing packages. China and India, for example, already have access to project finance from international capital markets and refuse to be subjected to what they consider onerous and intrusive external social and environmental standards for projects that benefit the investors as much as they benefit the host country. Objections have also been raised about the inspection mechanisms of these institutions, which (at least in theory) can be used to halt or delay projects deemed as violating their social, environmental and financial safeguard measures. The response of the World Bank and ADB has been to pare down their own – already minimal – safeguard measures to keep developing country governments happy and borrowing.

In early 2005, the World Bank initiated a pilot programme called 'country systems' through which the bank would apply a borrowing country's own environmental and social safeguard systems to assess the potential impacts of infrastructure and other projects.[20] Although couched in language such as 'expanding development impact', 'increasing country ownership', 'building capacity', 'facilitating harmonisation' and 'increasing cost effectiveness', the main impulse behind the programme seems to be to: a) ensure that the bank continues to have a presence in large infrastructure projects, either through direct financing or through 'advisory' services, and; b) transfer responsibility for negative social and environmental impacts onto host governments since it is now their safeguard measures that are to be followed. Environmental activists indicate that the institution may well be on a path of 'downward harmonisation' of project standards to ensure that it does not lose its infrastructure borrowing clientele.

The ADB has taken similar measures with regard to its public information, inspection and safeguard policies. The newly revised public information policy does not even recognise the 'public' as a principle target audience and is tailored to meet the information needs of the private sector and governments. The unfortunate story of the ADB's inspection policy bears telling. The very first project that the inspection policy was tested on was the Samut Prakarn Wastewater Management Project (SPWMP) in Thailand. Thai government officials and ADB staff responsible for the project not only rejected the grounds for inspection, but also refused to cooperate with the inspection team.

Despite numerous setbacks, the inspection team found grave violations of the ADB's operational policies and directives and made recommendations accordingly. Senior ADB management and staff by and large dismissed the findings of the inspection team and refused to acknowledge any wrongdoing on their part. Most unexpected, however, was the response of the ADB's executive directors to the inspection report, most of whom rejected the report. The strongest and most vociferous rejection came from Mr Zhao Xiaoyu, the executive director for China, who called the SPWMP inspection result skewed, biased and a 'lousy course of dish', and invoked the experience of the World Bank's inspection of China's Western Poverty Project as an example of how multilateral development bank staff can be demoralised by externally led investigation efforts. According to Director Zhao Xiaoyu, the World Bank inspection result induced bank staff to maintain 'big China maps on the wall with little red flags pinned here and there ... The marks stand for regions with ethnic residents and the staff are constantly reminded to keep

> *Chinese representatives in IFIs and other regional/global platforms are notorious for being aloof and unapproachable to civil society and other 'non-official' representatives.*

away from these places.'[21] As a result of the controversy surrounding the SPWMP inspection process and the rejection of the inspection report by the ADB's most influential borrowers, the ADB's inspection policy has become so watered down that it may as well cease to exist.

The readiness of IFIs to make adjustments to their lending and governance policies to suit borrowing governments poses important and tricky strategic questions for civil society organisations who are fooled into believing that IFIs are actually development institutions that can be made to stop bad projects by operational directives, safeguard measures, etc.

Conclusion

The above arguments are not intended to valourise China's dealings with IFIs or its role as an external donor and investor. From a constructive start possibly based on Southern solidarity politics several decades ago, China's current aid and foreign investment practices have begun to dangerously resemble colonialism. For numerous countries in Africa and Southeast Asia, China has been a donor, financier, investor, contractor, builder and market. Certainly, China's intentions, tactics and overall strategy should be closely monitored by civil society actors and challenged as needed, much as we would do in the case of any other country with colonial ambitions.

What is interesting in the case of the IFIs, however, is that China exposes them for what they are – bankers and financiers whose first and last priorities are to push loans and financing regardless of the costs, and recoup money and make profits for their shareholders.

China's relationship with the IFIs defies easy categories. On the one hand, China uses IFIs to leverage access to relatively cheap capital and technical support to meet its own growing infrastructure, human and social development, technological and institutional needs; here it is no different from other middle-income developing countries. On the other hand, China uses IFIs to expand its economic reach, and access markets and investment opportunities in other developing countries through IFIs projects and programmes; and here, it is no different from developed countries. In both cases, China is using IFIs to shore up its economic, financial, political and strategic advantages and potential.

China is too important a country in the world of development finance and financial institutions for civil society to ignore. Rather than look for clear 'for' or 'against' positions on China, we need to find and create opportunities to engage with this newly emerging economic super-power. Given the Chinese government's recalcitrance over engaging in dialogue with external civil society actors, this is indeed a daunting task. It is crucial that researchers, academics and representatives from workers and farmers' unions, indigenous peoples' organisations and other civil society organisations from outside China build strong collaborative relationships with their Chinese counterparts. In the long term, the voices of caution and conscience that Chinese policy makers are most likely to listen to are those of the Chinese public.

This paper is an adaptation of a presentation made by the author on the same subject at the conference in Shanghai in May 2007.

Notes

1 Walden Bello (2007) 'China's turbo-charged diplomacy sparks debate in Africa' <http://www.focusweb.org>.
2 William Wallis (2007) 'China to invest $5bn in Congo', *Financial Times*, 19 September.
3 CNN (2006) <http://money.cnn.com/2006/03/03/news/international/chinasaving_fortune/>.
4 *China News* (2006) 'High savings lead to trade surplus', 16 June <http://www.chinadaily.com.cn/china/2006-06/16/content_618330.htm>. See also, <http://www.rieti.go.jp/en/china/06122702.html>.
5 The SDR is the unit of account of the IMF; it is a potential claim on the freely usable currencies of IMF members. More information about how IMF quotas and SDRs are calculated is available on the IMF website.
6 The IBRD is one of the five institutions of the Wold Bank Group and makes loans at near

market interest rates to middle-income developing countries.

7 IDA is one of the five institutions of the Wold Bank Group. It provides grants and concessional loans (with low interest rates) to lower income developing countries.

8 Other major borrowers from the ADB in recent years have included Indonesia, India, Pakistan and Vietnam.

9 Hu Xuan (2005) *China Daily*, 7 July.

10 Jian-Ye Wang (2007) 'What drives China's growing role in Africa?'. *IMF Working Paper*. Washington, DC: International Monetary Fund, African Department.

11 Ibid.

12 W. Wallis (2007) 'China to invest $5bn in Congo', *Financial Times*, London, 19 September.

13 A. Hübschle (2007) *China's Whistle-Stop Tour of Africa*. Cape Town: Organised Crime and Money Laundering Programme, Institute for Security Studies <http://www.iss.co.za/index.php?link_id=4057&slink_id=4055&link_type=12&slink_type=12&tmpl_id=3>.

14 W. Bello (2006) 'Chain-gang economics: China, the US, and the global economy <http://www.focusweb.org/index2.php?option=com_content&do_pdf=1&id=1103> and p. 7 of this book.

15. By obtaining certified emission reductions (CERs) from projects in developing countries, developed countries can escape cutting down greenhouse gas emissions; CERs are usually generated through financing so called 'sustainable development projects' in developing countries.

16.< http://www.adb.org/Media/Articles/2006/10594-PRC-CDM-potential/>.

17 See the ADB web page for the PRC <www.adb.org/prc> and follow links.

18 MIGA (1988) Created in 1988, MIGA is the World Bank Group's newest member. It provides guarantees (political risk insurance) to foreign private investors against the risks of expropriation, transfer restriction, breach of contract, and war and civil disturbance. It also provides technical assistance to host governments on means to attract more foreign direct investment.

19 Chee Yoke Ling and Celine Tan (2007) 'China criticizes IMF decision on exchange-rate surveillance', *South-North Development Monitor (SUNS)*, no. 6283, 2 July.

20 World Bank (2005) <http://web.worldbank.org/WBSITE/EXTERNAL/NEWS/0,,contentMDK:20433658~menuPK:34480~pagePK:34370~piPK:116742~theSitePK:4607,00.html>.

21 The minutes of the board meeting in which the ADB executive directors discussed the inspection report was leaked to the public. Sections of it can be found in a May 2002 publication by Focus on the Global South: *Too Hot to Handle, The Samut Prakarn Wastewater Management Project Inspection Process* <www.focusweb.org>. Mr Zhao Xiaoyu's remarks can be found on pp. 39–42.

THE EQUATOR PRINCIPLES AND THE ENVIRONMENTAL RESPONSIBILITIES OF THE FINANCIAL INDUSTRY IN CHINA

YU XIAOGANG AND DING PIN

The Equator Principles are a benchmark developed by the financial industry for judging, evaluating and managing risk in project financing. Yu Xiaogang and Ding Pin describe how the principles have been used to try and ensure that financial assistance from Chinese banks goes to projects in China that minimise damage to the environment. He points out the crucial yet still developing role of Chinese NGOs in helping this happen.

Behind every large-scale environmentally risky project sit investors, private-owned and state-owned banks and financial institutions. In general, enterprises contribute around 30 per cent of funding of a given project, while banks contribute the remaining 70 per cent in the form of loans, and it is only with the bank's accreditation that projects can get loan funding and be implemented. Banks, therefore, are strong supporters of companies' behaviour.

Banking and financial institutions start from a consideration of the returns to be made on an investment, and look to the size, not the quality, of a given investment. However, environmental and social problems arising from investment projects bring bad publicity for banks and financial institutions. NGOs from both developed and developing countries have applied a lot of pressure on banks and financial institutions and pushed the financial industry to develop environmental and social policies.

Under developed market economy conditions, the importance of bank financing of projects outweighs the importance of government approval processes. For example, governments of all countries only invoke the right to approve investment projects above a certain threshold, whereas banks base loan decisions on considerations of loan risk and benefit, normally carrying out risk assessments for investments exceeding RMB10 million (or sometimes even RMB500,000).

Consequently, countries around the world are tending towards a consensus which treats financial assets as a scarce resource, and which seeks to improve the efficiency of loan use through strengthening the impact of finance on social investment, avoidance of risk, adjustment of the industrial structure and the encouragement of reasonable consumption. Under these circumstances, it is necessary to consider the social and environmental impact of investment projects and to perfect financial risk evaluation and early warning mechanisms. Therefore, when making and administering loans and managing projects, the financial industry, financiers and banks should take responsibility for the environmental and social impacts of the projects they support.

Let us look first at examples of the damaging environmental impacts of some major projects financed by the international financial industry.

The negative environmental impacts of projects

At the beginning of this century, Citibank's investment projects, notably the Camisea Natural Gas Project, became the focus of public criticism. In 2000, America's Hunt Oil and the SK Corporation of South Korea invested US$1.6 billion in Peru for the development of the Camisea natural gas project, including prospecting for oil in the Peruvian rainforest, setting up of four drilling platforms, installing two natural gas pipelines to transport gas to the Peruvian coast and building two natural gas processing plants on the coast near Lima. Three-quarters of the project area is located within the territory of indigenous peoples living in isolation from the rest of the world. In the 18 months after the project started producing oil, the pipeline ruptured four times and in at least three cases this caused major spills. In May of 2004, a report from the Epidemiology Office of the Peruvian Ministry of Health showed that 22 indigenous communities and a host of agricultural communities could not avoid being affected, either directly or indirectly, by the project. This impact includes the loss of fish species, landslides and exposure to communicable diseases. Citibank, as the financial backer of the Camisea project, also came in for fierce criticism from environmental NGOs, most notably from the Rainforest Action Network.

In addition to the Peruvian natural gas project, Citigroup is also involved in the logging of redwoods in California's Headwaters forest, pipeline construction in Ecuador, and the development of oilfields in Papua New Guinea, all of which investment projects damage already fragile forests and local communities as well as accelerating global warming.

Citibank has been the subject of fierce criticism from environmental NGOs for its role in providing investment to many such environmentally damaging projects. As a result of this, Citigroup has adopted comprehensive environmental protection policies, set new investment standards, carried out

---

When making and administering loans and managing projects, the financial industry, financiers and banks should take responsibility for the environmental and social impacts of the projects they support

---

capacity building with employees and industry partners, as well as setting and constantly improving its environmental and social policies. In 2005, of 21 projects in which there was a potential for significant environmental damage, Citibank approved only three, and these were carried out in strict accordance with the Equator Principles and environmental and social risk management policies.

The Japan Bank for International Cooperation was involved in a number of projects in Asia that had damaging environmental impacts. For example, as a result of the construction of the Kotopanjang Dam in Indonesia, residents lost their means of livelihood due to resettlement, and water and forest resources were damaged. In the construction of the San Roque Dam in the Phillipines, ethnic minority peoples were deprived of their means of livelihood, while in the case of the Samut Prakarn wastewater treatment project in Thailand, no prior evaluation was made of the impact on the fishery industry.

At this stage, international NGOs mounted an environmental campaign severely criticising projects funded by export credit agencies and calling for large-scale environmental and social reform. This campaign included not only developed-country NGOs, but also those from developing countries, such as Indonesia.

The Sakhalin-2 integrated oil and gas project was criticised by NGOs and indigenous peoples as a threat to the western grey whale (a species facing extinction), for damaging the habitats of rare fish and bird species and for pollution affecting the local fishing industry. Russian NGOs lodged complaints in the courts and in 2005 indigenous peoples of Sakhalin Island staged two protests against the project, garnering international attention. They believed that Credit Suisse First Boston should not play the role of financial consultant to a project which violates the Equator Principles in many places. Other banks, such as ABN AMRO, were also involved in this project. Under pressure, the project developers contracted the World Conservation Union (IUCN) to organise an independent scientific evaluation of the impact of the project on the western grey whale.

The Baku-Tblisi-Ceyhan crude oil pipeline (BTC) project was the first to be classified as a category A project under the Equator Principles, and was their first major test. The project was financed by nine banks, including the Royal Bank of Scotland. A number of NGOs (including the Worldwide Fund for Nature and Friends of the Earth) pointed out that the BTC project violated the Equator Principles in a total of 127 places, and that as a consequence, Equator Principles financial institutions should not be involved in its financing. At the same time, the banks were under pressure from the media, and NGOs appealed to the courts to protect human rights and the environment. As a result of this pressure, the consortium of banks financing the project commissioned an evaluation from an independent environmental consultant. In addition, and for further peace of mind, the financing consortium contracted a second environmental consultant to assist them in monitoring the project.

Due to resistance from local NGOs, ten years on the Asian Development Bank's Nam Theun 2 hydropower project (Laos) has still to get off the ground.

The safeguarding policies embodied in the Equator Principles

The adoption of sustainable development principles and related policies by the international financial industry is a historic trend of our times. The World Bank, the Asian Development Bank, the International Finance Corporation (IFC) and other multi-country regional development banks have already voluntarily produced, committed to, and implemented relevant environmental and social policies, and these are constantly being updated.

In January 2003, the Collevecchio Declaration on Financial Institutions and

Sustainability was released by more than a hunded NGOs. The declaration sets out six principles which it is hoped financial institutions will adhere to. These are commitments to sustainability, to do no harm, to responsibility, to accountability, to transparency and to sustainable markets and governance.

In 2005, of 21 projects in which there was a potential for significant environmental damage, Citibank approved only three, and these were carried out in strict accordance with the Equator Principles and environmental and social risk management policies

---

The influence of the declaration on the Equator Principles has been significant, and it has subsequently become a reference standard used by NGOs to evaluate the environmental and social impact of financial institutions.

In June 2003, ten major commercial banks from seven countries, including Citibank, ABN AMRO and WestLB AG led the way in voluntarily committing to respect norms for the sustainable development of the financial industry – the Equator Principles. Following this, more and more major banks gradually signed up to the principles, including HSBC, Standard Chartered and Bank of America. In 2003, export credit agencies of all countries adopted the Recommendation on Common Approaches on Environment and Officially Supported Export Credits.

To date, more than 40 major private banks, with a presence in more than a hundred countries have committed to respect the Equator Principles. These banks together contribute more than 80 per cent of the global market for project development financing, and include a number of banks from developing countries, including four major Brazilian banks. Seven out of ten South African banks and three out of twelve Nigerian banks have incorporated environmental, social and environmental pollution and management of ecological damage into their risk assessment procedures used in loan approval and some banks have adopted stricter environmental policies than those set out in the Equator Principles.

The Equator Principles are formulated in compliance with the policies of the major world financial institutions, the IFC and the World Bank, and are

an industry benchmark for judging, evaluating and managing risk in project financing. When banks make investment decisions, they should do so based on specific clauses and conditions, and these should include a basis for the classification of risk. This is the core of the document, set out in ten articles or principles. Principle 1 relates to the grounds for categorising project risk.

International NGOs mounted an environmental campaign severely criticising projects funded by export credit agencies and calling for large-scale environmental and social reform. This campaign included not only developed-country NGOs, but also those from developing countries

---

Principle 2 stipulates social and environmental assessment (SEA) requirements for category A and category B projects. Principle 3 specifies principal content of the SEA, while Principle 4 states requirements of the action plan. Principle 5 specifies a framework for open consultation with affected groups. Principle 6 gives information disclosure and public participation requirements and requires the establishment of grievance mechanisms. Principle 7 states the requirement for independent monitoring, while Principle 8 specifies that compliance covenants be included in financing documentation. Principle 9 mandates the appointment of independent environmental and social experts, and Principle 10 requires periodic and open reporting on the project.

The content of the principles deals mainly with the following areas: environmental assessment requirements of different types of projects (including environmental assessment, urban and engineering projects, resettlement, indigenous peoples, natural habitats, forestry, pest management, cultural property, safety of dams, roads and international waterways); environmental and social impact evaluation (including health); environmental management plan requirements (including reduction of environmental and social risk); action plans; monitoring (including timeframes); independent expert assessment; borrower covenants (including adherence to environmental management plans in the course of project set-up and operation, periodic reporting of the status of implementation, etc); grievance systems (including specifications for action to be taken by the bank in cases where the borrower fails to comply with environmental and social clauses) and periodic and open reporting by the bank.

Banks undertaking to comply with the Equator Principles formulate green statutes, guidelines and handbooks governing their behaviour, and establish environmentally and socially sustainable development departments, as well as pools of consultants on environmental and social questions.

The Equator Principles have helped strengthen communication and trust between banks, civil environmental organisations and the public, as well as increasing the attention of shareholders and external interests towards environmental and social safeguards. To a certain extent, they have also reduced the probability of negative environmental and social impacts of investment projects, reduced the overall volume of bad investments, and increased investment efficiency.

The Equator Principles are a historic landmark in the development of international finance, setting for the first time minimum environmental and social standards applicable in international project financing and succeeding in getting these applied.

In July 2006, banks from a number of countries jointly revised the Equator Principles to incorporate the performance standards of the IFC. These standards are an update of the World Bank's environmental and social safeguard policies, and target the private sector. In total, there are eight standards: social and environmental assessment and management systems, labour and working conditions, pollution prevention and abatement, community health, safety and security, land acquisition and involuntary resettlement, biodiversity conservation and sustainable natural resource management and indigenous peoples and cultural heritage. In addition, under Standard 3, rules relating to gas and wastewater emissions are taken from the *Pollution Prevention and Abatement Handbook* of the World Bank.

Status of implementation

To date, the financial organisations of essentially all OECD countries have formulated new environmental evaluation programmes, industry financing directions and similarly detailed rules, as well as establishing dedicated implementation organs and personnel. For example, chairs of the board of directors of banks, chief executive officers, other high-level bankers and directors frequently take corporate social responsibility seriously, and exert their influence at board meetings, believing that banks should place emphasis on environmental and social risk and reduce financial risk. In such cases, these high-level personnel actively take part in setting and implementing internal corporate social responsibility policies, undertake

---

Under pressure, the project developers
contracted the World Conservation Union
(IUCN) to organise an independent scientific
evaluation of the impact of the project
on the western grey whale

---

related training, personally approve environmental and social policies, read related government reports, and so on.

In addition to voluntarily implementing the Equator Principles, and in order to clearly delimit minimum loan amount and investment standards in environmentally sensitive industries, in 2004 HSBC's Sustainable Risk Advisory released the bank's first industry-specific financing guidelines, on forest land and forest products. Following this, the group released guidelines on freshwater infrastructure and on the chemicals industry sector, and risk policies on the energy sector and the mining and metals sector.

The energy sector risk policy, for example, specifies that HSBC should not provide loans to enterprises whose activities cause pollution in a number of specified areas, including UNESCO world heritage sites, locations on the Register of Wetlands of International Importance (of the Ramsar Convention on Wetlands), primary tropical moist forests, high conservation value forests and critical natural habitats. In addition, HSBC expects client companies in Kyoto Protocol Annex 1 countries to comply with the protocol and EU companies to comply with their allowances under the EU emissions trading scheme.

The policy also states:

HSBC is committed to supporting the energy sector. It will work with clients who meet its sustainability standards and those who are making credible progress towards meeting them. In line with its own commitment to reduce greenhouse gases and combat climate change, HSBC will also encourage its clients to consider similar measures and proactively support clients moving towards cleaner technology.

Problems with implementing the Equator Principles

Industry experts have raised the point that using the size of investment as the criterion for applying the Equator Principles is unreliable, because a small project, with an investment of only US$10 or 50 million or less can still produce a major negative impact in a sensitive area or developing country. The Equator Principles are also not always applied in earnest. Due to their voluntary nature and the lack of a body for their enforcement, there are some banks that do not operate in accordance with the principles.

Moreover, the principles are capable of being deliberately evaded. For example, a powerful project developer could potentially raise funds from shareholders and use these for project start-up until work was completed, at which point they could secure limited recourse debt for ongoing financing. Equally, a project developer can seek an alternative source of financing (or this could be arranged by banks), such as bonds or similar financial instruments, or the bank can use an alternative investment method, such as providing a company loan direct to the company developing the project under the guarantee of the project developer. Alternatively, the project developer can also carve up a large project into smaller projects so that they fall under the US$10 million threshold.

If the principles were strictly applied, category A projects would find it hard to raise funds at all. Further, investment banks have only a limited influence on the projects they finance. Because it is difficult to intervene in the initial stages, investment banks normally come in once a project has already been settled.

Other countries' expectations of China

Following China's 'Going global' strategy, the country is fast becoming a major financer of large-scale development projects, with much of this financing concentrated in Southeast Asia, sub-Saharan Africa and Latin America. China's Africa strategy is the most representative example of this trend. Of the projects in which China is investing, a large proportion are in fields with a major environmental impact, such as the extractive industries (oil, natural gas and minerals) and large-scale basic infrastructure projects (including dams and electricity projects).

China's largest providers of capital include the policy banks and the commercial banks, in which the state retains a controlling share. Policy banks include the Export-Import Bank of China, the China Export and Credit Insurance Corporation, and the China Development Bank. By 2010, the Export-Import Bank of China and the China Export and Credit Insurance Corporation will have turned China into the world's largest supplier of export

> *To date, more than 40 major private banks,*
> *with a presence in more than 100 countries have*
> *committed to respect the Equator Principles.*
> *These banks together contribute more than*
> *80 per cent of the global market for*
> *project development financing*

credit. By that time, long-term loans supplied by the Export-Import Bank of China are expected to reach between US$40 billion and US$80 billion, while insurance provided by the China Export and Credit Insurance Corporation is expected to reach US$1.2 trillion. The Export-Import Bank of China has already become one of the three largest credit exporting organisations in the world, alongside the Japan Bank for International Cooperation and the Export-Import Bank of the United States.

The China Export and Credit Insurance Corporation provides a combination of medium- and long-term investment to high-risk clients. For the most part, the Corporation concentrates on countries with underdeveloped economies, in which management is fairly lax, such as the Sudan, Cuba, Angola, Nigeria, the Phillippines, Pakistan and Brazil. For the most part, beneficiary countries are of the opinion that the Chinese banks provide loans at low interest rates, and with rapid approval processes.

Violating banking and financial industry norms can expose Chinese financial institutions to pressure and serious consequences. This has occurred in a number of overseas investment projects.

- A number of Chinese financial institutions and companies have plans to develop palm oil plantations in central Borneo. These number 18 in all, with an average area of 100,000 hectares, though such development could be a threat to seven rivers in the country, including the Rajang river, as well as damaging the habitats of 200 bird species, 150 species of insect and amphibian and 100 mammal species.
- The China International Marine Containers (Group) Ltd is engaged in logging hardwood in Surinam to produce trays for use in their containers, and this is likely to have a negative impact on the local black community.
- At the beginning of the century, Jilin Provincial government invested in the lumber business in Surinam, but due to their lack of understanding of local forest and environmental protection laws, more than RMB70 million invested in equipment was squandered.
- China National Machinery Import and Export Corporation is investing US$3 billion in an iron ore mine, a port, railway and two dams in the Belinga Mountains in Gabon. This could have an impact on a conservation area home to western lowland gorillas and chimpanzees.

In 2006, the then World Bank president, Paul Wolfowitz, warned Chinese banks that they must comply with the Equator Principles, and that they cannot make the same mistakes in Africa that France and the United States did. In Africa, there are people speaking out who want to drive China out in the same way that India was driven out in the 1960s. Pollution and environmental damage could well become an important reason for such attitudes.

The modernisation of Chinese banks and financial institutions

For a long time, Chinese banks have paid insufficient attention to environmental and social issues, and a number of banks and high-level banking figures do not understand the link between banking and these issues, seeing them as problems for the State Environmental Protection Administration (SEPA) or the Ministry of Labour and Social Security (MOLSS). In 2001, the IFC took shares in the Nanjing City Commercial Bank (NCCB, now Bank of Nanjing). The first point to be raised by the IFC during discussions was the requirement that the NCCB produce an environmental protection charter in line with international standards, and institute environmental management systems. For a domestic bank, there is no doubt that this was a conceptual innovation. Not only did the IFC require the NCCB to provide the names of two bank officials responsible for environmental issues, they also provided these officials with specialist training. This is a vivid lesson for both the NCCB and China's other major banks.

Following reforms in China's financial system, banks have independent decision-making power over loan allocation, and decisions are made based on the profitability of the company concerned. As banks' investment policies

> *The then World Bank president,*
> *Paul Wolfowitz, warned Chinese banks that*
> *they must comply with the Equator Principles,*
> *and that they cannot make the same mistakes in*
> *Africa that France and the United States did*

are centred on financial risk and the company's ability to make effective use of loaned funds, it is very easy for banks to chase quick returns, and pay insufficient attention to China's national situation and natural resource, environmental and social challenges, and this can lead to poor investments.

At present, the credit policies of the Chinese financial industry pay insufficient attention to environmental and social safeguards. This must change, and for a number of reasons. Firstly, as independent corporate legal entities, banks' credit policies must obey the principles of sustainability and demonstrate a commitment to social responsibility, in the same way as other such entities do. To not follow such principles would be to expose the bank to brand and reputational risk in the event of an environmental or social problem. Secondly, if there are problems with the environmental or social safeguards used by an investment bank investing in a given project, environmental or social compensation must be paid, and this can create a bad loan. Problems arise, not just because the borrower may be unable to repay capital or pay interest, but because the bank as creditor (and those associated with the bank) will face rising costs which they must cover. Today, therefore, all successful banks around the world start from a principle of sustainability and pay great attention to environmental and social safeguards in their investment policies.

Starting from 2007, China is coming into line with international banking and financial standards, including transparency standards, and is starting to apply the Equator Principles. All of China's large banks are starting to increase the size of loans for environmental protection projects; they are actively working to reduce credit risk, make loans more socially useful and raise awareness of social responsibility among companies in order to protect the global environment and ensure harmony between different countries and peoples of the world.

Following China's entry into the WTO, increased contact with the international financial industry and the building of a modern banking industry, China must establish green investment policies and investment policies for sustainable development. The government should legislate on the basis of investment policies and bring auditing of investment budgets into the orbit of the legal system. Banks must set up green auditing mechanisms, and allocate responsibility to departments and specialist personnel for environmental and social protection, and thereby put in place green safeguards on investment. Banks should also put in place mechanisms for public accountability and periodic reporting. These measures are extremely important for the strengthening of risk management, increasing competitiveness in world financial markets, maintaining the good name of Chinese banks and promoting the harmonious and sustainable development of China's financial industry.

Negative impacts of domestic investment projects

There are several examples of the harmful impacts of investment projects in China. In the 1990s, with the closure of enterprises engaged in 15 polluting industries in the Huai river basin, the Agricultural Bank of China found itself unable to recoup more than RMB1 billion in loans.

In January 2005, SEPA announced the closure of 30 projects guilty of illegally starting construction, and with a combined investment of almost RMB118 billion. Among these was the Xiluodu hydroelectric station on the Jinsha river, with a total investment exceeding RMB44 billion, only a little less than that of the Three Gorges Project. The projects were suspended for lack of official approval of their environmental impact assessments. The suspension or cancelling of these large and super-large projects must have had a huge impact on the banks financing them.

The ADB Lingjintan hydropower project started contributing power to the grid on 26 December 1998 when the first generator was put into operation. The project was completed in January 2001 and was judged by the ABD to be a technical and economic success. However, because of lack of funds and because resettlement plans had not been completed, the project had a negative impact on those displaced during its construction (3,687 people were formally resettled, though another 6,100 people were also affected). Subsequent evaluation found that the incomes of 50 per cent of those resettled suffered due to lack of land or other means of gaining a livelihood, while only 8 per cent expressed satisfaction with the resettlement. The majority said that it was hard to re-establish a livelihood following resettlement, and most were dissatisfied with the compensation offered for this.

The first generator was installed in the ADB Mianhuatan hydropower project in July 2001. The project was completed in March 2003, when it was judged to be a technical and economic success. Those displaced by the project were resettled according to China's resettlement regulations and a resettlement plan approved by the ADB. A total of 39,393 people were affected by the project, of whom 36,640 lost land and 36,913 lost houses. Although those resettled expressed satisfaction with the new houses provided after resettlement, they expressed dissatisfaction with their ability to re-establish a livelihood, and believed this was not adequately catered for in the resettlement policy or compensation given.

Positive impacts of domestic investment projects

There are also a number of examples where the impacts have been positive. The WWF (the global conservation organisation) and HSBC Yangtze river programme was started in 2002, with RMB30 million provided by HSBC. The project selected three lakes along the central section of the Yangtze river and cut off from the river as demonstration areas – the Hong lake, Zhangdu lake and Tian'e Zhou. The objective of the project was to restore seasonal linkages between the lakes and the central section of the river, improve water quality and help 296 pilot fishing households to develop sustainable fishing methods. Following the combined efforts of the WWF and the local government, 1.5 million nets and poles formerly used to demarcate fishing areas on Hong lake have been decommissioned and water quality has improved. According to calculations, 34 types of waterfowl have returned to the lake and in great numbers. To date, a total of 450km^2 of wetlands have been rehabilitated, greatly exceeding the original target of 200km^2

over five years, while the establishment of ecological wetland industries has resulted in a two- to threefold increase in the incomes of local peasants. In addition, HSBC distributed free 'I Love the Mother Lake' environmental education textbooks to more than 100,000 students at 258 schools in Hong Lake City.

Between 2003 and 2006, the World Bank provided loan funding worth several hundreds of millions of dollars for nearly 20 projects in Chongqing, including construction of a water plant, a water treatment plant, a waste disposal plant, railway, expressway, flood-prevention dykes and small towns. In addition, the World Bank used this as a trial of the Equator Principles in China. Following the requirements of the principles, the World Bank established a project supervisory consultative committee, composed of

---

For a long time, Chinese banks have paid insufficient attention to environmental and social issues, and a number of banks and high-level banking figures do not understand the link between banking and these issues

---

NGOs, academics and professors, accountants, village-level cadres, retirees, etc, with the remit of inspecting, overseeing and providing feedback on the project. The committee was headed by a member of the Green Volunteer League of Chongqing and received guidance from an international engineering consultancy firm.

The committee was diligent in its work and carried out in-depth on site investigations *in situ* and with people concerned with the project, and organised a consultation meeting attended by members of the public to evaluate the social and environmental impacts of the project. During this process, the committee discovered a number of problems: destruction of forests and protected dinosaur remains, forcible relocation of residents, wanton filling in of wells and cutting off of drinking water supplies, lack of compensation for appropriated land, artificially low relocation fees, poor quality relocation housing with cracked walls and leaking roofs and delays of several years between the demolition of residents' old houses and

building of new ones, etc. All of these problems made life difficult for those relocated during the project, which generated dissatisfaction and some protest. The problems uncovered by the committee were reported to the local government and to the World Bank, following which they were dealt with, greatly reducing the negative impacts of the loan.

At the same time as bringing to light problems in the World Bank programme, the committee discovered a number of problems relating to an ADB project in the province, including the lack of consideration given to the opinions of the people being relocated over where they were relocated to and the type of accommodation, the provision of poor quality housing, and the inadequate provision of necessary facilities such as natural gas systems,

---

As banks' investment policies are centred on financial risk and the company's ability to make effective use of loaned funds, it is very easy for banks to chase quick returns, and pay insufficient attention to China's national situation and natural resource, environmental and social challenges

---

toilets, rubbish dumps, sewerage facilities and paved roads. To date, some people have still not been allocated housing. The committee reported these problems and suggested measures to be taken to resolve them, as well as recommending that supervision be included in the design phase of the project in order to prevent such problems.

The World Bank Nantai island (Fuzhou) project resulted in a conflict between the need to restore a local road and the protection of several hundred hectares of wetlands. Following two years of negotiations between the World Bank and the local government, the wetlands, which are of great ecological and economic importance, have been preserved.

Assessment of the ADB's Wenzhou (Zhejiang) Shanxi water control resettlement project and plan were good. A total of 37,199 people were affected by the project, and they were relocated to 123 places in 10 counties of Wenzhou City. The main reason for the success of the relocation programme was the high degree of participation in its formulation, as well as the fact that people were largely relocated from mountainous areas to the coastal plains, where living conditions are better. In addition, many people were moved out of agriculture during the relocation, freeing up land and space for immigrants. Today, of those affected by the project, 89 per cent have managed to re-establish their livelihood or have achieved higher incomes following relocation. Of those affected by the project, 89 per cent expressed satisfaction.

China's 'green credit' policy

In mid-July, the SEPA, the People's Bank of China (PBOC) and the China Banking Regulatory Commission (CBRC) issued the 'Opinions on implementing environmental protection policies and rules and preventing credit risks'. According to this regulation, environmental protection agencies at all levels must investigate, publicly report on and deal with projects in the following categories: those that have been constructed without prior approval and those for which approval bypassed the correct level of government administration; those in which environmental facilities were not installed at the time of construction or those constructed having failed to pass environmental checks. Financial institutions should act according to the rules set out by SEPA, and carry out strict management of loan evaluation, disbursement and supervision, and they should provide no financial support to projects which have not passed an environmental assessment or whose environmental facilities have not been checked and accepted. Financial institutions should rigorously control applications for working capital from enterprises listed by environmental authorities at all levels as falling into the following categories: those having exceeded pollution indicators or permitted total discharge volumes; those that have not acquired pollution permits in accordance with the law, or which have not complied with their permit; and those companies which have not completed specified governance tasks within a set timeframe.

It has been reported that in the first half of this year, SEPA and the PBOC shared environmental information on companies, including those in the PBOC's national credit database.

As stipulated by the opinions and the 'Trial measures for the disclosure of environmental information', environmental protection

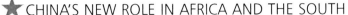
departments should provide financial institutions with the following information: results of evaluation of environmental impact assessment documents examined and results of the environmental assessment of finished projects; lists of enterprises discharging pollutants in excess of national or local standards, or whose total pollutant discharge exceeds control indicators established by local governments; lists of enterprises responsible for major environmental pollution accidents; lists of enterprises which refuse to comply with administrative penalties in force; enterprises which have received a warning, been required to mend their ways or been closed down; lists of environmentally friendly enterprises; appraisal of the environmental behaviour of enterprises; and other environmental supervision information as needed by the financial institutions.

The opinions also make specific demands of the PBOC, the bank supervision and management organisations, and the commercial banks: commercial banks have a duty to contribute environmental information to the national credit database, and this is to be overseen by branches of the PBOC at all levels. Banking regulatory bureaus at all levels should ensure that commercial banks refer to documents detailing companies' compliance

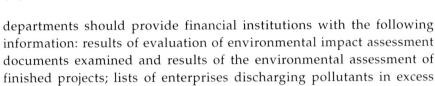

All of China's large banks are starting to increase the size of loans for environmental protection projects; they are actively working to reduce credit risk, make loans more socially useful and raise awareness of social responsibility among companies

with environmental law when making lending decisions and ensure that commercial banks work together with the environmental protection authorities to control the credit risk of polluting companies and bring them within the supervision system. Regulators should thoroughly investigate cases in which companies' poor environmental performance has led to bad loans. All commercial banks must place utmost importance on companies' compliance with environmental law when making lending decisions, and use control of credit to polluting enterprises as a means to fulfil their social responsibility and to avoid credit risk.

The opinions clearly specify the establishment of a meeting framework jointly chaired by both the environmental and financial regulatory bureaus, and that this should periodically convene coordination meetings for the exchange of information. The opinions also specify research into the establishment of environmental guidelines for credit management, the provision of training, and consulting on new environmental policies, laws and regulations in order to increase financial institutions' abilities to judge environmental risk. The opinions also specify investigation and punishment of commercial banks which lend to projects in breach of environmental regulations.

The CBRC must publicise to all commercial banks the list of enterprises blacklisted by SEPA and the list of all river basins that are subject to restrictions on development. The banks are required to rigorously control loans to these companies and for work in these areas. In addition, the CBRC should organise investigation into cases in which environmental violations by enterprises have resulted in bad loans. In areas in which it has not been possible to reach energy-saving and emissions reduction targets and in restricted river basins, the CBRC should guide the banks and financial institutions to adjust the loan structure. In areas in which it has been possible to reach these targets, the CBRC should encourage banks and financial institutions to further improve their credit services.

At the same time, the CBRC requires that banks and financial institutions strengthen their systems for evaluating enterprises in energy-intensive and highly polluting industries at all stages in the loan cycle, as well as periodically checking the final destination of investment funds, and attempting to make energy-saving, emissions-reduction and related loan work an important part of the performance evaluation of banks and financial institutions.

Figures show that by the end of May 2007, growth in medium- and long-term loans provided to the petroleum processing, coking, chemical and other high-energy and highly-polluting industries by the main financial institutions was down RMB52.7 billion year-on-year (or down 9 per cent from the end of 2006). However, in the first half of 2007, loans still grew by RMB150 million.

By the time the opinions were released, the PBOC had already received the names of more than 10,000 infringing enterprises, but because of the inadequacy of technical equipment used by the reporting environmental bureaus around the country, these lists of names did not include company identification codes and could not be processed by the bank's systems, meaning that it was impossible to identify the offending enterprises. This problem still awaits resolution.

At the same time, SEPA released the 'Guidelines on environmental assessment of companies applying for first stock market listing or refinancing listed companies', which extend to 36 months the period of examination for companies applying to list or to refinance using credit markets.

Following on from the green credit policy, SEPA has also been collaborating with the Ministry of Finance, the China Insurance Regulatory Commission, the China Securities Regulatory Commission and similar government departments in order to carry out policy research and experiments in green taxation, green insurance and green securities, and promoting these as they become ready. In addition, they have been setting laws and policies to progressively establish systems for green credit and environmental risk management, green risk investment, ecological funds, environmental financing tools, environmental insurance, environmental performance

The projects were suspended for lack of official approval of their environmental impact assessments. The suspension or cancelling of these large and super-large projects must have had a huge impact on the banks financing them

evaluation, environmental accounting and reporting for listed companies, etc. Financial industry experts have even suggested the establishment of a new system to more faithfully reflect the effectiveness of national savings, gross social credit and bank efficiency, based on environmental considerations.

The China Development Bank's environmental policy mandates that only projects included in SEPA approval lists are eligible for credit. The governor of China Development Bank, Chen Yuan, has said that the bank will from now on refuse credit to projects that violate international norms.

Starting in June 2007, the Shenzhen branch of the PBOC committed to periodically make public lists of names supplied by SEPA specifying environmentally sound and unsound companies, and to incorporate this information in their credit information systems used to evaluate loan applications and into the national credit database. The Shenzhen branch of the PBOC has already circulated notices to all financial institutions in the city requiring them to refuse credit to environmental offenders included in the database. Enterprises included on SEPA's list of offenders should be the subject of influence and control on the part of banks when they apply for funds or government support, when they bid for public procurement contracts, engage in import and export, renew their registration with the State Administration of Industry and Commerce, and list on stock exchanges. Financial institutions can make use of the national credit database to check companies' environmental status and from there adjust their lending behaviour and mitigate credit risk.

During the first two months of Shenzhen's credit information system, the Shenzhen Environmental Protection Administration had provided a list of names and information on 90 companies with exemplary environmental records and 82 offending companies. Of the latter, three companies have been subjected to administrative punishment for illegal polluting and one company has been punished for direct discharge of wastewater. Both of these companies have been ordered to correct their behaviour within a specified period. After the inclusion of these two companies in Shenzhen's credit information system, the city branch of the PBOC ordered that all loans to the companies be frozen – a total of more than RMB11 million and US$13.6 million. In order to regain their creditworthiness, the four companies have invested a total of RMB7.31 million and carried out comprehensive reforms.

Under Shanxi province's evaluation indicators, all financial institutions in the province have made environmental factors an important indicator used in loan applications. In July 2007, five enterprises had already been blacklisted by the Shanxi province branch of the Industrial and Commercial Bank of China (ICBC), and the Taiyuan branch of the Huaxia Bank refused a project loan worth several tens of millions of RMB for a coking plant. In the entire province, 50 enterprises have so far been denied loans as a result of the new practices.

According to incomplete statistics, following the implementation of the 'Stop credit, prevent pollution' programme, Shanxi province has closed down more than 1,200 enterprises and facilities of different types, has reduced electricity consumption by around 1 billion units, provincial transport by around 30 million tonnes, pollution fees by RMB1.55 billion and losses arising from bank loans by around RMB2.3 billion.

Rural credit cooperatives (RCCs) in Wuxi, Suzhou and similar locations are offering credit support to industry leaders and outstanding companies with sound financial means, saleable products and low levels of debt which meet environmental standards. At the same time, the RCCs are carrying out strict supervision of polluting companies lacking 'three waste' treatment facilities (waste gas, water and industrial residues), on the one hand urging them to join the government's integrated wastewater treatment system, while on the other establishing high-risk management methods, increasing credit guarantee measures, and decreasing loan risk. Regarding those enterprises that must be subject to strict government control and that must be shut down, the RCCs are resolute in withdrawing credit and in using legal means when necessary in order to guarantee the security of their loan capital.

Wujiang Rural Commercial Bank lending emphasises support for green agriculture, flax growing and other independent innovative industries, while stopping credit to small-scale chemical, printing and dyeing, and jet weaving enterprises. Rural cooperative financial institutions of Changzhou, Zhenjiang and such places have set entry conditions and withdrawal measures for enterprise loans in the chemical and textiles industries, in accordance with national industrial policy and specific government control measures applicable to the chemical industry, etc. The 'One infraction refusal system' applies to highly polluting industries and enterprises that do not pass environmental standards or which have a poor record. Highly polluting industries such as the chemical industry and smelting are to be refused loans, without exception. For those enterprises found to be polluting in contravention of regulations, loans will be recalled and they will be banned from receiving further credit. As soon as the Yixing Rural Cooperative Bank received the government's list of chemical companies to be closed, have their operations suspended, merged or made to switch industries, they acted forcefully, taking legal action against enterprises with bad loans, realising their assets, etc.

After the outbreak of blue-green algae in Lake Taihu, the Jiangsu Rural Credit Cooperative immediately released the 'Opinions on the work of credit guidance' for the implementation of environmental policy. Rural cooperative financial institutions in Wuxi, Suzhou and other places ringing Lake Taihu also instigated emergency forecasts.

In August and September, Jiangsu provincial government circulated the 'Opinions regarding financial institutions' guidance of the integrated clean-up of Lake Taihu of the Nanjing branch of the PBOC', according to which Jiangsu financial institutions should use multiple methods and channels to support the clean-up of pollution in Lake Taihu. The opinions require that all financial institutions support adjustment of the industrial structure and optimise their credit structure in order to achieve socially and economically beneficial results. As concerns major projects for prevention and control of water pollution and environmental rehabilitation, financial institutions should be actively involved in the early stages of planning and debate in order to understand the project's organisation and financing needs and to be able to provide integrated financing plans in a timely manner, and support

The China Banking Regulatory Commission
requires that banks and financial institutions
strengthen their systems for evaluating enterprises
in energy-intensive and highly polluting
industries at all stages in the loan cycle

increases in technological capacity. Pollution projects with a public benefit which comply with national industrial and credit policies, and are listed in national or provincial key support plans, should be supported through 'green credit channels' and should benefit from preferential interest rates and diversified financial products.

In the case of large-scale investment projects like the Yangtze-Taihu diversion, a variety of methods should be used to satisfy the financing needs of pollution control projects, including bank consortium loans, trusts, loans with toll fees as collateral, issuance of bills and securities, etc. In the case of smaller investment projects, such as the extension or building of wastewater treatment plants, laying of auxiliary pipe networks, construction of ecological screens, etc, methods such as grouped financing with standardised costs should be used. All financial institutions, especially the Jiangsu Bank, the Bank of Nanjing and the rural credit cooperatives should increase the coverage of their guaranteed small loans service, and make these available to peasants who have lost their land as a result of programmes for restoring farmlands to forest, lake and wetlands. Financial institutions should make use of their individual strengths to support projects that fulfil the relevant conditions and raise funds through multiple channels.

The opinions require that all financial institutions of Jiangsu province should do their utmost to support the clean up of Lake Taihu. Financial institutions should optimise their credit structure and increase support to high-tech, high-efficiency, resource-extensive and non-polluting industries. They should make it more difficult for industrial enterprises to get credit, weed out backward production capacity, promote the optimisation of the industrial structure in the Lake Taihu basin and put in place rigorous environmental evaluation systems.

Credit demands of projects that cannot pass environmental evaluations should be subject to the 'One infraction refusal system'. Banks should implement strict supervision systems following loan disbursement, and new loans should be refused to projects that do not reach environmental standards and do not improve within a specified time period. Those enterprises in the Lake Taihu basin which have been closed, merged, transformed or declared bankrupt should be rigorously checked, and appropriate credit policies should be instituted. Banks should support the policy of relocation of industry from cities to development zones, should encourage technical

The problems uncovered by the committee were reported to the local government and to the World Bank, following which they were dealt with, greatly reducing the negative impacts of the loan

upgrading and should give appropriate financial support to water treatment and separation systems and pollution reduction and elimination projects and treatment of non-point source pollution. They should withdraw credit from small-scale textile, printing and dyeing and chemical plants and other similar energy-intensive and polluting industries.

The opinions stress the pressing need to protect financial assets and to establish a reporting system containing information on the pollution status of enterprises. Environmental protection agencies at all levels should strengthen their working relationship with financial institutions, and provide information on enterprises' pollution emissions status to the local branch of the PBOC in a timely manner for input into the credit rating system and circulation to financial institutions, and systems should be instituted to report those enterprises that have ceased activity. Related government departments at all levels should set up and perfect information distribution platforms and circulate information on enterprises that have closed, merged, transformed or been declared bankrupt to financial institutions in a timely manner, allowing them to formulate relevant policies to deal with these.

Media and expert criticisms of the opinions

Following the release of the 'Opinions on implementing environmental protection policies and rules and preventing credit risks' by SEPA, the PBOC and the CBRC, media evaluations made a number of points, the first of which was that banks were to be commended for starting to marketise, after many years of effort and after long maintaining only a poor separation between their official and commercial functions.

After the stormy process of capital injection, restructuring and listing that Chinese banks have been going through, it is perhaps the incompleteness of recent reforms that has given rise to two problems, similar in the short term, but divergent in the long term. On the one hand, for listed banks, the effectiveness of corporate governance is mainly expressed in the share price, which becomes the most direct indicator for measuring managers' performance, with the result that high growth, high profits and high dividends basically become the sole objective of these banks. On the other hand, the highly monopolistic nature of the banking market in China and the high degree of control under which it operates, combined with an abundance of cheap capital and high demand make it easy for banks to achieve high returns. The greatest consternation arising from this is that not only do banks not perform the gatekeeper function they should in a market economy, but they also compete to invest cheap money in already overheated industries.

For example, fixed asset investment in aluminium smelting and similar industries recently rebounded. Meanwhile, as the rapid rise in China's trade surplus is closely related to the great growth in exports of electrolytic aluminium, steel and similar energy-intensive industries, this has the effect of worsening China's already loose money supply situation.

On the other hand, there is no shortage of places in which individual company taxes are of great importance to the locality. If the local government does not dare offend the enterprises, how can the banks? If the bank says 'No' and their formerly functioning loan suddenly becomes a bad debt, what happens then? What's the real legal authority of so-called 'opinions' from these three government departments? Are foreign-invested banks going to abide by them? And what about domestic banks? Are they going to be punished if they do not correctly implement the opinions?

A proportion of Chinese financial institutions undervalue future risk, and under these conditions it is hard to control their tendency to blindly provide credit. All in all, this makes macro adjustments, such as the green credit policy, hard to carry out. Such imperfectly commercial behaviour on the part of commercial banks should be nipped in the bud.

A number of points are made by industry experts. First, the Equator Principles are currently only applicable to project financing. While there

---

*Highly polluting industries such as
the chemical industry and smelting are to be
refused loans, without exception*

---

are a number of financial institutions that apply the principles to company financing and in other contexts, this practice has not been extended throughout the industry.

Secondly, in contrast to the voluntary nature of the Equator Principles, the opinions are a key policy document issued jointly by the banking industry management and supervisory institutions and are a form of governmental administrative intervention. The opinions, however, are mainly concerned with setting up systems allowing environmental agencies to report enterprises' compliance with environmental laws and regulations to banking institutions, but there are no regulations specifying the acceptable degree of financial institutions' exposure to project financing, concrete provisions for disciplining commercial banks, etc, and this is a weak point in the opinions.

Consequently, experts suggest the need to make the opinions more implementable and operational. Simply having the Equator Principles and green credit policy is not enough; there is also a need for supporting frameworks and measures to ensure their implementation. For example, first there is a need to legally require commercial banks to publicly disclose information on their investment projects in order to open this up to shareholder and public scrutiny. Second, a number of significant listed banks could publicly launch and sign voluntary green credit declarations, declaring to the public and to shareholders their promise to uphold their social responsibility, and thereby create a good image and reputation both domestically and internationally.

Third, banks and financial institutions pay insufficient attention to reports from the environmental agencies. These institutions should set up their own environmental and social protection departments and publicise their internal social and environmental policies and auditing systems, in addition to setting up databases and dossiers allowing tracking of all stages of a given project, from investment and construction to production, consumption and pollution discharge. In addition, the banks and financial institutions should expedite the setting up of industry-wide effective modern systems to tackle these concerns.

Fourth, a system for third-party authentification of corporate social responsibility in the banking industry should be set up, and industry standards such as the Equator Principles should be written into national law and specific regulations should be formulated to address the social responsibility of financial institutions, etc. Fifth, there is a need to speed up legislative action on the Government Investment Law, the Overseas Investment Law and the Interim Measures for Examining and Recording Enterprise Investment Projects, and to develop policies on issuance of green stocks and bonds and green industry funds and to develop green land, green tax, green pricing, and green industries and funds policies. Only in this way will it be possible to fully bring into play the green credit policy.

Participation and oversight by Chinese NGOs

In the last ten plus years, Chinese NGOs have developed significantly and made great progress, and they are increasingly becoming a third force, independent of government and enterprise and able to perform a supervisory role in reflecting the general public mood and opinion. This is apparent from the following examples.

At the beginning of the 1990s, environmental volunteers, Yang Yong and Yang Xin walked around 1,000km (along with the head of the Ertan branch of the China Construction Bank, Chen Lianyue, and another member of staff, Liao Guohong) to carry out two inspections of forest resources upstream from the Ertan hydropower plant on the Yalong river. The results of the investigation showed that from the start of large-scale logging in the 1960s, the forests upstream of the dam had been largely destroyed, and that the construction of a mechanical log pass in the dam, at great expense to the Ertan plant, would prove to be useless. Subsequently, related government departments convened a meeting to discuss the results of the investigation and decided to stop the logging (with an annual volume of 800,000m³) in the higher reaches of the Yalong river, and to stop the building of the log pass, with a saving of RMB300 million in construction fees. Those who took part in the investigation were awarded prizes for their work.

In 2001, the Chongqing Green Volunteers Union wrote to the city branch of the Industrial and Commercial Bank, calling on the bank not to provide loans for the construction of an environmentally destructive cableway on Jinshan mountain.

In June 2003, the Chongqing Green Volunteers Union called on the city government to halt renovation and extension of Chongqing's 300 MW Jiulongpo power plant and safeguard the city's air quality. In August, the project was discontinued for failing to pass SEPA's environmental impact assessment. As a result, the RMB20 million loan contract between the Pudong Development Bank (Shanghai) and the plant was dissolved, though the previous loan of several tens of millions of RMB, for laying foundations, underground pipes, etc, was effectively squandered.

The examples above show domestic NGOs starting to participate in or assume a supervisory role with regard to investment projects of the financial industry.

Chinese NGOs first found out about green credit at the Greater Mekong subregion summit of the Asian Development Bank, held in Phnom Penh in 2002. From then onwards, Chinese NGOs started to actively collaborate with Mekong basin NGOs in lobbying the ADB Greater Mekong subregion on sustainable development. In 2004, Green Watershed translated and officially published the 'Handbook on the environmental and social guidelines of the Japan Bank for International Cooperation' (JBIC), produced in collaboration with Mekong Watch (Japan). The book systematically sets out the environmental and social responsibilities of JBIC, alongside means of public supervision and complaint against the bank in case of need. At NGO meetings and training sessions following this, Green Watershed advocated for NGOs to pay more attention to the financial and banking industries. At the meeting of Chinese NGOs held in October 2006 by the All China Environmental Federation, Green Watershed took the opportunity to present an NGO perspective on green credit to domestic environmental NGOs.

In December 2006, Green Watershed, Friends of Nature, Mekong Watch and Oxfam Hong Kong jointly organised the China Finance, Environment and Harmonious Society conference in Beijing. This was the first international conference on green credit to be held in China, and gave Chinese government departments, NGOs and the academic world a chance to systematically understand this topic. The conference not only invited NGOs with many years of experience of lobbying banks about green credit to share their experience, but also invited the World Bank as representative of the multilateral banks, the JBIC as representative of the international import-export credit banks and Japan's Mizuho Bank as representative of commercial banks signed up to the Equator Principles and then chair of the Equator Principles.

At the meeting, the case was made that Chinese environmental NGOs' advocacy activities should be more broadly targeted. First, activities should include the domestically financed policy banks, foreign-funded banks with

---

Industry standards such as the Equator Principles should be written into national law and specific regulations should be formulated to address the social responsibility of financial institutions

---

activities in China, and the multilateral development banks, as the projects financed by these banks, and the impacts of these projects, are close at hand and easy to monitor. Second, the overseas investments of Chinese banks should be included. This implies the setting up of channels of communication between Chinese NGOs, international NGOs and NGOs in countries in which China invests in order to jointly monitor overseas investment, to make China's 'Going global' strategy more sustainable and to ensure that it contributes to the development of a more harmonious world.

NGOs should call on government to perfect investment auditing systems, while also calling on banks and the financial industry to actively take up their social responsibilities and help banks develop environmental and social policies to put limits on their own behaviour, as was the case with cooperation between Mekong Watch and the Japan bank for International Cooperation, whose environmental and social safeguards policy is a very good example.

Conclusions

Green credit policies, as well as advocacy for and promotion of these policies, have opened a window of activity for environmental NGOs. Improving investment evaluation procedures and banks' internal environmental and social safeguard policies is dependent on public supervision. In order to make this possible, not only should government and banks make available relevant environmental and social impact assessment information, but they should also create the necessary conditions, including information disclosure, necessary outlays and genuinely equal dialogue mechanisms. Second, capacity building for NGOs themselves is also sorely needed. Third, NGOs are relatively unfamiliar with the banking and financial industries. Advocacy around green credit not only requires a basic understanding of loan policies and programmes and risk management, but also requires an understanding of the macro development concepts that lie behind investment. It is especially important when overseas investment and diplomacy are interwoven (which greatly increases the complexity of issues) to understand environmental diplomacy and distinguish long-term strategic national interest and short-term realist calculations of national interest.

SINO-AFRICAN RELATIONS: NEW TRANSFORMATIONS AND CHALLENGES

XU WEIZHONG

China's relationship with Africa has changed over the past 50 years from the period when China was viewed as a supporter of Africa's independence movements. Xu Weizhong considers the challenges to implementing the shift to its current role and argues that careful management of the changing Sino-African relationship is crucial to its healthy development.

Wide-ranging Sino-African relations

At the beginning of 2006, the Chinese government published 'China's African Policy', which represents a milestone in Sino-African relations, symbolising a period of comprehensive development of relations between China and Africa. The policy offers a retrospective of friendly Sino-African relations and sets out China's views on the position and status of Africa. It also plans for a new era in Sino-African cooperation across a range of spheres, including the political, economic, cultural and social. The document makes clear that the Chinese government's point of departure is the basic interests of both the Chinese and African people. The Chinese government is working to establish and develop a new type of Sino-African cooperative relations built on political equality and mutual trust, win–win economic cooperation and reciprocal cultural cooperation, in order to further consolidate relations between China and Africa.

In recent years, Sino-African relations have been developing fast. As well as the release in early 2006 of 'China's African Policy', President Hu Jintao visited Morocco, Nigeria and Kenya in April. During these visits, President Hu advanced five proposals for the strengthening of Sino-African cooperation: strengthening mutual political confidence; expanding mutually beneficial economic activity; taking one another as cultural reference points; strengthening security cooperation; and close international coordination. In June, Premier Wen Jiabao carried out formal visits to Egypt, Ghana, Congo-Brazzaville, Angola, South Africa, Tanzania and Uganda. During his visits, Premier Wen signed implementation outlines for deepening strategic and cooperative relations with Egypt and South Africa, as well as issuing joint statements with the other five countries included in his visit. In addition, China signed a total of 71 agreements with the seven African countries,

---

Throughout their visits to Africa, President Hu and Premier Wen expressed the consistently high degree of importance the Chinese government and leadership attached to Africa

---

covering political, economic and trade ties and the construction of basic infrastructure, as well as agreements in the fields of culture, education and science and technology. Throughout their visits to Africa, President Hu and Premier Wen expressed the consistently high degree of importance the Chinese government and leadership attach to Africa and African relations and the important place occupied in China's foreign relations by the development of traditionally friendly and cooperative Sino-African relations.

According to statistics, between 2000 and 2007, more than 100 African leaders visited China, while Chinese leaders visited 35 African countries, giving impetus to the comprehensive development of Sino-African ties. In November 2006, the Third Ministerial Conference of the Forum on China–Africa Cooperation was convened in Beijing, at which both sides expressed their commitment to strengthening a 'new type of strategic partnership', while at a meeting of heads of state, President Hu put forward eight policy measures for the strengthening of Sino-African cooperation. The main themes of the conference were 'friendship, peace, cooperation and development', and the Conference passed the 'Declaration of the Beijing Summit of the Forum on China–Africa Cooperation' and the 'Forum on China–Africa Cooperation Beijing Action Plan (2007–2009)'. This meeting took place under changed conditions for China, Africa and the international community, lending it added significance and influence.

In 2007, Sino-African relations continued to deepen. Early in the year, President Hu paid state visits to eight African countries, in a trip that covered almost 40,000km and took in Cameroon, Liberia, Sudan, Zambia, Namibia, South Africa, Mozambique and the Seychelles. This African tour marked President Hu's first foreign visit in 2007 and was his third goodwill visit to Africa since taking up office, clearly showing the importance attached by China to developing relations with Africa. This visit served to consolidate the traditional ties of friendship between China and Africa, concretise the results of the Beijing summit, expand practical cooperation and advance the goal of shared development. As such, it represents an important chapter in the annals of Sino-African ties.

Economic and trade ties

Alongside the strengthening of political ties between China and Africa, economic and trade ties have been given a significant boost. According to statistics from Chinese Customs, in 1950 trade between China and Africa stood at only US$12.14 million. By 1990 and 2000, this figure had increased to US$935 million and US$10.6 billion, respectively. In 2005, the figure hit US$39.75 billion, making China Africa's third largest trading partner, while in 2006, total trade reached US$55.5 billion. Chinese products are reasonably priced and have brought benefits to African consumers, while breaking the stranglehold of Western countries' high-priced products in these markets. According to Ministry of Commerce figures, Chinese trade with Africa at present contributes around 20 per cent to Africa's economic growth, and it is estimated that by 2010 total bilateral trade will hit the US$100 billion mark. Rapid development of Sino-African trade has been accompanied by rapid development of Chinese investment in Africa. By the end of 2006, China had an accumulated total investment of US$11.7 billion in Africa, across many different industries, but with a particular focus on agricultural development, value-added manufacturing, transport, telecommunications, water conservancy, power generation and other basic infrastructure projects.

To date, China has signed trade agreements with 41 African countries, and has set up bilateral economic and trade mechanisms with 37 more. China has also signed bilateral accords for the promotion and protection of investment with 29 African countries as well as bilateral double-tax avoidance agreements and tax evasion prevention agreements with nine countries. Twenty-three African countries have granted China full market economy status. In addition, in the last 50 years, China has assisted Africa with a total of 900 projects. In the coming three years, China will assist Africa by building 30 hospitals, 100 rural schools, 30 malaria prevention centres and 10 agricultural demonstration centres. In addition, China will broaden the scope of its aid work in Africa, reduce and write-off debts, and open markets.

In the field of engineering contracting, in May and November of 2006, Chinese companies not only signed framework contracts worth US$6.25 billion for part construction of the East-West Algerian Highway, but also signed a contract worth US$8.3 billion for the modernisation of Nigeria's railway. These two projects are the largest ever won by Chinese companies on the international market, and are simultaneously the most high-tech and have the shortest timeframe of any large-scale Chinese international design and build contract projects to date.

On 4–5 November 2006, Chinese and African leaders and high-level representatives of the business community convened the second Conference of Chinese and African Entrepreneurs in Beijing. During the conference, the establishment of the China–Africa Joint Chamber of Commerce was officially announced and African governments and companies signed 14 contracts and agreements worth a total of US$1.9 billion with 11 Chinese companies. Projects range from basic infrastructure construction, telecommunications

---

Chinese citizens' understanding of Africa is relatively one-sided. Equally, African citizens' understanding of China is not well rounded

---

and equipment export to resource exploitation and financial insurance, to be carried out in a total of 11 countries, including Ethiopia, Egypt, South Africa, Nigeria, Kenya, Ghana, Zambia, Uganda, the Seychelles, Lesotho and Cape Verde.

The year 2007 saw the further development of Sino-African economic and trade ties, with the holding of the annual meeting of the governors of the African Development Bank group in Shanghai in May. The opening ceremony was attended by Wen Jiabao, China's premier, who also delivered a speech. Due to the importance attached to this meeting by both sides, this year it was the largest and of the highest standard ever, with more than 2,000 representatives of national and international organisations – more than three times the number of participants in 2006 – making it a milestone in the history of Sino-African economic relations.

On 26 June, the China–Africa Development Fund Company (hereafter, China–Africa Development Fund), financed and presided over by the China Development Bank, was inaugurated in Beijing, symbolising the increased deepening of Sino-African economic and trade relations. The China–Africa Development Fund is a specialist fund dedicated to support Chinese companies' establishment and development in Africa. The focus of the fund's activities is assisting companies intending to invest, or engage in economic and trade activities in Africa by taking shares in these companies and helping them overcome capital limitations, while at the same time helping them make effective investments and providing consultancy services to those companies intending to invest in Africa. The fund will have an important role in the economic and social development of African countries, continually helping them improve their basic infrastructure, basic industries, agriculture, manufacturing, etc.

Educational and cultural exchanges

In recent years, Sino-African social, cultural and educational exchange have seen breakthroughs of quantity, scale and form. China has always attached great importance to cultural cooperation with Africa. According to incomplete statistics, from 1955 to the end of 2005, China signed 65 cultural accords with African countries and 151 implementation plans, while more than 50 government cultural delegations have visited Africa and more than 160 African cultural groups have visited China. In recent years, Sino-African cultural and artistic exchange has increased in frequency. One example is the holding of the Meet in Beijing International Art Festival, at which Africa was the 'guest of honour continent'. Other examples have included the Chinese Cultural Tour of Africa, covering 11 countries, a China–Africa Youth Festival, as well as a television series entitled *The Road of Friendship*, shot to commemorate the 40th anniversary of Premier Zhou Enlai's visit to Africa.

China has already established educational exchange relations with more than 50 African countries. The Chinese government has also provided around 20,000 (person/time) government scholarships to 50 African countries. In the next five years, the number of overseas African students expected to receive Chinese government scholarships is expected to double from its current figure of 1,200. China has established a total of six Chinese cultural centres overseas, of which three are in Africa. A total of 26 African countries have become tourist destinations for Chinese people, while last year the number of Chinese people visiting Africa for private (i.e. not official) reasons was twice that of the preceding year. According to plans of the Forum on China–Africa Cooperation, the Chinese government will increase its involvement in Africa in fields such as human resources training and educational and health cooperation, thereby broadening and deepening the development of Sino-African ties.

Three changes in Sino-African relations

The release of Chinese government documents dealing with Africa and the holding of the Beijing Summit of the Forum on China–Africa Cooperation have provided powerful policy guidance and strengthened the 'platform for cooperation' between China and Africa, thereby favouring 'friendly and cooperative relations' and strengthening the 'new type of strategic partnership' between China and the African continent. The principles of 'enhancing friendship, treating each other as equals and extending mutual support and promoting common development' are bringing new impetus to Sino-African relations. The period following the closing of the Beijing Summit of the Forum on China–Africa Cooperation is a key time for the strengthening of Sino-African relations. The three largest challenges facing China in its relations with Africa are the three major transformations in Sino-African relations: a transformation from elite to mass diplomacy, from official to civilian diplomacy and from bilateral to multilateral ties.

The first transformation is the broadening of diplomacy from elite to mass activities. For a considerable period of time, Sino-African diplomacy has largely been constrained to elite figures from both sides, giving little scope for the participation of ordinary citizens in diplomatic processes. However, following the continued deepening of Sino-African ties, the increase in business activities of small and medium enterprises as well as businesspeople and traders in Africa and the increase in the numbers of ordinary Chinese citizens travelling to Africa, the influence of ordinary citizens on Sino-African relations is increasing.

For a variety of reasons, however, mutual understanding between ordinary Chinese and African citizens has remained at a relatively low level. For example, the channels through which Chinese citizens can acquire knowledge about Africa are relatively few, and Chinese citizens' understanding of Africa is relatively one-sided. Equally, African citizens' understanding of China is not well rounded. Taking a long-term view, insufficient understanding on both sides, and the distorted perspectives resulting from this are unfavourable to the development of Sino-African ties. If in the future, both

---

The government needs to introduce Chinese enterprises to current international norms in order to prevent the inappropriate behaviour of some enterprises having a negative influence on Sino-African economic and trade ties

---

China and Africa pay insufficient attention to 'mass diplomacy', and do not broaden their knowledge of one another's history, culture and customs, the danger is that cultural misunderstandings and a gulf between the citizens of both sides will develop, which could set back the continued development of Sino-African ties. For this reason, we should increase the degree of exchange between both sides and put in place a solid basis of popular support for the healthy development of Sino-African relations.

The second transformation is to extend Sino-African relations from official to civilian diplomacy. The fact that enterprises are playing an ever greater role in Sino-African relations is no longer disputed. Wu Bangguo, chairman of the National People's Congress, when visiting Africa this year, explicitly made the point that:

> We should make strengthening cooperation between enterprises the priority direction of Sino-African economic and trade cooperation. Enterprises make up the main body of the market and of investment, and they are also the main body of economic and trade cooperation. It is only with the full cooperation of enterprises that the full potential of Sino-African economic and trade cooperation can be fully realised.

Henceforth, with the enlargement of Sino-African cooperation, a large number of Chinese enterprises and individuals are travelling to Africa. However, due to differences in background, aims and concepts of management, a number of problems have arisen, with some people even being opposed to the continued deepening of economic and trade ties, due to a poor understanding of the nature of the new economic and trade cooperation that exists between the two regions. The Chinese government should therefore broaden its conception of diplomacy to include civilians in future. This should include inculcating respect for market rules, bringing into play the motivating power of enterprises and absorbing the advanced experience of foreign governments in dealing with enterprises. The government needs to introduce Chinese enterprises to current international norms in order to prevent the inappropriate behaviour of some enterprises having a negative influence on Sino-African economic and trade ties.

In addition, future exchanges between non-governmental organisations is likely to be more and more frequent. Africa is an area of intense NGO activity, and NGOs from all countries have done a lot of work in the continent in areas such as poverty alleviation, environmental protection and education. With the deepening of Sino-African relations, it is possible that more NGO members

---

Western countries have to recognise that China has proved perhaps more popular than them in Africa and they envy the successes achieved in Sino-African relations

---

and volunteers will take part in Sino-African exchange. In this scenario, the Chinese government needs to think about how to incorporate NGOs into its diplomatic position, and how better to develop the effectiveness of NGOs in bilateral relations. In fact, the activities of Chinese NGOs, volunteers and charitable organisations are becoming stronger and stronger. For example, China has been carrying out aid activities in Ethiopia, providing voluntary assistance to Ethiopian youth volunteers in studying Chinese, computer and network education, agricultural and herding skills, health and hygiene and industrial techniques. This is a pioneering programme in the area of Chinese volunteering. In May 2007, the China Foundation for Poverty Alleviation's 'Action 120 for the Safety of Mother and Baby' programme included, alongside the plan for assistance to impoverished mothers and babies in Tibetan areas one for assistance to mothers and babies in impoverished areas in Africa. In the course of this project, the China Foundation for Poverty Alleviation and Care action Macau donated RMB6 million worth of goods to Guinea-Bissau.

The third transformation is to extend Sino-African relations from bilateral ties (those involving Chinese and African participation only) to multilateral diplomacy. For a long time, Western countries have paid very little attention to Sino-African relations; however, this has changed in the last two to three years, especially with the holding of the Beijing Summit of the Forum on China–Africa Cooperation. Now Sino-African relations have become a very hot topic in the West and China's diplomacy towards Africa has been increasingly coming under the spotlight of Western scholars and politicians. On the one hand, the increased attention of Western countries to Sino-African relations stems from an anxiety that these could damage Western interests in Africa; it is seen as important to be on guard amid fears of the threat of a rising China. On the other hand, Western countries have to recognise that China has proved perhaps more popular than them in Africa and they envy the successes achieved in Sino-African relations. They wish to strengthen cooperation with China on African issues in an attempt to bring China into the Western orbit and make China play by the West's rules and share the costs of work in Africa. In fact, a number of Western experts already see Sino-African relations as a touchstone of future relations between China and the world.

Opportunities provided be these changes

In light of the above, Sino-African diplomacy should be broadened from bilateral diplomacy to multilateral diplomacy; China should strengthen multilateral cooperation with Western countries and with the UN agencies on African issues. Although Sino-African relations should not be completely within the Western orbit, China should neither exclude third parties. The Chinese government should think about how to make Western countries better understand its policies towards Africa, while the Chinese government should also study the good methods used by Western countries in dealing with Africa – there are obviously lessons to be learned from Western experience. It is only in these ways that the space for dialogue on African issues between China and Western countries can be expanded. In fact, the opportunities for cooperation between China and Western countries on African issues are considerable. For example, in future projects in Africa,

say in poverty alleviation, a cooperative model could be employed in which Western countries contribute more in funding, while China contributes more in people. In ways such as this, cooperation can be strengthened.

China can adopt a more open attitude towards other big powers and international organisations on African issues, thereby creating greater scope for cooperation for the benefit of all parties. In recent years, with the high-speed and continued development of the economy, China has increasingly been cooperating with a range of international organisations. In May 2004, the World Bank organised the Shanghai Conference on Poverty Reduction, which was run by the Chinese government. China's Premier Wen Jiabao attended the opening ceremony and gave an address. This was a high-level and large-scale international meeting focusing on global poverty reduction, the objectives of which were to exchange international poverty reduction experience, bring forward new poverty reduction measures, mobilise international development finance and the overall development of global poverty alleviation efforts. This meeting demonstrates the willingness of the Chinese government to engage more actively in multilateral cooperation for poverty alleviation. The China–Africa Joint Chamber of Commerce was set

---

In future projects in Africa, say in poverty alleviation, a cooperative model could be employed in which Western countries contribute more in funding, while China contributes more in people

---

up in 2005 with the support of UNDP for the purpose of encouraging Sino-African economic and trade activity. It has offices in a number of African countries, including Nigeria, Ghana, Tanzania, Mozambique, Cameroon and Kenya. A number of Western organisations are currently in contact with relevant Chinese government agencies and are preparing to establish greater cooperation with them in several fields of work in Africa.

The three major transformations currently facing Sino-African relations are a source of opportunity for greater development, but also pose challenges. Therefore, as well as effectively carrying out the work arising from the Beijing Summit of the Forum on China–Africa Cooperation, the Chinese government should strengthen the education of Chinese citizens and meet the need for greater mass, and civilian, diplomacy. To achieve this, China needs to strengthen cooperation with the African media and also strengthen educational cooperation with African countries. In this way it will increase mutual sympathies and through greater media and educational exchange take Sino-African mutual understanding to a new level. In the process of extension

Giving play to the positive role of NGOs and volunteers will give life to Sino-African relations

from official to civilian diplomacy, it is necessary to strengthen external economic legislation and to guide the behaviour of Chinese enterprises and individuals in Africa, thereby promoting the healthy development of Sino-African relations. At the same time, giving play to the positive role of NGOs and volunteers will give life to Sino-African relations.

In the process of transformation from bilateral to multilateral diplomacy, China and Western countries should increase their mutual understanding and cooperation on African issues. One Western scholar has pointed out that China and Western countries competing to increase investment in, trade with, and aid to, Africa is a good thing, but an even better thing would be for both parties to cooperate on these issues. The 21st century will be a period of great development of Sino-African relations, but it will also throw up considerable challenges. However, if China can successfully manage these three major transformations, then it will be possible to develop a new type of healthy and stable Sino-African strategic partnership.

THE ROLE AND IMPACT OF CHINESE ECONOMIC OPERATIONS IN AFRICA

DOT KEET

Civil society organisations are beginning to ask critical questions about the effects of Chinese enterprises operating in Africa. What are China's real intentions in Africa and how do China's economic operations in Africa differ from those of the imperialist West?

China's activities in Africa

Evidence and information is gradually accumulating in Africa of the full extent of China's interest in the continent. China's growing role is not only evident in its export penetration of African markets (as elsewhere in the world) but also in many other sectors such as the following:

- Domestic consumer commerce, that is in the wholesale trade through large-scale Chinese importers and suppliers located within Africa, and in the retail trade, through the growing presence of small Chinese traders, street vendors, etc
- Extractive mining, focused mainly on fuel supplies, above all oil (and coal-to-fuel technology from South Africa) and uranium, and in industrial minerals such as platinum, chrome, manganese, cobalt, nickel, tin, lead, zinc, copper
- Construction, such as in large-scale infrastructural projects, including roads, railways, dams, hydro-schemes and power lines, and major social projects, such as public housing, hospitals, clinics, schools and sports stadiums
- Capital equipment supply, including large-scale heavy construction machinery and transport equipment, and information and communication equipment
- Production, that is in some agricultural projects especially in basic food

crops, which is expected to increase, and the start of some processing related to minerals, which is promised to increase
- Finance, including large-scale interest-free grants to governments and parastatal bodies, and concessional or 'soft' loans attached to many of the above projects.

There are also some Chinese projects in Africa that combine many of these areas in complex integrated projects on a very large scale (such as in Gabon). Others operate in special economic zones set up for them by African governments (for example in Zambia).

Chinese organisations

Further research is needed on the precise nature of the Chinese entities that operate in Africa. This is complicated by the fact that most governments in Africa are not open and transparent about their international economic relations and investment agreements. The Chinese government and economy are similarly, or even more, opaque and difficult to access and assess.

Many questions face analysts in Africa who are concerned about the current methods and aims of the Chinese government in Africa and what the 'accountability' of Chinese enterprises might be. Such questions relate to whether:

- These companies are independent private enterprises operating on the same bases as their counterparts in the 'West', and which can therefore be expected to operate on the same straight 'profitability' criteria in Africa
- These are private companies but heavily subsidised by national (or provincial) governments in China, which therefore gives them important competitive advantages over African companies
- Apparently 'independent' enterprises are, in fact, directly supported and assisted in their operations abroad by Beijing through political accords and through 'tied' financial agreements with African governments
- Some are semi-state or state enterprises that are not only backed by the Chinese government but could, in significant ways, be potentially accountable to political/economic directives, conditionalities and requirements set by the Chinese authorities.

Given the very active, one might even say directive, role of the Chinese authorities in their own domestic economy, these points, particularly the last, could be significant. The significance relates to the degree to which, or even whether, it is strategically worthwhile and feasible for African activists to engage with African governments, separately or together through the African Union (AU), and with other continental African bodies (such as the African Development Bank – AfDB), in order to approach the Chinese authorities to influence or determine the nature of, and criteria for, Chinese company operations within Africa

The effects of Chinese activities

Civil society organisations – and even some governments – are beginning to ask critical questions about the effects on Africa of such Chinese activities in Africa. The main questions and criticisms concern:

- Commerce – where Chinese imports and Chinese traders on the ground are ousting small local traders, which is, in turn, resulting in pronounced anti-Chinese feelings or xenophobia
- Mining – where little attention is given to health and safety standards and workers rights, or to damaging pollution of neighbouring communities,[1] and broader environmental effects
- Forestry – where vast extractive operations of precious woods and timber are being carried out by Chinese companies with no local processing and with highly destructive effects
- Construction – where many such projects rely on imported Chinese workers, skilled and unskilled, and therefore do not create much local employment and do not transfer production/management skills
- Capital equipment supplies being brought in from China – which therefore exclude possible local suppliers – and, being subsidised in China, discourages the local production of capital goods
- Manufactured goods – which are flooding into African markets and displacing small, and even relatively larger producers that do not enjoy the (direct and indirect) subsidies that Chinese industries receive from their authorities.

Questions also need to be asked about financial flows from China to Africa.

These flows take various forms:

- Enterprise investment in the above projects, which raise questions about the capital transfer rights back to China attached to such investments. How will the growing scale of such investments affect African countries' international reserves and financial security and stability?
- Unconditional government grants given to unaccountable and even corrupt governments, which will strengthen such governments, reinforce these characteristics and help to entrench such abusive or authoritarian regimes in power
- 'Soft' loans, provided to these governments or attached to projects, as above, which will over time inevitably accumulate into growing African indebtedness to the Chinese government and Chinese banks, repeating the patterns of indebtedness that were previously created by Western governments and banks.

What are China's intentions?

In the light of this, fundamental questions are being posed about the so-called partnership and 'brotherly' relationships declared between the Chinese and African governments, as in the Forum on China–Africa Cooperation (FOCAC) in Beijing in November 2006. Looking past the formal declarations and South–South rhetoric, the overriding question is whether the rapidly growing role of China in Africa is one of partnership and cooperation, or more akin to colonial or neocolonial patterns, or reflective of a new imperialism. Alternatively, is China trying to contribute towards new South–South tactical and strategic alliances with regard to the North?

The first point is that, whatever good intentions the Chinese government may say it has, the objective and fundamental problem is that these relations are based upon highly uneven levels of development and a very different capacity to benefit from such interactions and cooperation. This pronounced inequality will result in China making very much greater gains from what it obtains from Africa, even *if* this is undertaken 'fairly' and with some generous gestures. Africa may indeed receive (some) quantitative returns, but it is China that will achieve the further vast qualitative transformation of its economy, using the material and financial resources it gains from Africa.

There cannot be genuine win–win development scenarios in such a situation. These grossly uneven gains are not necessarily the result of deliberate bad intentions but are intrinsic to relations between such very uneven 'partners', unless deliberate efforts are made to compensate for such very different situations and capacities, to consciously counter the unbalanced effects, and to conscientiously avoid (or undo) damaging social and environmental impacts.

In the political sphere, major problems reside in Beijing's assurance that it does not interfere in the internal affairs of other countries. This, of course, means that it does not concern itself with the nature of the governments with which it enters into large-scale economic and 'aid' relations. But this by

Most governments in Africa are not open and transparent about their international economic relations and investment agreements. The Chinese government and economy are similarly, or even more, opaque and difficult to access and assess

itself constitutes an 'interference' in the internal affairs of African countries through the financial and other support provided to highly questionable regimes, thus helping them to entrench themselves in power. Without the full democratisation of African countries, the kind of domestic role that civil society organisations want their governments to play, and the kind of 'developmental' proposals that they want their governments to put to the Chinese authorities (see below) will be prevented.

Other questions must be posed about China's perceptions of Africa and the location of Africa within its own geo-economic and geopolitical strategies, and in relation to the powers of the North. This is posed particularly clearly with regard to China's role in the World Trade Organisation, especially within the G20 and the G33 groupings of developing countries. Both groupings reflect tactical alliances of resistance against the majors, but they also reflect differing economic/social interests and strategies vis-à vis the North within and between the respective groupings/countries.

The major question is why China has identified with both these groupings, even though not very actively and certainly not in any leadership roles. Such positioning by Beijing may reflect not only China's specific economic interests and international aims – which all the world is focusing on – but also some possible emerging geopolitical positioning with the rest of the South in relation to the interests of the North. The question is whether this represents mere tactical positioning to gain political allies in the South in what are bound to become increasing rivalries between China and the older industrialised economies in new versions of wider inter-imperialist rivalries. The alternative question is whether this could be used to the advantage of the South in general, and how civil society organisations can intervene and influence this geopolitical potential, if at all?

It is similarly important to obtain some insights into China's role in relation to the G77 in the UN. For a start why does China insist on the 'G77 plus China' designation rather than simply joining the G77? Also, of course, have China's role and veto powers in the Security Council been used in ways that reflect concerns to politically support Africa or other countries of the South? Such analyses would inform a more nuanced perception of China's positioning and political role in the world today as a purported emerging super-power. It is not only its economic interests and role that are important.

Developmental challenges by civil society

The political and economic dimensions go together. The Chinese political authorities have to be challenged about their practice in political and essential human rights and social issues, abroad as at home. There are also, however, developmental demands that independent African analysts need to make of African governments, and that official African institutions have to present to the Chinese authorities. These relate to the economic, environmental, and social terms and conditions under which Chinese companies operate in Africa.

During the 'development era' of the 1960s and 1970s the common demand from development analysts and activists was that Western foreign investors in the Third World should include some significant undertakings that would increase the 'gains' from their investment for the host countries, and minimise or reduce the losses or negative effects. The investment conditions that were applied by many Third World governments in various combinations included:

- Defined durations for such investment projects
- Agreed reinvestment of (a proportion of) profits, for defined periods
- Agreed return of foreign exchange earnings from exports from the host country

- Payment of company and other taxes, and appropriate royalties
- Limitations on the geographical areas/zones and spheres open to foreign investment
- A defined proportion of shares to be held by the host government and/or local shareholders
- Joint ventures or partnerships with local enterprises and/or parastatal bodies
- A defined proportion of production inputs, and services, to be acquired from local companies
- Payment of import taxes on equipment and other imported production inputs
- Transfer of technology with accompanying training and maintenance/services capacities
- Employment of local management and active transfer of management skills
- Employment of local technicians and active skills transfers
- Employment creation for local labour, and active skills development
- Observance of specified wage rates, health and safety regulations.

The much weaker – or non-existent – requirement that foreign investors observe full trade union organisational and collective bargaining rights, at best reflected the frequently paternalistic and substitutionist nature of many of the 'developmental' governments of the time; or in some cases their active suppression of such rights. Similarly, the almost total silence on the observance of gender rights and appropriate environmental regulations also reflected the shortcomings of the development paradigm of that era. Overall, the terms of the development paradigm sought to 'improve' the benefits of

---

'Soft' loans … will over time inevitably accumulate into growing African indebtedness to the Chinese government and Chinese banks, repeating the patterns of indebtedness that were previously created by Western governments and banks

---

foreign investment in Africa, as in other Third World countries, but those terms could not fundamentally substitute for internally generated capacities and resources. Some African governments saw these foreign investment policies and terms as providing an interim basis for industrial take off in their countries, although, in practice, the major gains still accrued to the foreign investors and their home economies.

Nonetheless, even those regulatory investment conditions that some of the more determined African governments (such as Tanzania) implemented have been largely swept away in recent decades under the International Monetary Fund and World Bank structural adjustment programmes (SAPs) imposed in most African countries. This onslaught has also been reinforced by various World Trade Organisation trade and trade-related agreements,

---

Africa may indeed receive (some) quantitative returns, but it is China that will achieve the further vast qualitative transformation of its economy, using the material and financial resources it gains from Africa

---

and through the even more demanding liberalisation terms within bilateral trade and investment treaties between African governments and the home governments of the major international investors. These, together, are central to the neoliberal counter-offensive that has displaced the so-called development partnerships of earlier decades, limited and inadequate though those were.

However, a very important 'test' question to be put to Chinese investors and to the Chinese government is whether they accept that it would be justifiable for African governments to require the above terms and conditions of them, and whether they would be prepared to agree, instruct and require all Chinese projects and investments in Africa to abide by all these terms. In this scenario, much will depend, of course, on the will and capacity of African governments, supported by institutions such as the AfDB and the United Nations Economic Commission for Africa (UN-ECA), to establish and to monitor such terms. Without them, African governments and countries will simply be exchanging one set of long-standing Western neocolonial

'partners' for a new set of South 'partners'.

If, indeed, these new partners from the South are, or intend to be, different to the established masters from the North, then the question to be put by African civil society organisations to African governments and, through them, to the Chinese authorities, is whether Beijing will accept and actively commit to all these very reasonable developmental terms. Failing this, the further question must then be asked: How do China's economic operations in Africa differ from those of the imperialist West?

These issues also pose a significant challenge to emerging Chinese civil society. However, this is not just about their responsibility to and solidarity with their counterparts in Africa – important though that is. It is also about their responsibility to themselves and their own people. The terms and conditions posed within the development paradigm of earlier years – and now being revived in many debates in the South – can be posed, just as importantly, within China itself. These questions have to be asked about China's own economy, about the damaging effects and impacts of international investors in China, and about the regulatory terms and developmental conditions that the Chinese authorities should be presenting to internal and international corporations operating within China.

The author wrote this paper in her capacity as a fellow of the Transnational Institute and as part of TNI's Asia Programme <www.tni.org>.

Note
1 The very neo liberal government in Zambia was even recently forced to close down a Chinese manganese mining operation in that country owing to the outrageous pollution in the neighbouring community.

FRIENDS AND INTERESTS: CHINA'S DISTINCTIVE LINKS WITH AFRICA

BARRY SAUTMAN AND YAN HAIRONG

China's expanded links to Africa have created much debate on how to characterise those ties. Western political forces and media have criticised every aspect of China's activities in Africa, while the Chinese, with significant support from Africans, have mounted a spirited defence. Barry Sautman and Yan Hairong examine two sets of factors that make distinctive China's links with Africa: the Chinese model and Beijing consensus, and aid and migration. They argue that distinctive aspects of China's links with Africa make the People's Republic of China seem a lesser evil than the West on key issues in Africa's development and African dignity.

Between countries, there are no friends, only interests.
Senegalese President Abodoulaye Wade, paraphrasing Lord Palmerston, in a 2005 letter to President Chen Shui-bian, announcing Senegal's de-recognition of Taiwan and establishment of diplomatic relations with China (Chang and Ko 2005).[1]

China has no friends, only interests.
African diplomat, commenting on President Hu Jintao's 2004 visit to oil-rich Gabon (Cheng 2004: 5)

Introduction

A remarkable and telling exchange on Chinese policies in Africa occurred in 2006 between the United States Council on Foreign Relations (CFR) and the Chinese government. A CFR report on enhancing US influence in Africa devoted a chapter to the People's Republic of China. It charged that China protects 'rogue states' like Zimbabwe and Sudan, deploys its influence to counter Western pressures on African states to improve human rights and governance, and unfairly competes with US firms in contract bids in Africa (CFR 2006: 49–52). These same points have been made by veteran critics of China in the US Congress and US analysts who see China as a competitor (Smith 2005; Eisenman and Kurlantzick 2006).[2]

China's elites have long regarded the CFR as a 'superpower brain-trust' and 'invisible government' shaping the US global role (Shambaugh 1993: 195–197). They responded in a paper that argued that China has a 'strategic partnership with Africa that features political equality and mutual trust, economic win–win cooperation and cultural exchange' (PRCMOFA 2006).

China's practice then of supporting developing state initiatives and giving aid that did not enrich elites still resonates with Africans today, even though, since the 1990s, China's activism on behalf of developing states has waned and much of what it does in Africa is now profit-centred

---

The paper backed Africa's desire for a more democratic international order and detailed the aid activities of the Forum on China–Africa Cooperation (FOCAC), which convened African and Chinese ministers in Beijing in 2000, Addis Ababa in 2003, and Beijing again in 2006 (see UN 2003; Liu 2004).

The CFR report and China's paper present single-minded visions. One Western stock idea is that China practices neocolonialism in Africa (Norberg 2006). The CFR paper fosters this notion by presenting China's actions as deleterious to African interests in ways that it does not acknowledge with regard to the West: it singles out China's activities as uniquely supportive of illiberal regimes and harmful to the environment through purchases of illegal African timber. Elsewhere, China is accused of especially promoting corruption in Africa and trade that damages African anti-poverty efforts (Lyman 2005; Widdershoven 2004). Western powers, however, have long supported authoritarian regimes in Africa, as does Taiwan with states that recognise it, rather than the People's Republic of China (AC 2005; Kaplan 2005).[3] The most-praised African US ally, Yoweri Museveni, for example, incarnates 'competitive authoritarianism', having tried his main opponent for rape and treason and changed the constitution to stay in office after 20 years as Uganda's president (*Economist* 2006; Levitsky 2002). China's support for Zimbabwe and Sudan is much discussed in the West (Mawdsley 2007).[4] Less is said about US support for authoritarian African states, especially oil producers such as Gabon, Angola, Chad and Equatorial Guinea (Peel 2003; Max 1997). That support extends to Sudan, through intelligence and other military cooperation (*Economist* 2005; Hari 2005).[5]

There is no indication African regimes have become more corrupt since China's presence began to rise around 2000 (Goldstein 2006: 53). Both China and the European Union (EU) buy much illegal African timber and Western drug firms engage in bio-piracy in Africa.[6] Chinese exports compete with African exports almost solely in textiles and clothing (Kurlantzick 2006).[7] China supplies most of the cloth African firms need to compete in their main market, the US. Some 60 per cent of China's exports, moreover, are produced by foreign-owned firms. Cheap China-made household goods brought to Africa by Chinese and Africans do inhibit light industry formation and may harm the poor as potential producers; yet, machinery, electronic equipment and 'high- and new-tech products' made up nearly half China's 2005 exports to Africa (Barboza 2006; XH 2006a).[8] Chinese goods are much cheaper than Western imports and many local products, benefiting the poor as consumers. Only seven sub-Saharan states receive a significant share (5–14 per cent) of their imports from China (Edwards and Jenkins 2005; Kennan and Stevens 2005). African industrialisation was already severely damaged by Western imports following imposition in the 1980s and 1990s of World Bank/ International Monetary Fund (IMF) structural adjustment programmes (SAPs) (Melamed 2005; Woods 2006: 141–178).

The CFR report is representative of the common Western moral binary in discourses of China's Africa policies, exemplified by a German foundation's ad for its panel on 'China in Africa' at the NGO forum of the World Trade Organisation (WTO) 2005 ministerial meeting. It queried:

Are China–Africa trade investment relations following a pattern of South–South cooperation, guided by development needs of both sides? Or are [they] just replications of the classical North–South model, where Africa's hope of building a manufacturing sector gets another beating? Will the Chinese 'no political strings attached' approach help the African development state regain posture or is it a recipe for closed-door business with autocrats to get a competitive edge over Western economic interests (FES 2005).

In its own paper, China presented it policies as unlike the West's ignoring of African aspirations for a more equitable international distribution of wealth and power. It eschewed, however, the obligation of states to indicate the rights of especially oppressed people. The paper also indicated China will follow the West's path of forging bilateral free trade agreements (FTAs) in Africa that go beyond WTO requirements in opening developing states to higher levels of penetration by overwhelming external economic forces (see Draper and le Pere 2005; Cockayne 2005).[9]

This paper focuses on two sets of China–Africa links that contrast with what the West has had on offer through the Washington consensus and post-Washington consensus, which adds to Washington-consensus neoliberalism a discourse of democracy, good governance, and poverty reduction (Fine and Jomo 2005). These links make China soft power a lodestone for African elites, including 1) a 'Chinese model of development' and a 'Beijing consensus' that supposedly takes seriously developing state aspirations ignored by the West and 2) China–Africa aid and migration policies which, unlike those of the West, many Africans see as not exclusively serving foreign and elite interests.

These distinctive links stem from China's semi-colonial and socialist legacies and developing country status, as well as from its late entry into Africa as a resource-seeking state, in the midst of a decades-long decline in African fortunes associated with Washington consensus privatisation,

---

Chinese bids for resources fare well because they are packaged with investments and infrastructure loans typically at zero or near-zero interest. Such loans are often repaid in natural resources, if they are not entirely cancelled

---

liberalisation, deregulation, and austerity policies (Teunissen and Akkerman 2004; Ahmed 2004; Broad 2004). Chinese leaders are usually depicted as having an instrumental approach to dealings with foreigners and are said to have interests, but no friends abroad (Lorenz 2005). The distinctive features of its links with Africa, however, often position China as a perceived lesser evil among powers that interact with the continent, a perception that may allow Chinese leaders to make good on their claim to have Africans among their 'all-weather friends' (Liu 2005).

China's Africa policies should not be reduced to either 'China is the best' or 'China is just like the rest.' China is now a trade-driven industrial power integrated into the world system and practices a realpolitik of aggrandising national wealth and power (Guang 2005). It implements a 'neoliberalism with Chinese characteristics' (Harvey 2005: 120–151). China thus increasingly replicates in key ways longstanding developed-state policies in Africa of disadvantageous terms of trade, exploitation of natural resources, oppressive labour regimes, and support for authoritarian rulers. The commonalities of Chinese and Western approaches are now fundamental, but important distinctions also exist.

The 'Chinese model' in context

Before the 1990s, China's Africa policy was purely political: China fostered anti-colonial and post-colonial solidarity (Hutchinson 1976). Such efforts were repaid through African states' recognition of China (Nwugo 1977). The symbol of China–Africa links from the 1960s to 1980s was the Tanzania–Zambia railway (Tazara) built by 50,000 Chinese (Hall and Peyman 1976; Monson 2004–2005). China's practice then of supporting developing state initiatives and giving aid that did not enrich elites still resonates with Africans today, even though, since the 1990s, China's activism on behalf of developing states has waned and much of what it does in Africa is now profit-centred (Chen 2001; Alden 2005).

Post-colonial Africa is often understood as burdened by civil wars, epidemics, and venal regimes that aggravate endemic poverty, a perception that led to a post-Cold War Afro-pessimism or even Afrophobia and to Africa's downgrading as a concern for developed world policymakers and investors (Rieff 1998; *Economist* 1997; Andreasson 2005). In part because of China's increased presence which, over the 1990s, saw China–Africa trade grow by 700 per cent, Western leaders began to again give attention to the continent. Yet, even as China's activities compete with British, French and US interests, many Africans still find Africa remains in many respects invisible, especially to the US (Jaffer 2004; Pan 2006). That is so even though it is the second largest continent and has the fastest-growing population:

with 900 million people in 2005, less than a seventh of the world's people, it is projected to have nearly a quarter of global population by 2050. Africa's economy may double in a generation (*EH* 2005; Dyer 2007).

Africa is the most resource-laden continent, with every primary product required for industry, including 10 million (m) of the globe's 84m barrels per day (bpd) oil production in 2005. Most is light, sweet, highly profitable crude and much is off-shore, away from politics. Some 85 per cent of new oil reserves found in 2001–04 were on west/central African coasts. Strong competition for African oil exists because 90 per cent of the world's untapped conventional oil reserves are owned by states, 75 per cent of known reserves are in states that exclude or sharply limit outside investment in oil, and world demand may hit 115m bpd by 2030. The US imported 60 per cent of its 20m bpd of oil used in 2005, 16 per cent from Africa. In 2006, however, US imports of oil from Africa slightly surpassed those from the Middle East, with both at 22 per cent of total imports (2.23m bpd). Oil accounts for more than 70 per cent of all US imports from Africa.[10] China imported 48 per cent of the 7.2m bpd it used in 2005, with 38 per cent of imports from Africa (1.33m bpd). By 2025, its imports should reach 10.7m bpd, 75 per cent of consumption. More than 60 per cent of the output of Sudan, Africa's third largest oil producer, went to China and supplied 5 per cent of China's oil needs. Angola and Nigeria, the next largest producers, each sent a quarter of their production to China and in 2006 Angola overtook Saudi Arabia as China's greatest source, supplying 15 per cent of China's oil imports. Overall, however, China consumed less than a tenth of oil exported from Africa.[11]

Chinese bids for resources fare well because they are packaged with investments and infrastructure loans typically at zero or near-zero interest. Such loans are often repaid in natural resources, if they are not entirely cancelled (Brautigam 2007). In Angola, China offered $2 billion (b) in aid for infrastructure projects and secured a former Shell oil block that the largest Indian company had sought (Hurst 2006: 10). In Nigeria, a promised $7b in investments and rehabilitation of power stations secured for Chinese firms oil areas sought by Western multinationals (Alden and Davies 2006). Chinese companies outbid Brazilian and French firms for a $3b iron ore project in Gabon after pledging to build a rail line, dam and deepwater port (CI 2007; *SCMP* 2007).

There were more than 800 Chinese enterprises in Africa in 2006, 100 of them medium and large state-owned firms (XH 2007a). China recently accounted for only a tiny part of Africa's foreign direct investment (FDI).

Its firms invested $135m and $280m in Africa in 2004 and 2005, of $3.6b and $6.9b in total Chinese overseas direct investment. Africa's average annual 2001–04 FDI intake was only $15–18b, despite the continent providing the world's highest FDI returns, averaging 29 per cent in the 1990s and 40 per cent by 2005. FDI in Africa in 2005 jumped to $29b (of $897b in global FDI), but China's FDI stock in Africa was still only $1b of Africa's $96b in FDI (two-thirds of it European – half British or French – and one-fifth North American). By late 2006, however, China's investments in Africa were pegged

---

Even such US allies as Museveni see Africa's 'donating' of unprocessed raw materials to the West as allowing a small part of humanity to live well at Africans' expense; they contend Africans need investment that will permit them to sell coffee and not just beans, steel and not just iron ore

---

at almost $8b, as pledged investments were actualised. China will soon become one of Africa's top three FDI providers. Since the 2006 FOCAC, that effort has been aided by a $5b China–Africa Development Fund to spur China investment. Trade with Africa was a tiny part of China's 2006 $1.76 trillion in world trade, but had grown from $3b in 1995 to $10b in 2000, $40b in 2005 and $55b in 2006, balanced slightly in Africa's favour. Yet, while China is the third largest trader with Africa, after the US and France, its trade was well-behind the US's $91b and only a tenth of Africa's world trade, most of which remains with the EU and US.[12]

In the 1970s, Africa's share of world trade was 5 per cent and of global FDI inflows 6 per cent; in 2005 the figures were 1.5 per cent and 3 per cent (AFP 2006a; *Herald* 2005; RTE 2005; UNCTAD 2006: 40). Chinese and African analysts contend that increased Chinese trade and investment eases Africa's dependence on the West and is highly complementary (Losing Africa 2006; Itano 2005; Li Yong 2003). The UN Development Programme agrees and underwrites a China–Africa Business Council that promotes China's investment in Africa (CABC 2006).

Talk of a 'Chinese model' in which trade and investment play prominent roles, is common in Africa.[13] Some analysts argue that most facets of the model cannot apply to Africa (*Addis Fortune* 2004; *BD* 2005). Many Africans find aspects of it appealing, however. The UK Centre for Foreign Policy Analysis' director has observed that:

> [T]he phenomenal growth rates in China and the fact that hundreds of millions have been lifted out of poverty is an attractive model for Africans, and not just the elderly leadership. Young, intelligent, well-educated Africans are attracted to the Chinese model, even though Beijing is not trying to spread democracy (Moorcraft 2007; see also Zhang 2006).

The African Development Bank's president has said of the Chinese that 'we can learn from them how to organise our trade policy, to move from low to middle income status, to educate our children in skills and areas that pay off in just a couple years' (WEF 2006).

Many Africans view China's political economy as differing from that of the West in ways that matter to Africa. A Nigerian journalist has argued that China's strategy:

> is not informed by the Washington Consensus. China has not allowed any [IMF] or World Bank to impose on it some neoliberal package of reforms … [T]heir strategy has not been a neoliberal overdose of deregulation, cutting social expenditure, privatising everything under the sun and jettisoning the public good. They have not branded subsidy a dirty word (*TD* 2005).

African analysts contrast the Chinese government's massive investment in infrastructure and support services within China with their governments' failure to provide these requisites of development and contend the difference stems from 'strictures imposed by multilateral and bilateral financiers' (*TN* 2006). Some note that China has had high growth rates and reduced poverty without adopting Western liberal democracy (Vanguard 2006).

Many Africans find Chinese and Western economic practices distinctive. They decry Western states' use of 'unequal and disparate exchange' to lock in underdevelopment (Williams 1985; Raffer 1987; Srkar 2001).[14] Some accuse Western firms of destructive actions, such as buying natural resources, but selling weapons (Colombant 2004). African analysts agree that China wants Africa's oil, but argue that 'the way in which China's demand for oil is framed in Western media – in breathy, suspense-filled undertones ... smacks of racist double standards' (Wanyeki 2006; see also *M&G* 2006). Indeed, while three-fourths of US FDI in Africa has been in oil, 64 per cent of China's FDI in Africa from 1979 to 2000 was in manufacturing and 28 per cent in resources (Ferguson 2003; WBGAR 2004: 63).[15]

Lack of infrastructure inhibits FDI and Africa's exports (UN 2007: 105). China, it is said, pre-eminently invests 'in long-neglected infrastructure projects and hardly viable industries' (*NE* 2006). Its firms had $6.3b in

---

Examples of US, UK and French direct exercises of hegemony in Africa are legion. In contrast, China is said to allow African states to vote as they please at the UN and it deploys troops only as peacekeepers

---

construction contracts in 2005 (Singh 2006) and now employ many African workers.[16] A Nigerian official has also noted that 'the Western world is never prepared to transfer technology – but the Chinese do [and] while China's technology may not be as sophisticated as some Western governments', it is better to have Chinese technology than to have none at all' (*FT* 2006a).

Even such US allies as Museveni see Africa's 'donating' of unprocessed raw materials to the West as allowing a small part of humanity to live well at Africans' expense; they contend Africans need investment that will permit them to sell coffee and not just beans, steel and not just iron ore. They regard China's surging demand for African exports – China's share as a destination rose from 1.3 per cent in 1995 to 10 per cent in 2005 – as aiding that effort (Goldstein 2006; Broadman 2006:11; *NV* 2005).[17] Africans also find Chinese goods to be cheaper than Western imports and, often, local goods: a 50kg bag of local cement costs $10 in Angola, but imported Chinese cement costs $4 (Donnelly 2005).

Talk of Chinese colonialism or imperialism in Africa is thus inapt. 'Imperialism' is often 'indiscriminately applied to any foreign policy ... to which the user happens to be opposed' (Morgenthau 1960: 45), but is commonly equated with 'informal empire', where a stronger state determines a weaker one's external policies and influences domestic matters (Motyl 1999).[18] Yet, claims that China has 'substantial influence' over several African states, notably Sudan and Zimbabwe (*FT* 2006b; *Observer* 2007; *WP* 2007), remain unproven.[19] China's influence is limited by its sovereigntist stance. Its actions also differ from those of longstanding practitioners of imperialism. Examples of US, UK and French direct exercises of hegemony in Africa are legion (Jarrett 1996; Milburn 2004; Ayittey 2007).[20] In contrast, China is said to allow African states to vote as they please at the UN and it deploys troops only as peacekeepers (Lafargue 2005).

Other characteristics that Africans attribute to China concern her position in the international system. A South African scholar has noted that China is

the first country from the so-called marginalised developing fold to occupy centre stage in the global political economy. In terms of political ideology and approaches to socio-economic development, China is closely aligned to countries of the south … creat[ing] a somewhat idealistic impression of the distant partner or big brother in the East that is still evident on the continent today (Whi 2006).

For many Africans then, there is a 'Chinese model' and not just of FDI/export-led rapid industrial expansion (Li 2005; Cao 2005). It is also an image of a developing state that does not fully implement Washington consensus prescriptions, does not impose onerous conditions on African states' policies and is more willing than the West to help develop predicates of industrialism in the global South, including by opening many factories in Africa.[21] Whether this positive view of a 'Chinese model' is warranted is less important than the fact it exists and plays a role in how Africans appraise the policies of the main Western states. This perception is now part of an image often labelled 'the Beijing consensus'.

The Beijing consensus as a 'competing framework'

China's self-representation as Africa's helpmate is often dismissed as propaganda designed to curry favour with African elites. The Washington consensus/post-Washington consensus, however, has a more than two-decade history in Africa (Sandbrook 2005) and the Beijing consensus is now seen as competing with Washington consensus/post-Washington consensus instruments set up by the EU, US and South Africa around the year 2000.[22]

The Cotonou agreement of 2000, the EU framework with 77 African, Caribbean and Pacific (ACP) states, is based on free trade (WTO compliance and sub-continental regionalism), private enterprise, export production, FDI, austerity measures, and conditioned aid. It gives a leading role to the European Commission and individual political, not group and socio-economic, rights.

In the global South, there is a sense of grievance with neoliberalism, seen as an aggravated form of worldwide unequal exchange and embodied in the EU, US and NEPAD mechanism

---

Poverty reduction is seen as a concomitant of trade and capital liberalisation and FDI secured by compliant labour. Quintennial conferences serve to renegotiate the EU–ACP relationship, which also includes bilateral and regional free trade economic partnership agreements. These pacts, like those the US negotiates, weaken solidarity among developing states in the WTO (Nunn and Price 2004; Hurt 2003; Bensah 2003).

The US African Growth and Opportunity Act (AGOA) of 2000 provides that states that marketise, liberalise, privatise, de-subsidise, deregulate and do not undermine US foreign policy interests may receive trade preferences. Some 37 African countries, many of them authoritarian, have been declared eligible. US and African ministers meet every two years in an AGOA forum. AGOA trade concessions only go slightly beyond the US General System of Preferences, in part because oil and minerals are more than 80 per cent of the value of African exports to the US. Only a few countries have gained under AGOA, mainly by exporting agricultural products not plentiful in the US, such as cut flowers. Most African products remain barred by competition from subsidised US agriculture and non-tariff health and safety barriers, while Asian firms produce many goods entering the US from Africa. AGOA is also a platform for free trade agreements between the US and African regional entities (UNCTAD 2003:1–2; Rice 2004; Melber 2005; Lall 2005). Its appeal for African rulers lies not so much in direct benefits, as in closer political ties to the US, resulting in aid, including military training useful in quelling oppositions (Hallinan 2006).[23]

Since 2001, neoliberal principles also have been embodied in the New Partnership for African Development (NEPAD). NEPAD is based on the idea that there is no alternative to neoliberalism and that integration into the world market is the antidote to poverty. It is African Union-endorsed and backed by global and South African firms. Critics compare NEPAD as implemented to IMF/World Bank SAPs (Lesufi 2004; Adesina 2004, 2006; Bond 2005). Its representation as 'by Africans for Africans', however, provides another mechanism for implementing developed countries' Washington consensus/ post-Washington consensus frameworks. US firms in Africa link AGOA and NEPAD (Hayes 2002) and US leaders praise NEPAD as 'extend[ing] democracy and free markets and transparency across the continent' (WH 2003). EU endorsements of NEPAD link it to the Cotonou agreement (Lake 2003). China too voices support and says it implements NEPAD through FOCAC (Liu 2004).

In the global South, there is a sense of grievance with neoliberalism, seen as an aggravated form of worldwide unequal exchange and embodied in the EU, US and NEPAD mechanisms. At the 2000 FOCAC opening ceremony, Zambia's president stated:

[Developed countries] are not prepared to discuss the issues of justice and fair play concerning the international trade and commercial sector, which imposes considerable suffering and privation on developing countries … [T]he developing world continues to subsidise consumption of the developed world, through an iniquitous trade system. The existing structure is designed to consign us to perpetual poverty and underdevelopment … It is unrealistic to expect support, relief or respite from those who benefit from the status quo (Chiluba 2000).

Those Africans who are disenchanted with Western neoliberalism plausibly regard China as an alternative, based on experiences and needs it shares with Africa (Tull 2006).

China's creation of an attractive (although not necessarily accurate) image, termed the Beijing consensus, itself distinguishes China's links with Africa. The Beijing consensus notion originated with Joshua Cooper Ramo, ex-*Time* magazine foreign affairs editor and Goldman Sachs China advisor, and now managing director of Kissinger Associates. While there is no consensus on the Beijing consensus (A. Leonard 2006), it is often discussed as China's investments, aid, and trade not conditioned by demands of Western states and international institutions. US neoconservatives, who are especially exercised by it, reduce the Beijing consensus to 'economic growth without the constraints of democratic institutions' or 'economic development without political change' (Wortzel and Stewart 2005; Craner 2005). Others

---

*US neoconservatives, who are especially
exercised by it, reduce the Beijing consensus to
'economic growth without the constraints
of democratic institutions' or 'economic
development without political change'*

---

describe it as liberal trade and finance with strong state leadership (Alert Unit 2004: 117), a strong state role in industrial development, but caution toward liberalisation and deregulation (Dauderstadt and Stetten 2005: 7) or state guided development and concern with stability (Lieberthal 2006).

Washington consensus/post-Washington consensus 'market fundamentalism' is about Western prescriptions for the world's economies and politics and the ordering of global power relations. The Beijing consensus is about lessons of articulation of state and economy in China and her approach to international relations. Ramo presents it as a multifaceted policy set forefronting constant innovation as a development strategy (instead of one-size-fits-all neoliberal orthodoxy) and using quality-of-life measures, such as equality and environment (not just GDP) in formulating the strategy. He asserts that it opposes the hierarchy of nations embodied in the Washington consensus-related international financial institutions (IFIs) and WTO (Ramo 2004a).[24] China's leaders are said to reject 'a US-style power, bristling with arms and intolerant of others' world views', in favour of 'power based on the example of their own model, the strength of their economic system, and their rigid defence of ... national sovereignty' (Ramo 2004b).

Ramo himself cannot be written off as 'radical.' He is a CFR member and was declared a 'Global Leader of Tomorrow' by the neoliberal World Economic Forum. Ramo is affiliated with the Tony Blair-founded Foreign Policy Centre in London and the World Bank has praised his book on the Beijing consensus (FPC 2005). Not surprisingly, the Beijing consensus, as

Ramo conceives it, is a 'model' within the neoliberal paradigm, yet he approvingly quotes an Indian sociologist who has stated that 'China's experiment should be the most admired in human history. China has its own path' (Ramo 2004c).

China's government denies it touts any model (French 2005). Asked about Rwanda's development, the Chinese ambassador said only that Chinese experience shows Rwanda should encourage local and foreign investment (Akanga 2006).[25] Yet soon after Ramo coined the Beijing consensus concept and world economic forum chair Klaus Schwab contrasted it with the Washington consensus (RW 2004), a leading Chinese economic journal published an article by Ramo and a TV programme on his book was telecast in China (FPC 2005). His work was circulated to the top 5,000 Chinese leaders. Some of China's media argued that the Beijing consensus is challenging the Washington consensus (Jing Bao 2004; BR 2006). China's leading newspaper carried an article in which economists Wu Shuqing (former head of Beijing University and now a Ministry of Education advisor) and Cheng Enfu (Academy of Marxism head and proponent of

Africans go to China to learn how to build the infrastructure themselves or how to work in it as doctors, teachers, officials

the 'socialist market economy' as a world model) endorsed the 'theoretical scientificity and practical superiority' of the Beijing consensus. Opposing it to the Washington consensus, they spoke of its 'growing influence in the world, particularly among developing countries' (Wu and Cheng 2005). Other Chinese works counterpose the Beijing consensus and Washington consensus (Zhang 2004; Huang and Cui 2005; Wang 2005; Mao 2005).[26] That contrast has also been taken up by US analysts (Nye 2005; Thompson 2005). Since 2006, Chinese writers have praised Africans' supposed move from Washington consensus to Beijing consensus (Liu 2006; 21SJBD 2006). Their enthusiasm for the Beijing consensus reflects a desire to make China the world's leading state, while in some Western circles it may stem from the view that the Beijing consensus is a more saleable variant of the post-

Washington consensus or that any 'consensus' is better than one enforced by the US.[27]

The Beijing consensus appears as an alternative to strictly neoliberal 'consensuses'. China's aid comes without the strings attached by AGOA and other programmes. China approves African states focusing their investment on infrastructure and human capital, rather than just primary products. It supports the state addressing development problems not solved by neoliberalism's favoured corporate initiatives. Jim McDermott, the US Congressman known as the 'Father of AGOA', has implicitly drawn this contrast:

> [T]he US cannot rely solely on the private sector to help support Africa's endeavour to develop. Private companies may invest in new manufacturing plants or mineral extracting facilities, but they usually do not drill water in remote villages, or build schools to educate young Africans. Do you know of many venture capitalists who buy malaria or TB drugs for the world's poor to enhance their trade opportunities (de Figueiredo 2003)?

To some analysts, Washington consensus–Beijing consensus differences amount to a US–China ideological struggle, e.g. between a 'neoliberal Anglo-Saxon credo' and an Asian-derived 'socially oriented' approach (Cheow 2006). A UK journalist has said the Washington consensus–Beijing consensus confrontation is 'the biggest ideological threat the West has felt since the end of the cold war.' Expressing no doubt about which 'model' will prevail, he opined that in two decades 'the press will be full of articles about "Asian values" and the "Beijing consensus"' (M. Leonard 2005a, 2005b). Arif Dirlik, who emphasises the Beijing consensus's lack of ideological coherence, has argued, however, that its appeal may be its acknowledgement of the desirability of a global order 'founded, not upon homogenising universalisms that inevitably lead to hegemonism, but on a simultaneous recognition of commonality and difference' (Dirlik 2006). That recognition magnifies China's soft power in Africa, the putative Beijing consensus's main testing ground. Yet, while China is seen as offering a new approach, its institutions related to Africa do mirror the form and some of the content of developed country frameworks.[28]

Distinctive aid and migration

Chinese aid to Africa, as well as patterns of Chinese migration to Africa and African migration to China, differ from Western practices, but relate to each other. Infrastructure development, the centrepiece of China's aid, facilitates China–Africa migration. Over several decades, China has sent 16,000 medical personnel to Africa to develop hospitals and clinics and treat 240m patients (XH 2006c). Chinese have long aided African agricultural development (Brautigam 1998): 10,000 Chinese agro-technicians have been sent to Africa since the 1960s and worked on 200 projects, including setting up farms and agricultural stations and personnel training (*BD* 2004a). For example, in Tanzania, Chinese-built Ubungo Farm Implements Factory (UFI) turned out 85 per cent of hand tools, while the Mbarali Farm produced a quarter of

> *The US is now heavily involved in African politics, for example through multimillion dollar programmes to support or undermine the governments of Angola, Burundi, Sudan and Zimbabwe, carried out by the self-described 'overtly political' Office of Transition Initiatives of the US Agency for International Development*

the rice eaten by Tanzanians (Ai 1999). China is to train 10,000 agricultural technicians for Africa in 2007–10 (Macauhub 2007). Some 530 Chinese teachers have worked in African schools and many Chinese are in Africa to train government staff (XH 2005; Ryu, 2004; Kuada, 2005). Many more go for contract labour service – building railways, roads, telecommunications systems, hospitals, schools and dams – or to do business that uses that infrastructure.

Africans go to China to learn how to build the infrastructure themselves or how to work in it as doctors, teachers, officials, etc. Some 16,000 African professionals were trained in China in 2000–06; 15,000 will do so in 2007–09

(XH 2006d; *TD* 2007). From 1956 to 1999, 5,582 Africans studied in Chinese universities. By late 2004, 17,860 Africans had received Chinese scholarships and 15,000 had graduated, two-thirds within the preceding decade. China provided 1,500 scholarships to Africans in 2005 and 2,000 in 2006; there are to be 4,000 a year by 2010. By 2007, more than 20,000 Africans had graduated, including several political leaders.[29] Despite difficulties presented by a commonplace racism, a few Africans remain in China after graduation, some engaging in China–Africa business (Leu 2007; Nyamwana 2004; Gillespie 2001: 98–108, 169–179; interviews with Africans in Beijing, Shanghai, Shenzhen, 2006; Guangzhou, 2007).

China's aid to Africa, while not disinterested, is not used as a political tool in the same way as aid from Western political actors to Africa is. This approach is longstanding: Tanzania's first leader Julius Nyerere (1974:235), commenting on the loan for building Tazara stated that 'The Chinese people have not asked us to become communists in order to qualify for this loan … they have never at any point suggested that we should change any of our policies – internal or external.' In contrast, during the Cold War, the US and UK pressured Tanzania to take the West's side and later to accept IMF/World Bank SPAs. The US is now heavily involved in African politics, for example through multimillion dollar programmes to support or undermine the governments of Angola, Burundi, Sudan and Zimbabwe, carried out by the self-described 'overtly political' Office of Transition Initiatives of the US Agency for International Development (USACOC 2005; USAID 2005; USAID/OTI 2005; McGreal 2002; *CSM* 2006).

Chinese aid has also differed from US aid in terms of whether the recipient or donor decides the projects on which aid monies are spent. China's approach is more commercial than formerly, but contrasts with US and UK insistence on aiding only private enterprise development. For example, the UK Commission on Africa 2005 report states that Africa should adopt the Private Finance Initiative: all major projects should be built in conjunction with the private sector (Nelson 2005). China continues to support state-run projects in industry and agriculture. There is no evidence China politically conditions its aid, except that recipients must maintain full diplomatic relations with the People's Republic of China, rather than Taiwan, as all but five African countries do (Mukandala 1999; Liu 2001).

Tied and untied aid

Much developed state aid is subject to conditions that benefit the donor economically and politically, including its security interests. A study notes that:

> Tied aid is a particularly inefficient form of development assistance because it does not help poor countries develop their economies. Instead of creating new businesses and jobs in recipient countries, most of the benefits remain in the donor nations. Tied aid is also inefficient because often goods and services would be available at a lower price from local producers or world markets (Hirvonen 2005: 8, 12).

About 80 per cent of US grants and contracts to developing countries must be used to buy goods and services from US firms and NGOs. Some 90 per cent of Italy's aid benefits Italian companies and experts; 60–65 per cent of Canada's aid and much of that of Germany, Japan and France is tied to purchases from those states. A UN study found such ties cut by 25–40 per cent the value of aid to Africans, who are required to buy non-competitively priced imports (IPS 2004; Pawson 2005). Actual costs of tied direct food aid transfers are 50 per cent higher than local food purchases and a third higher than buying third-country food (OECD 2005).

The popular view in the West nevertheless is that it is generous with Africa, in response to NGOs seeking to help Africa through debt relief and increased aid (IPS 2005).[30] Yet, from 1970 to 2002, Africa received $530b in aid and loans and repaid $540b. The G8 and IFIs subsequently cancelled the debt of only 14 states and Africa's debt still stands at about US$300b. An additional $50b in aid was promised in 2005, but more than half was either double-counted or involved money already pledged. Debt relief and refugee-related expenditures in developed countries are also counted by them as part of increased development assistance (Hertz 2005; Hirvonen 2005; Abila 2005).

China's aid to Africa provides it with political benefits, such as support on sovereignty issues and for China gaining 'market economy status' that will enable it to better resist anti-dumping actions in WTO (Ching 2005). If China were ever to directly confront Western states in international forums, support could be expected from African states. China, however, does not need other states' support for such activities as control of international institutions or war-making, in contrast to the US, which in 2003 pressured the three African UN Security Council members to endorse the war in Iraq (IPS 2004).

Chinese firms secure many contracts on projects in Africa financed by China's soft loans. An analyst speaks of 'indirect conditionalities', an understanding that Chinese firms will secure a portion of work financed by Chinese loans (Kuada 2005). The $2b credit line China extended to Angola in 2004, used for railroad repair, road building, office construction, a fibre-optic network and oil exploration, was guaranteed by a contract for the sale of oil from a field that generates 10,000 bpd. The loan, originally at 1.5 per

---

China's winning bids are based on low labour costs and profit margins and quick turn-around. Most Western firms expect 15–25 per cent profits rates; most Chinese firms expect less than 10 per cent and many accept 3–5 per cent

---

cent interest, but lowered to 0.25 per cent, is to be recouped over 17 years, including a five-year interest free period. Its terms reserved for Angolans 30 per cent of the value of contracts paid for with its funds. Angolans feared Chinese firms would win the other 70 per cent, engendering resentment among them (APA 2004, 2006c; IRIN 2005a, 2005b; CCS 2006).[31] Chinese firms do in fact secure many contracts, even apart from those financed by China's aid: in Botswana by 2005 they were winning 80 per cent (UPI 2005a). A study of 505 contracts opened by African states for international bids in 2004 showed Chinese firms won 2.6 per cent of the total, but these amounted to 18 per cent of the value of all contracts (ADB 2005: 23). In 2001, Africa-based contracts were 17 per cent of all contracts Chinese firms had outside China, but by 2005, they were 28 per cent and in 2006, 31 per cent. In that year, Chinese-won contracts ranked first in new contract value among the totality of contracts secured by foreigners in Africa (Zhu and Xu 2007). In 2006, there were over 600 Chinese infrastructure projects in Africa and financing by China's Exim Bank for African infrastructure had increased to $12.6b, much more than the developed countries' total infrastructure aid to the continent (*NA* 2006; White 2006).

China's winning bids are based on low labour costs and profit margins and quick turn-around (Kurlantzick 2006). Most Western firms expect 15–25 per cent profits rates; most Chinese firms expect less than 10 per cent and many accept 3–5 per cent (CCS 2006). In Ethiopia, some Chinese firms have been instructed by their government to make unprofitable bids to get a foot in the door. Lower salaries and profits margins also arise from China's state-owned firms competing with each other. Chinese contractors building Ethiopia's roads seek a 3 per cent profit; Western businesses seek 15 per cent or more (Shinn 2005; Lyman 2005; Leggett 2005). Efficient, low-cost Chinese construction softens the image of China's participation in the overall unequal trade and investment relationships between Africa and more developed states, including China.

While China's aid to Africa is thus not entirely untied, it is distinct from Western aid in a key way that stands at the intersection of aid and migration. As one analyst explains:

> Chinese aid is often dispensed in such a way that corrupt rulers cannot somehow use it to buy Mercedes Benzes … [It] is often in the form of infrastructure, such as a railroad network in Nigeria or roads in Kenya and Rwanda. Or in the form of doctors and nurses to provide health care to people who otherwise would not have access … China provides scholarships for African students to study in its universities and, increasingly, funds to encourage its businessmen to invest in Africa (Ching 2005).[32]

Speaking of China's activities in Africa, Sierra Leone's ambassador to China has said 'The Chinese are investing in Africa and are seeing results, while the G8 countries are putting in huge sums of money and they don't see very much' (UPI 2005b). This difference advantages China in African eyes even when altruistic motives are discounted.

Draining and gaining migrations

Migration patterns set another key distinction between China–Africa links and Western connections with the continent. Africans generally perceive Chinese who work in Africa as less privileged and exploitative than Western expatriates (Wainaina 2006).[33] Chinese construction personnel and agricultural advisors live more like their African counterparts than do expats,

106

Table 1 Number of Chinese in select African countries, circa 2001 and 2003–07

Country	Ohio U. Database 2001	Estimate for 200X	
Algeria	2,000	20,000	(2007)
Angola	500	20,000 –30,000	(2006)
Benin	—	4,000	(2007)
Botswana	40	3,000–10,000	(2006–07)
Burkina Faso	—	1,000	(2007)
Cameroon	50	1,000 – 3,000	(2005)
Cape Verde	—	600–1,000	(2007)
Congo (Democratic Rep.)	200	500	(2007)
Cote d'Ivoire	200	10,000	(2007)
Egypt	110	6,000–10,000	(2007)
Ethiopia	100	3,000–4,000	(2006)
Ghana	500	6,000	(2005)
Guinea	—	5,000	(2007)
Kenya	190	5,000	(2007)
Lesotho	1,000	5,000	(2005)
Liberia	120	600	(2006)
Madagascar	30,000	60,000	(2003)
Malawi	40	2,000	(2007)
Mali	—	2,000	(2007)
Mozambique	700	1,500	(2006)
Namibia	—	5,000–40,000	(2006)
Nigeria	2,000	100,000	(2007)
Senegal	—	2,000	(2007)
South Africa	30,000	200,000 – 300,000	(2007)
Sudan	45	5,000–10,000	(2004–05)
Tanzania	600	3,000–20,000	(2006)
Togo	50	3,000	(2007)
Uganda	100	5,000–10,000	(2007)
Zambia	150	4,000 – 6,000	(2007)
Zimbabwe	300	5,300–10,000	(2005 – 07)

Sources: Ohio University 2001; Becker 2004; Chen 2003; AFP 2005; Tull 2005, fn. 98; Sudan Tribune 2005; Xinhuanet 2007; *Daily News* (Gaborone) 2006; AFP 2006d; *PD* 2002; *DTe* 2005; Weidlich 2006; Namibian 2006a; IRIN 2006b; Ren 2007; DPA 2007; XH 2007b; Tian 2007; Hoffmann 2007; CCS 2006:19; Guineenews 2007; interviews with Chinese in Ghana, 2005, Tanzania, 2006; information from Chinese embassies in Mozambique, Liberia, Ethiopia, 2006; communications with Chinese living in Benin, Botswana, Burkina Faso, Cape Verde, DR Congo, Egypt, Malawi, Mali, Senegal, Kenya, Togo, Uganda and Zambia, March–August 2007 (for S. Africa, see next fn).

in keeping with the eighth Principle on External Economic and Technical Assistance set out by Premier Zhou Enlai during a 1964 trip to Africa: 'The experts dispatched by the Chinese government to help construction in the recipient country should enjoy the same living conditions as the experts of the recipient country. The Chinese experts are not allowed to make any special demands and ask for any special amenities' (Donnelly 2005).[34] Similarly, the small, mostly short-term, African migrations to China are seen as benefiting Africa, while many Africans view the large, permanent migration of African professionals to the West as harming Africa's development.

A surge in Chinese migration to Africa began in the mid-1990s and accelerated in the present decade, soon rendering population estimates obsolete. An Ohio University (OU) database shows 137,000 Chinese in Africa, the same figure provided for 2001 by Taiwan's government.[35] Its estimates for 34 African states are now very out-of-date. While some discrepancies may reflect differing conceptions of residence, the magnitude of the differences indicates a very rapid growth in Africa's Chinese communities.[36]

The growth of South Africa's Chinese population is especially significant. The 10,000 'indigenous' or 'South-African born Chinese' (SABCs) were almost the whole Chinese population until 1980, when an immigrant community, 90 per cent from Taiwan, began to form. By 1993, there were 36,000 Chinese in South Africa. A decade later, the Chinese embassy in South Africa stated there were perhaps 80,000 Chinese residents, while South Africa's ambassador to China has said there are many more than 100,000. Almost all the increase since 1993 has come from Chinese mainland migrants, as the Taiwan-origin community shrank by half to 10,000 and the SABC population declined. Estimates in 2004–07 ranged from 100,000 to 400,000 legal and illegal Chinese residents.[37]

A Belgian diplomat in Tanzania once told a Japanese diplomat in the 1970s that his African employee had queried, 'Why are there two kinds of Chinese in Tanzania? One kind wears dirty clothes, looks poor, but works very hard; another kind wears a good suit, rides in a modern car with a camera on his shoulder, and looks like an American.' The African worker was conflating as 'Chinese' those who had come from China to build Tazara and Japanese visiting Tanzania for very different purposes (Michiaki 1979).[38] Only a small number of Chinese in Africa today perform service of the kind rendered by their 1970s compatriots, yet substantial differences remain between the positions of Chinese and citizens of developed countries in Africa. A South African university official has advanced a common, implicitly comparative view in noting that China provides low-cost technology and its people are willing to work in inhospitable places (Muekalia 2004).

Most developed country citizens in Africa are managers or professionals. Some work for large corporations, others are among 40,000 NGO-employed expats (Ayodele 2003). They generally command salaries that allow a lifestyle very different from most Africans and usually better than local occupational peers. Larger Chinese communities in Africa also have well-off members, usually business people. Most long-term Chinese residents in Africa, however, are small merchants, with little capital, who sell what one Kenyan has called 'down-street merchandise' (*TN* 2005; *TP* 2005; Mayanja 2005). In Zimbabwe, Zambia and South Africa, there are also Chinese farmers (*Asianews* 2006;

Africans generally perceive Chinese who work in Africa as less privileged and exploitative than Western expatriates

---

Ncube 2005; Ryu 2004).[39] Some Chinese study in Africa, mostly in South Africa: in 1999, there were only 19, but by 2004, 3,300 Chinese had attended South African tertiary institutions, where in late 2005, 3,196 Chinese were studying (PRCMOC 2006).

Many Chinese work in Africa under labour service contracts.[40] They are paid much less and live more frugally than Western expats doing comparable work. In 1992, Africa employed 100,000 developed country expats at a cost of $4b per year, i.e. $40,000 per expat or nearly $800 per week (Kollehlon and Eule 2003). They generally work for African governments or NGOs; Westerners employed by multinational firms have even higher salaries. Chinese wages are even now not nearly so high. Chinese 'workers' (i.e. managers, engineers and skilled craftsmen) for one construction firm in Angola receive $500 a month, live two to three to a room, and cook for themselves, while Europeans each rent a house and eat out. Chinese supervising African workers on construction sites dig along with them (Donnelly 2005; BBCRF 2006). China's largest contract in Africa, worth $650m, is to build Sudan's Merowe Dam, where in 2003–05, 1,800 Chinese and 1,600 Sudanese worked. A Chinese firm won the bid because it kept expected profit margins and Chinese staff costs low. All project managers, 90 per cent of engineers and 75 per cent of technicians are Chinese; locals are 20 per cent of skilled workers and all general labour.

Expats earn $220–$600 per week, Sudanese $22–$350 (XH 2006f; Reina 2004). Chinese firms in Africa 'reportedly provide good quality projects at a price discount of 25–50 per cent compared to other foreign investors' due to lower profit margins, access to cheap capital, and low wages and living standards for Chinese employees (Kaplinsky 2006: 18–19).

While many Chinese now live in Africa, a growing number of Africans live in China. Guangzhou had 10,000 or more Africans in 2006, mainly China–Africa traders and students (BD 2006; Zatt 2007).[41] Beijing in 2005–06 was said to have at least 600 Africans, Shanghai 500, and Shenzhen 100 (Simpson 2006).[42] Most were students of medicine, engineering or natural science, expected to return to Africa in four or five years. That small brain gain

China provides a model for developing states based on rapid industrialisation fuelled by a high-level of investment and concentration on exports and, unlike the West, its low-tariff, low-subsidy regime allows other developing countries to export freely to China and compete with it in world markets

contrasts with Africa's brain drain to the West that originated with structural adjustment programmes that required deep reductions of state expenditures. Up to 1980, Africa had a dozen high growth countries, averaging 6 per cent. A third of African states had savings rates higher than 25 per cent, which sustained human resource development. Structural adjustment programmes curtailed state funding, including for universities, and costly expats had to replace local intellectuals. Savings rates plummeted to 10 per cent, too low for industrialisation or adequate education (Mamdani 2002). Thus, Africa yearly produces 83 engineers per one million people; China graduates 750 and developed countries 1,000 (NMI 2006; NA 2006). Many African engineers emigrate: more are in the US than in Africa (ACBF 2004: 15).

From 1985 to1990, 60,000 African professionals emigrated. In 2000, 3.6 per cent of Africans, but 31.4 per cent of Africa's emigrants, had a tertiary education. By 2005, 300,000–500,000 professionals, including 30,000 doctoral degree holders, had left and 20,000 more emigrate each year to the US or

Europe. The half million figure would mean a third of African professionals had left. On average each represents a loss of $184,000 to Africa.[43]

Of 400,000 African immigrants age 16 and above in the US in 2000, 36 per cent were managers or professionals. Many were brought in through the Diversity Visa Program ('Green Card Lottery'), most of whose winners are Africans. By 2005, 50,000 Africans a year were migrating to the US, with perhaps four times that number entering illegally. While such migrants send remittances home, a leading African scientist in the US estimates Africans there contribute 40 times more to America than to Africa's economy (Mazrui and Kaba 2004; Herbert 2005; Roberts 2005; Manda 2004).[44] Others stay on after graduation from US universities, which had 34,000 African students in 2000–01, 6.25 per cent of their international students (Coffman and Brennan 2006). Most were graduate students and a survey of Africans who received US PhDs from 1986 to 1996 showed that 37 per cent remained there after graduation. The percentages staying were higher in fields key to development: engineering (54 per cent), physical sciences (44 per cent), health sciences (44 per cent) and management (67 per cent), and higher also for two of the three top PhD-receiving peoples, Nigerians (62 per cent) and Ghanaians (61 per cent) (Pires 1999). Because education levels among entrepreneurs correlate with private enterprise growth and human capital is a key determinant of FDI inflows, the brain drain plays a role in continued poverty in Africa (Kapur and McHale 2005: 102). For example, austerity measures and faculty out-migration have collapsed Nigerian tertiary institutions, rendering the country's 50,000 engineers severely under-trained (*TD* 2006b).

Africa, with 14 per cent of world population has 24 per cent of the global burden of disease (WHO 2006), so poaching of Africa's human resources is most apparent among medical workers, of which Africa has 1.4 per 1,000 people, while North America has 9.9 (Mallaby 2004). Of Africa's estimated 800,000 'trained medical staff', 23,000 a year leave for developed countries. The doctors among them cost on average $100,000 to train (Jack 2005). Their immigration saves a receiving country like Britain $340,000–$430,000 in costs of training a doctor. Ghana, with six doctors for each 100,000 people, has lost 30 per cent of the MDs it educated to the US, UK, Canada and Australia, all of which have more than 220 doctors per 100,000. South Africa, Ethiopia and Uganda have lost 14–19 per cent of their doctors. In 2001, Zimbabwe graduated 737 nurses; 437 left for Britain (Eastwood et. al 2005; Mullan 2005; Mallaby 2004). There are more Ethiopian-trained doctors in Chicago than in Ethiopia and more Beninese doctors in France than in Benin (*DTr* 2004; IOM 2003).[45]

111

Conclusion

In 2005, a Chinese official working on WTO affairs, Wu Jiahuang, made a presentation to a UN agency on industrialisation, trade and poverty alleviation through South–South cooperation (Wu 2005). He argued that China's high growth rate was fuelled by Chinese saving 44 per cent of their income and encouragement of FDI (half from Hong Kong and Taiwan), which contributed 28 per cent of value added to industry in 2004. He said China's industrial and trade growth are related, with over half of industrial exports produced by foreign investors. Wu noted China does not over-protect domestic industry: average Chinese tariffs dropped from 43 per cent in 1992 to 10 per cent in 2005, lower than those of its trading partners.[46] Primary agricultural products and textiles tariffs averaged 15.5 per cent and 12.9 per cent, while those of China's trading partners averaged 24.5 per cent and 17.7 per cent. China provides world-class resources and 'the

---

As one scholar has observed, Africa is for the West a 'haven for terrorists', the 'cradle of HIV/Aids', and a 'source of instability', but for China it is a 'strategically significant region' and place of opportunity

---

cheapest domestic labour', so its businesses can market the world's most competitive products, leading to greater incomes, state revenue and social welfare. Wu called on WTO to remove trade-distorting subsidies to farmers in the North to enable farmers in the South to sell their products at a higher price. He explained that Chinese farms are very small, averaging 0.7ha of land, compared to Europeans' 20ha and US farmers' 200ha. Wu noted that China's agricultural tariffs averaged 15.8 per cent, compared to 23 per cent in the US and 73 per cent in Europe. Meanwhile, state support for China's farmers was only 1.5 per cent of their income, while in the US it was 18 per cent and in the EU, 33 per cent. China and other developing states were thus in the same boat in needing cuts in developed world agricultural subsidies.

Wu's presentation summed up a commonly-held perception of Chinese practices that relates to distinct China–Africa links: China provides a model for developing states based on rapid industrialisation fuelled by a high-level of investment and concentration on exports and, unlike the West, its low-tariff, low-subsidy regime allows other developing countries to export freely to China and compete with her in world markets. The official thus essentially argued that Chinese policymakers are more consistent economic liberals than those of the West and that this greater liberality fulfills the common needs of Chinese and citizens of other developing countries. Wu did not explain how China's extraordinary savings rate and its FDI inflow mainly from co-ethnics on its periphery can be duplicated by most developing states. Nor did he recognise that these states are scarcely positioned to take advantage of China's economic liberality by competing with Chinese producers, either in their domestic market or the world. Still, one point was doubtless convincing: that China, unlike Western states, is not obstructing development in the world's poorer countries. That point, whether it relates to the Beijing consensus or aid and migration, epitomises the distinctiveness of the China–Africa link for many Africans.

It is the practices of Western states associated with past colonialism or present imperialism that make Chinese practices appear distinctive to Africans. Most prominent among these are impositions of neoliberal structural adjustment programmes that have resulted in diminished growth, huge debt, declining incomes, and curtailed social welfare for most Africans;[47] the use of aid to compel compliance with structural adjustment programmes and the foreign policies of Western powers; protectionism (despite free trade rhetoric) in developed states that inhibits African exports; and support for authoritarian leaders (despite talk of democracy and human rights) to secure resources and combat 'radicals'. Western disparagement of Africa, through an unremitting negative discourse overlaid with strong implications of African incompetence, remains prevalent (Araya 2007).[48] The ideas that on balance colonialism benefited 'the natives' and that Africa's troubles have all been post-colonial, are popular among elites of the ex-colonial Western states (Sautman and Yan 2007; Nyang 2005).

The experience of Africans in China has been less than positive due to popular racism, which Chinese in Africa also often display (Segal 2006).[49] The Chinese government bears some responsibility, due to its propagation of social Darwinism (the richer, the fitter) and representations of Africa as uniformly poor. It is nevertheless careful to recognise the main cause of

Africa's problems as the legacy of colonialism, broadly construed to include states captured for elite enrichment (*BD* 2004b; Li Xing 2003). Chinese leaders would never term Africa a 'hopeless continent,' as did *The Economist* (2000). They would never state, as a US House Subcommittee on Africa member did to a Rwandan human rights activist during the 1994 genocide, that 'America has no friends in Africa, only interests, and it has no interests in Rwanda' (*Ghosts of Rwanda* 2005).

Chinese leaders, officially at least, celebrate Africa's culture and achievements and China's 65 cultural agreements with 46 African states have led to hundreds of exchanges (*PD* 2004; *DTr* 2006b). Meanwhile, the culture and achievements of Africa are often implicitly denigrated by Western politicians. As one scholar has observed, Africa is for the West a 'haven for terrorists', the 'cradle of HIV/Aids', and a 'source of instability', but for China it is a 'strategically significant region' and place of opportunity (Gu 2006). China, moreover, acknowledges its political indebtedness to Africa for her support of China's entry into the UN and continued backing in international forums. That contrasts with Western states' total lack of acknowledgement of their indebtedness to Africa for its contributions to the West's industrialisation and cultural development (see Inikori 2002).

Unlike during the Mao era, China today provides no radical solutions to Africa's predicament and its 'neoliberalism with Chinese characteristics' likely provides no solutions at all. China instead avails itself of the historically determined disadvantages of Africa in trade (Holslag 2006), although much of what it sells to Africa is useful to developing manufacturing and providing affordable consumer goods (Soderbom and Teal 2004). While China differs from the West in that a greater proportion of its investment seemingly goes to non-oil sectors, part of that is imbricated with the continent's harsh labour regimens, in places like Zambia's Copperbelt (Lungu and Mulenga 2005; *TZ* 2006). China nevertheless is perceived as different in providing some investments of direct benefit beyond elite circles, in not insisting that Africa's political economy steer a required course, and in contributing to, not draining Africa's talent pool. For that reason, US neoconservatives have increasingly expressed alarm about China's gains in Africa (Brookes and Ji 2006; Bartholomew 2006).

It is not clear whether the differences outlined here will persist over the long-term. Among major powers at any given time, there are always differences in approach to subaltern states. The very process of differentiating superordinate and subordinate states and dominant and subaltern peoples tends over time, however, to make the conduct of great powers and their elites more similar than different. In a decade or two we should be able to determine whether that will be the case as well with China in Africa.

This research has been generously funded by the Hong Kong Research Grants Council.

References
Abila, Patrick (2005) 'It is Trade, Not Aid that Will Lift Continent from Poverty', *East African*, 8 November
AC (2005) 'Chinese Walls', 46(2): 8
ACBF (2004) *An Analysis of the Market for Skilled African Development Management Professionals*, s.1 <www.acbfpact.org/knowledge/operations.asp>
ADB (2005) *2004 Annual Procurement Report*. Tunis: ADB
Addis Fortune (Ethiopia) (2004) 'NEPAD and the challenge of Africa's Development: toward the Political Economy of a Discourse', *Society in Transition*, 35(1): 125–44
__(2006) 'Development and the Challenge of Poverty: NEPAD, Post-Washington Consensus and Beyond', in J.O. Adesina et al (eds) *Africa and Development Challenges in the New Millennium: the NEPAD Debate*. London: Zed
AFX News (2007) 'China's Hisense to Build Industrial Park in South Africa', 21 January
AFP (2005) 'Two Arrested in Cameroon Over Murder of Chinese Shopkeeper', 23 February
___(2006a) 'Africa Pays the Highest Price for Globalization', 18 January
___(2006b) 'US Watches China's Rising Star with Anxiety', 27 January
___(2006c) 'South Africa Fetes Chinese New Year with Dragons and Bollywood', 30 January
___(2006d) 'Chinese Businesses Workers in Demand in Algeria', 2 November
AHD (2000) New York: Houghton Miflin, 4th ed.
Ahmed, AKN (2004) *Washington Consensus: How and Why it Failed the Poor*. Dhaka: Shahitya Prakash
Ai Ping (1999) 'From Proletarian Internationalism to Mutual Development: China's Cooperation with Tanzania, 1965–95', in Goran Hyden and R. Muknadala (eds), *Agencies in Foreign Aid: Comparing China, Sweden and the United States in Tanzania* 169. Houndsmill: Macmillan
Akanga, E. (2006) 'China's Economic Development: a Good Lesson to Rwanda', *New Times*, 19 January <www.new.times.co.rw/index.php?option=com_content&task+view&id=3072&Itemid=58>
Akinjide, Richard (2005) 'Africa, China and Oil and Gas Supplies', *Alexander's Gas & Oil Connections* 10(17), 15 September <www.gasandoil.com/goc/news/nta53701.htm>
Alden, Chris (2005) 'China in Africa', *Survival* 47(3): 147–164
Alden, Chris and Martyn Davies (2006) 'A Profile of the Operations of Chinese Multinationals in Africa', *South African Journal of International Affairs* 13(1): 83–96
Alert Unit (2004) *Alert 2004: Report on Conflicts, Human Rights, and Peace-Building*, School of Peace Culture. Pau, Spain: Escola de Cultura de Pau
AllAfrica.com. (2006) 'The Scramble for African Oil', 25 May
AMPlify Wharton (2003) 'Into Africa: Doing Business on the Forgotten Continent' <http://exced-web.wharton.upenn.edu /Amplify/0312/amperspective.html>
Andreasson, Stefan (2005) 'Orientalism and African Development Studies: the "Reductive

Repetition", Motif in Theories of African Underdevelopment', *TWQ* 26(6): 971–986

APA 2004 'Angola/China: an Example of South–South Cooperation', 25 March

___(2006a) 'President Opens US$8 Million Luanda General Hospital', 2 March

___(2006b) 'Government to Build 200,000 Houses Countrywide Until 2008', 7 March

___(2006c) 'China Grants Additional USD 2 Billion Loan', 22 June

AP (2006) 'France's Ties with African Leaders Fading', 21 April

Araya, Selome (2007) 'The Misrepresentation of Africa', *Pambazuka News*, 14 February <http://www.pambazuka.org/en/category/comment/39756>

Asianews (2006) 'China–Africa Ties Grow and Tip Global Balance', 3 January <www.asianews.it/view_p.php?l= en&art=5023>

Ayers, Alison (2006) 'Demystifying Democratization: the Global Constitution of (Neo-) Liberal Polities in Africa', *TWQ* 27(2): 331–338

Ayittey, George (2007) 'Dr George Ayittey on China (France) and Africa' <www.ekosso.com/2006/11/dr_george_ayitt.html>

Ayodele, Thompson (2003) *Aid, Trade, Subsidies and Development in Africa*, Institute of Public Policy Analysis, <http:ippanigeria.org/page.php?instructions=page&page_id=323&nav_id=87>

Bagachwa, M.S.D. and Amy Mbelle (1995) 'Tanzania', in Samuel Wangwe (ed) *Exporting Africa: Technology, Trade and Industrialization in Sub-Saharan Africa*. London: Routledge

Barboza, David (2006) 'Some Assembly Needed: China as Asia Factory', *NYT*, 9 February

Bartholomew, Carolyn et al. (2006) 'Beijing Safari: the Challenge of China's Growing Ties to Africa', panel at American Enterprise Institute, 1 November

BBCMIR (2006) 'Text of Chinese President's Speech to Nigerian National Assembly, 27 April, 28 April

BBCRF (2006) 'World This Weekend', broadcast 4 June, 12:00 GMT

BD (2004a) 'Focus is on Aid and Support for Africa', 1 October

___(2004b) 'Quiet Superpower Seduces Africa', 30 November

___(2005) 'No Chance of SA Becoming US's Working Class', 2 August

___(2006) 'Out of Guangzhou, Africa Trade Booms', 23 May

Becker, J. (2004) 'China Fights UN Sanctions on Sudan to Safeguard Oil', *Independent*, 15 October

Bensah, E.K. (2003) 'The Cotonou Agreement: Who is Agreeing?', *Review of International Social Questions*, 22 May <www.risq.or/modules.php? name=News&file=print&sid=92>

Bhagwati, Jagdish and Arvin Panagariya (2003) 'Bilateral Trade Treaties are a Sham', *FT*, 13 July

Black, Panther (1969) 'Peking Builds Largest Tanzania Textile Mill', 15 January <www.etext.org/Politics/bpp/bpp19690115_3_tanzania.html>

Birchall, Jonathan (2006) 'Thousands Die as World Defines Genocide', *FT*, 6 July

Bond, Patrick (ed) (2005) *Fanon's Warning: A Civil Society Reader on the New Partnership for Africa's Development*. Trenton: Africa World Press

Booker, Salih and Ann-Louise Colgan (2006) 'Africa Policy Outlook 2006', *FPIF*, 17 March

BR (2006) 'Pervasive Unease', 49(6): 20–21, 9 February

Brautigam, Deborah (1998) *Chinese Aid and African Development: Exporting Green Revolution*. Basingstoke: Macmillan

___(2007) 'China and African Governance', *CFR* 14 February

Broad, Robin (2004) 'The Washington Consensus Meets the Global Backlash: Shifting Debates and Policies', *Globalizations* 1(2): 129–154

Broadman, Harry (2006) *Africa's Silk Road: China and India's New Economic Frontier*. Washington: WB

Brookes, Peter and Ji Hye Shin (2006) 'China's Influence in Africa: Implications for the

United States', Heritage Foundation Backgrounder #1916, 22 February, <www.heritage.org>

Butler, Tina (2005) 'Growing Pains and Growing Alliances: China, Timber and Africa', 20 April, <http://news/mongabay.com/2005.com/2005/0420x-tina_butler.html>

CABC (2006) 'Brief Introduction to the China–Africa Business Council', <www.cabc.org.cn/english/introduce.asp>

Cao Tian Yu (ed) (2005) *The Chinese Model of Modern Development*. New York: Routledge

Carroll, Rory (2004) 'Sudan Massacres are not Genocide, says EU', *Guardian*, 10 August

CCS (2006) *China's Interest and Activity in Africa's Construction and Infrastructure Sectors*. Stellenbosch University

CD (2006a) 'China's Direct Investment Overseas Rises to US$6.9b', 23 January

___(2006b) 'Scholarships for Africans Set to Double', 3 November

___(2007) 'They (the Toilets) Look Good, and Make US Feel Like Urbanites', 4 January

CF&F (2005) 'Foreign Economic Relations' <www.china.org.cn/english/en-sz2005/jj/jj-dw.htm>

CFR (2006) *More than Humanitarianism: a Strategic US Approach Toward Africa*, <www.cfr.org/publication/9302/>

Chandra, Nirmal Kumar (1999) 'FDI and Domestic Economy: Neoliberalism in China', *Economic & Political Weekly*, 6 November

Chang, Ha-Joon (2002) *Kicking Away the Ladder: Development Strategy in Historical Perspective*. London: Anthem

Chang, Yun-ping and Ko, Shu-ling (2005) 'Taiwan Foreign Minister Offers to Quit Over Senegal's Severance of Ties', *Taipei Times*, 27 October

Chen, Elaine (1996) 'Hopelessly De-Vote-ed', *Taiwan Panorama*, 2(76), <www.taiwan-panorama.com/en/show_issue.php3?id=199628502076E.TXT&page=1>

Chen Yiding (2003) 'Shi lun jingji quanqiuhua dui Feizhou Huaren jingji de yinxiang' (Tentative discussion of the impact of economic globalization on Africa's ethnic Chinese economy), Shijie Dili Yanjiu 12(3), 14–19 September

Chen, Zongde (2001) *Feizhou jingji quan yu Zhongguo qiye* (Africa's globalisation and China's industry). Beijing: Beijing chubanshe

Cheng, Allen (2004) 'Thirst for Oil Knows No Bounds', *SCMP*, 26 June

Cheow, Eric Teo Chu (2006) 'US-China Ideological Rivalry Heats Up', *Japan Times*, 5 January

Chiluba, Frederick (2000) 'Statement by the President of the Republic of Zambia', 27 December <www.statehouse.gov.zm/press/news/viewnews.cgi?category=3&id=977917598>

Ching, Frank 2005 'Cosy Ties, but China Needs to do more for Africa', *BT*, 13 July

CI (2007) 'Red China Meets Black Africa', Vol. 7:13, March

Clemens, Michael (2006) 'Medical Leave: A New Database of Health Professional Emigration from Africa'. Washington: Center for Global Development, Working Paper No. 95, August

Cockayne, R. (2005) 'SACU Needs Free Trade Agreement with the US', 12 June, <www.tralac.org/scripts/content.php?id=4324>

Coffman, Jennifer and Kevin Brennan (2006) 'African Studies Abroad: Meaning and Impact of America's Burgeoning Export Industy', *Frontiers: Interdisciplinary Journal of Study Abroad*, 9:139–147

Colombant, Nico (2004) 'China's New African Oil Ties Create Concerns', *VOA*, 29 September, <http://energybulletin.net/2340.html>

Commey, Pusch (2003) 'Biopiracy: the New Scramble for Africa', *NA*, 21 December

Cornwell, Rupert (2005) 'Darfur Killings Not Genocide, Says UN Group', *Independent*, 31 January

Craner, Lorne (2005) 'Economic Development without Political Liberalization: will the Chinese Model Prevail over the 'Global March of Freedom?', presentation, American Enterprise Institute, 14 December, <http://www.aei.org/events/filter.all,eventID.1206/transcript.asp>

CSM (2006) 'Democracy's "Special Forces" Face Heat', 6 February

___(2007) 'Chinese Leader's Almost Triumphal Trip to Africa', 9 February

Curtis, Mark and Claire Hickson (2006) 'Arming and Alarming: Arms Exports, Peace and Security', in David Mepham (ed) *The New Sino-Sphere: China in Africa*, 37–46. London: IPPR

Custers, Peter (2002) 'Unequal Exchange and Poverty in African Countries Exporting Primary Commodities', European Conference of People's Global Action, 2 September, <www.nadir.org/nadir/iniativ/agp/pgaeurope/leiden/poverty_africa.htm>

Daily News (Gaborone) (2006) 'Close to 3,000 Chinese in Botswana', 4 September, <http://www.gov.bw/cgi-bin/news.cgi?d=20060904>

Dauderstadt, Michael and Jurgen Stetten (2005) *China and Globalization*. Bonn: FES

Davies, Martin (2007) 'Yin and Yang', *Financial Mail*, 2 February

DC (2006) 'Nigeria-China Relations', 5 May

De Figueiredo, Antonio (2003) 'Africa's Relations with the West', *NA*, No. 416: 24–25, March

DeLisle, Jacques (2007) 'Into Africa: China's Quest for Resources and Influence', *Foreign Policy Research Institute E-Notes*, 19 February

Dirlik, Arif (2006) 'Beijing Consensus: Beijing "Gongshi": Who Recognizes Whom and to What End', <http://anscombe.mcmaster.ca/global1/servlet/Position2pdf?fn=PP_Dirlik_BeijingConsensus>

Dixon, Robyn (2007) 'Africa Holds Attractions for China Leaders', *LAT*, 31 January

DN (2006) 'Chinese Lured by Freedom into Africa', 12 December

Docquier, Frederic and Abdeslam Marfouk (2004) 'Measuring the International Mobility of Skilled Workers (1990-2000)', Working Paper 3381, Washington: WB

Donnelly, John (2005) 'China Scooping Up Deals in Africa as US Firms Hesitate', *Boston Globe*, 24 December

Dowden, Richard (2005) 'It's Good to Talk', *New Statesman*, 17 October

___(2006) 'Rebirth of the African University', *Prospect*, 26 January

DPA (2007) 'Chinese-Owned Small Businesses Bring Beijing to Nairobi', 12 February

Draper, Peter and Garth le Pere (eds) (2005) *Enter the Dragon – Towards a Free Trade Agreement Between China and the Southern African Customs Union*. Johannesburg: SIIA

DTe (2005) 'Beijing Greets Mugabe with New Aid Deal', 27 July

DTr (2004) 'Aids Ravaged Africa Hit by Mass Exodus', 2 November

___ (2005) 'The Long March to China', 20 October

___(2006a) 'Is Africa the New Oil Haven', 14 June

___ (2006b) 'Problems of Africa-China Co-operation', 8 November

Dyer, Gwynne (2007) 'Africa's Population Bomb', *IHT*, Mar 15: A15

EAS (2006) 'Kituyi's Vision for Africa's Place in Global Trade', 30 May

Eastwood, JB, et al. (2005) 'Loss of Health Professionals from Sub-Saharan Africa: the Pivotal Role of the UK', *Lancet*, 365, 28 May: 1893–1900

ECA (2006) 'International Migration and the Achievement of MDGs in Africa', paper present at the International Symposium on International Migration and Development, Turin, Italy, 28–30 June

Economist (1997) 'America Loses its Afrophobia', 26 April: 23–24

___(2000) 'Africa: the Hopeless Continent', 14 April

___(2004) 'A New Scramble', 27 November: 84–85

___(2005) 'It'll Do what it Can Get Away With', 3 December

___(2006) 'Democracy or Dictatorship?: Museveni's Re-election in Uganda,' 4 March

Edwards, Chris and Rhys Jenkins (2005) *The Effect of China and India's Growth and Trade Liberalisation on Poverty in Africa*, UK Department of International Development <www.eldis.org/static/ DOC19251.htm>

EH (2005) 'Ethiopia: Country Second Most Populous in Africa', *AN*, 13 October

___(2007) 'China's Trade with Africa Expanding Swiftly', *Ethiopian Herald*, 7 February

Eisenman, Joshua and Joshua Kurlantzick (2006) 'China's Africa Strategy', *CH*, 105(691): 219–224

Federici, Silvia and George Caffentzis (2004) 'Globalization and Professionalization in Africa', *Social Text*, 22(2): 81–99

Ferguson, Ian (2003) *US Trade & Investment Relations with Sub-Saharan Africa: the AGOA and Beyond*. Washington: Congressional Research Service

FES (2005) 'Panel on: 'China in Africa: focus on trade and investment', Leaflet distributed at WTO NGO forum, Hong Kong, 13 December

Fine, Ben and Jomo, K.S. (2005) *The New Development Economics: Post Washington Consensus Neoliberal Thinking*. London: Zed

FPC (2005) 'China and Globalisation', July <http://fpc.org.uk/fisblob/665.pdf>

French, Howard (2005) 'China Wages Classroom Struggle to Win Friends in Africa', *NYT*, 20 November

FT (2006a) 'Friend or Forager?', 23 February

___ (2006b) 'China Issues Zambian Election Threat', 6 September

___(2007) 'Ethiopia Looks East to Slip Reins of Western Orthodoxy', 6 February

Ghosts of Rwanda (2005) Alexandria, VA: PBS Home Video

Gillespie, Sandra (2001) *South-South Transfer: Study of Sino-African Exchanges*. New York: Garland

Goldstein, Andrea et al. (2006) *China and India: What's in it for Africa?*. Paris: OECD

Greenpeace (2000) 'Four Activists Arrested as Greenpeace Continues its Protests', 14 July <http://archive.greenpeace.org/forests/news/index.htm>

Gu Xuewu (2006) 'China Returns to Africa', *Trends East Asia*, Studie nr. 9: 8 Bochum: Sektion Politik Ostasiens: Ruhr-Universitat

Guang, Lei (2005) 'Realpolitik Nationalism: International Sources of Chinese Nationalism', *Modern China*, 31(4): 487–514

Hagopian, Amy (2004) 'The Migrations of Physicians from Sub-Saharan Africa to the United States of America: Measures of the African Brain Drain', *Human Resources for Health*, 2(17): 1–10

Hall, Richard and Hugh Peyman (1976) *The Great Uhuru Railway: China's Showpiece in Africa*. New York: Gollancz

Hallinan, Conn (2006) 'Desert Faux: The Sahara's Mirage of Terrorism', *FPIF*, 2 March

Hari, Johann (2005) 'The Century's First Genocide is Nearly Over', *Independent*, 4 October

Harrison, Graham (2005) 'Economic Faith, Social Protest and a Misreading of African Society: the Travails of Neoliberalism in Africa', *TWQ* 26(8): 1303–20

___ (2006) 'Neo-liberalism and the Persistence of Clientalism in Africa', in Richard Robison (ed) *The Neo-Liberal Revolution: Forging the Market State*. New York: Palgrave

Harsch, Ernest (2003) 'Foreign Investment on Africa's Agenda,' *African Recovery*, 17(2): 12–16

Hartung, William and Frida Berrigan (2005) 'Militarisation of US Africa Policy, 2000–05', <http://worldpolicy.org/projects/arms/reports/AfricaMarch2005.html>

Harvey, David (2005) *A Brief History of Neoliberalism*. Oxford: Oxford University Press

Hayes, Stephen (2002) 'Statement of Stephen Hayes, President, Corporate Council on Africa', in *The New Partnership for Africa's Development: an African Initiative*, hearing before the Subcommittee on Africa, US House of Representatives Serial no. 107–114: 18–20

Herald (Zimbabwe) (2005) '2005: Year of Major Strides for Africa', 22 December

Herbert, Nandi (2005) 'Africa: Killing us Softly', *NA*. No. 445: 8–12, November

Hertz, Noreena (2005) 'We Achieved Next to Nothing', *NS*, 12 December: 14–16

Hilsum, Lindsey (2006) 'We Love China', *Granta*, no. 92

Hirvonen, Pekka (2005) 'Stingy Samaritans: Why Recent Increases in Development Aid Fail to Help the Poor', Global Policy Forum, <http://www.eldis.org/static/DOC20305.htm>

Hoffman, Katharina (2007) *Challenges for International Development Cooperation: the Case of China*. Berlin: Friedrich Ebert Stiftung

Holslag, Jonathan (2006) 'China's New Mercantilism in Central Africa', *African and Asian Studies*, 5(2): 133–169

Houston Chronicle (2007) 'Africa Tops Mid-East for US Crude', 25 February <http://www.aei.org/events/filter.all.eventID.1416/transcript.asp>

Huang Ping and Cui Zhiyuan (2005) *Zhongguo yu quanqiuhua: Huasheng gongshi haishi Beijing gongshi* (China and globalisation: Washington Consensus or Beijing Consensus). Beijing: Shehui xuexe wenxian chubanshe

Hurst, Cindy (2006) *China's Oil Rush in Africa*, s.l.: IAGS Energy Security

Hurt, Stephen (2003) 'Cooperation and Coercions? The Cotonou Agreement Between the European Union and ACP States and the End of the Lome Convention', *TWQ*, 24(1): 161–176

Hutchinson, Alan (1976) *China's African Revolution*. Boulder: Westview

IADB (2006) 'How China and Latin America Compete in the Global Marketplace' <www.iadb.org/INT/Trade/1_english/2_WhatWeDo/Documents/cOtherPubs/AdditionalPubs/China/Chapter%205.pdf>

IEA (2004) 'World Energy Outlook 2004', <www.iea.org/Textbase/publications/free_new_Desc.asp?PUBS_ID=1266>

'Illegal Logging Europe Page – Germany' (2006) <www.illegal-logging.info/approachesLev3.php?approachId=20&approachSub Name=germany>

Indian Express (2006) ' Loosing Africa to China', 15 January

Inikori, Joseph (2002) *Africans and the Industrial Revolution in England: a Study in International Trade and Economic Development*. Cambridge: Cambridge University Press

IOM (2003) 'The Brain Drain' <www.iom.int/mida/mida_health.shtml>

IPS (2004) 'Tied Aid Strangling Nations, Says UN', 6 July <www.ipsnews.net/interna.asp?idnews=24509>

___(2005) 'Fifty Years Later, a Powerful China Basks in the Bandung Spirit', 20 April

IRIN (2005a) 'Angola: Oil Backed Loan Will Finance Recovery Projects' 21 February, <www.irinnews.org/ report.asp?ReportID=45688>

___(2005b) 'Angola: Cautious Optimism for 2005' 14 January <www.irinnews.org/report.asp?ReportID=45077>

___(2006a) 'China Entrenches Position in Booming Economy', 17 April

___(2006b) 'Zambia: Citizens Wary of "Exploitative" Chinese Employers', 23 November

Itano, Nicole (2005) 'Demand and Supply', *Newsday*, 4 October

Jack, Andrew (2005) '"Brain Drain" puts Africa's Hospitals on the Critical List', *FT*, 7 July: 20

Jaffer, Z. (2004) 'US Election and the World', *YG*, 15 November <http://yaleglobal.yale.edu/display.article?id=4868>

Jarrett, Albert (1996) *The Underdevelopment of Africa: Colonialism, Neo-Colonialism and Socialism*. Lanham: University Press of America

Jeune Afrique.com (2006) 'Ils ont Choisi l'Afrique' (They have chosen Africa), 12 November, <www.jeuneafrique.com/jeune_afrique/ article_jeune_afrique.asp?art_cle=LIN1216ilsoneuquirf0>

Jing, B. (2004) '2004 nian shijie yan zhong de zhongguo: quan shijie turan dou xiang jiang zhongwen', <http://news.tom.com/1002/20041231-1708037.html>

Johannesburg Star (2004) 'Chinese People Need a Channel so they can have a Say', 10 May

Kaplan, Robert (2005) 'America's African Rifles', Atlantic, 295(3): 91–94, April

Kaplinsky, Raphael, et al (2006) The Impact of China on Sub-Saharan Africa. Sussex: Institute of Development Studies, <http://www.ids.ac.uk/ids/global/Asiandriversbackgroundpapers.html>

Kapur, Devesh and John McHale (2005) Give Us your Best and Brightest: the Global Hunt for Talent and Its Impact on the Developing World. Washington: Center for Global Development

Kennan, Jane and Christopher Stevens (2005) Opening the Package: the Asian Drivers and Poor-Country Trade, Institute of Development Studies Sussex: IDS <www.ids.ac.uk/ids/global/pdfs/CSAsian%20DriversTrade.pdf>

Klare, Michael (2006) 'Fuelling the Dragon: China's Strategic Energy Dilemma,' CH 105(690): 180–185

Kleine-Ahlbrandt, Stephanie and Andrew Small (2007) 'Beijing Cools on Mugabe,' IHT, 4 May

Knight, Richard (2002) 'Expanding Petroleum Production in Africa', ACAS Bulletin, No. 64

Kollehlon, Konia and Edward Eule (2003) 'The Socioeconomic Attainment Patterns of Africans in the United States', International Migration Review 37(4): 1163–90

Konopo, Joel (2005) 'Chinese Economy Stimulates African Markets', Reporter (Botswana), 21 February

Kramer, Andrew (2007) 'Markets Suffer After Russia Bans Immigrant Vendors', NYT, 14 April

Kuada, John (2005) 'Learning from Asia: Chinese Investment Inflows to Africa and their Possible Impact on African Management Practices', African Renaissance, July–August: 36–41

Kurlantzick, Joshua (2006) 'Beijing's Safari: China's Move into Africa and Its Implications for Aid, Development and Governance', Policy Outlook, November <http://www.carnegieendowment.org/publications/index.cfm?fa=view&id=18833&prog=zch>

L'Express (2005) 'Textile Sector: AGOA – its Future in Africa', L'Express (Mauritius), 3 August

Lafargue, Francois (2005) 'China's Presence in Africa', China Perspectives, no. 61: 2–9

Lake, Michael (2003) 'NEPAD, the AU and the EU: the Challenges of a Relationship', workshop on 'Putting the Partnership into NEPAD', Pretoria, 22 May <www.eusa.org.za>

Lall, Sanjay (2005) 'FDI, AGOA and Manufactured Exports by a Landlocked, Least Developed African Economy: Lesotho', JDS, 41(6): 998–1022

Lardy, Nicholas (2007) 'China Economy: Problems and Prospects', Footnotes (Foreign Policy Research Institute) 12(4), February <http://www.fpri.org/footnotes/124.200702.lardy.chinaseconomy.html>

Lee, Don (2006) 'China Making Big Oil Moves', LAT, 23 January

Leggett, Karbyt (2005) 'China Forges Ties Alliances with War-Torn Nations', WSJ, 30 March

Leonard, Andrew (2006) 'No Consensus on the Beijing Consensus', Salon, 15 September

Leonard, Mark (2005a) 'The Road Obscured', FT, 9 July

___(2005b) 'The Geopolitics of 2026', Economist, November 16, <www.cer.org.uk/articles/leonard_economist_16nov05.html>

Leonard, Terry (2006) 'Africa Looks East for Economic, Political Salvation', Standard (Hong Kong), 4 August

Lesufi, Ishmael (2004) 'South Africa and the Rest of the Continent: Toward a Critique of the Political Economy of NEPAD', Current Sociology, 52(5): 809–829

Leu, Siew Ying (2006) 'Guangdong Seeks Tougher Rules for Foreign Residents', SCMP, 20 September

___(2007) 'Guangzhou Residents at Odds with Increase in Foreigners', *SCMP*, 22 February

Levitsky, Steven (2002) 'The Rise of Competitive Authoritarianism' *Journal of Democracy* 13(2): 51

Li He (2005) 'The Chinese Path of Economic Reform and Its Implications', *Asian Affairs: an American Review*, 31(4): 195–211

Li Xing (2003) 'The Power of the Logo: The Implication of the Chinese Revolution for Pan-African Movement', in Mammo Muchie (ed) *The Making of the Africa-Nation: Pan Africanism and the African Renaissance*, 147–68. London: Adonis & Abbey

Li Yong (2003) 'The Impact of FDI on Trade: Evidence from China's Bilateral Trade', *Journal of the Academy of Business and Economics* 2(2) <http://www.allbusiness.com/legal/international-law-foreign-investment-finance/752278-1.html>

Lieberthal, Kenneth (2006) 'Why the US Malaise over China?' *YG*, 19 January, <http://yaleglobal.yale.edu/article.print?id=6842>

Liu Bo (2006) 'Feizhou zhanwang dongfang: cong 'Huashengdun gongshi' dao 'Beijing gongshi' (Africa looks east: from the 'Washington Consensus' to the 'Beijing Consensus'), *21SJBD*, 7 November

Liu Guijin (2003) 'Great Prospects for Sino-African Cooperation', 11 December <www.china.org.cn/english/ features/China-Africa/82197>

___ (2004) 'China–Africa Relations: Equality, Cooperation and Mutual Development', speech, Institute of Security Studies, Pretoria, South Africa, 9 November <www.iss.co.za/SEMINARS/2004/0911chinaspeech.pdf>

___ (2005) 'All-Weather Friends in Need and Indeed: China–Africa Relations Seen from the Eyes of a Chinese Diplomat', *African Renaissance*, July/August

Liu, Phillip (2001) 'Cross-Strait Scramble for Africa: a Hidden Agenda in China–Africa Cooperation Forum', *Harvard Asia Quarterly*, Spring: 39–45

Lorenz, Andreas (2005) 'A Technocrat Riding a Wild Tiger', *Der Spiegel*, no. 45, 10 November <www.spiegel.de/international/spiegel/0,1518,384155,00.html>

Lungu, J. and Mulenga, C. (2005) *Corporate Social Responsibility Practices in the Extractive Industry in Zambia*, NIZA Institute for Southern African Affairs, <www.niza.nl/docs/200505301137193579.pdf>

Lyman, Princeton (2005) 'China's Rising Role in Africa: Presentation to the US–China Commission', 21 July <www.uscc.gov/hearings/2005hearings/written_testimonies/05_07_21_22wrts/lyman_princeton_wrts.pdf>

M&G (2006) 'Don't Fear the Dragon', 23 June

Macauhub (2007) 'Chinese Specialists Prepare Agricultural Development Program in Angola', 12 April <www.macauhub.com/mo/en/print.php?pageurl=en/news.php?ID=3150>

MacGregor, Karen (2005) 'Out of Africa', *Times Higher Education Supplement*, 1 July

Makokha, Kwamchestsi (2005) 'Who'd Take a $500 Job in Africa', *NS*, 14 March: 29–30.

Mallaby, Sebastian (2004) 'How Africa Subsidises US Health Care', *WP*, 29 November

Mamdani, Mahmood (2002) 'Misrule Britannia', *Guardian* (UK), 8 February

_____(2007) 'The Politics of Naming: Genocide, Civil War, Insurgency', *London Review of Books*, 8 March

Manda, Gilbert (2004) 'Brain Drain or Brain Gain?' *NA* 197(1): 74, December

Mao Zengyu (2005) *Sidigelici yu zhuan gui jing ji xue: cong 'Huashengdun gongshi' dao 'Hou Huashengdun gongshi' zai dao 'Beijing gongshi'* (Stiglitz and transition economics: from the 'Washington Consensus' to the 'Post Washington Consensus and again to the Beijing Consensus). Beijing: Zhongguo jingji chubanshe

Mawdsley, Emma (2007) 'China and Africa: Emerging Challenges to the Geographies of Power', *Geographic Compass* 1:1–17.

Max, Liniger-Goumaz (1997) *The United States, France and Equatorial Guinea: the Dubious 'Friendships'*. Geneva: Les Editions du Temps

Mayanja, Abu (2005) 'Uganda Should Invite "Real" Chinese Investors', *NV* (Uganda), 10 May

Mazrui, Ali and Amadu Kaba (2004) 'Between the Brain Drain and the Brain Bonus: the African Diaspora as a Nation Afloat', Africa's Brain Gain Conference, Nairobi, 19–22 December, <www.africasbraingain.org/ conference/report/ali_mazrui.pdf>

McDonald, Scott and Terry Walmsley (2003) 'Bilateral Free Trade Agreements and Customs Unions: the Impact of the EU/Republic of South Africa Free Trade Agreement on Botswana' <http://econpapers.repec.org/paper/gtaworkpp/1644.htm>

McGreal, Chris (2002) 'US Funds Penetrate Zimbabwe Airwaves', *Guardian*, 24 January: 17

Melamed, Claire (2005) *The Economics of Failure: the Real Cost of 'Free' Trade for Poor Countries*. London: Christian Aid <www.christian-aid.org.uk/indepth/506liberalisation/Economics%20of%20failure.pdf>

Melber, Henning (2005) 'Globalisation Blocks Regional Integration', *Development and Cooperation* 32(3): 116–11, <www.inwent.org/ E+Z/content/archive-eng/03-2005/tribune_art1.html>

Michiaki, Suma (1979) 'The Japanese – Still Unknown: Address by Ambassador of Japan to Canada, to the Empire Club', 26 April: 281–376, <www.empireclubfoundation.com/details/asp?SpeechID=1701&FT=yes>

Milanovic, Branko (2005) *Worlds Apart: Measuring International and Global Inequality*. Princeton: Princeton University Press

Milburn, Sarah (2004) 'Toujours la Chasse Gardee? French Power and Influence in Late 20th Century Francophone Central Africa (*c.* 1970-1995)', in Edward Rhodes et al (eds), *Presence, Prevention and Persuasion: A Historical Analysis of Military Force and Political Influence*, New York: Lexington Books

Mittelman, James (2006) 'Globalization and Development: Learning from Debates in China', forthcoming in *Globalizations* 3(3): 377–91, September <www.csglobalization.org/2.pdf>

MOE (2003) *Zhongguo Feizhou jiaoyu jiaoliu yu hezuo* (China–Africa Educational Exchange & Cooperation). Beijing: MOE

Monson, Jamie (2004–05) 'Freedom Railway', *Boston Review* <www.bostonreview.net/BR29.6/monson.html>

Moorcraft, Paul (2007) 'Why Beijing is Winning in Africa', *BD*, 2 February

Morgenthau, Hans (1960) *Politics Among Nations*. New York: Knopf. 3rd ed

Motyl, Alexander (1999) *Revolutions, Nations, Empires: Conceptual Limits and Theoretical Possibility*. New York: Columbia University Press

Muekalia, Domingos Jardos (2004) 'Africa and China's Strategic Partnership', *African Security Review* 13(1): 5–11

Mukandala, Rwekaza (1999) 'From Proud Defiance to Beggary: a Recipient's Tale', in Hyden & Mukandala, 31–67

Mullan, Fitzhugh (2005) 'The Metrics of Physician Brain Drain', *New England Journal of Medicine*, 353(17): 1810–18, 27 October

NA (2006) 'Go East My Son', December: 8–9

Namibian (2006a) 'Govt Should Wise Up to Benefits of "Chinese Invasion"', 11 August

___(2006b) 'Sub-Saharan Leadership to Nowhere', 5 May

Nankani, Gobind (2005) 'Enhancing Africa's Development Through an "Export Push": Prospects and Challenges', 14 September, <http://worldbank.org/wbsite/external/countries/africaext/0,,contentMDK>

Ncube, Archbishop Pius (2005) 'Zimbabwe's Chinese Puzzle', *Embassy* (Canada), 3 August, <www.embassymag.ca/html/index/php?display=story&full_path=2005/august/3/

123

zimbabwe/>

Nelson, Fraser (2005) 'How African Aid Can Be the New Imperialism', *Scotsman*, 8 June, 26

NE (2006) 'The Chinese are in Africa – This Time to Stay', 13 March

Ni Yangshuo (2006) 'Servir d'intermediaire pour faciliter les rapports entre la Chine et le Nigeria' (To serve as an intermediary to facilitate rapport between China and Africa), Chinafrique, no. 10, <www.chinafrique.com/zf-2005/2006-10/2006.10-hz-1.htm>

NMI (2006) 'African Institute of Science & Technology', <www.nmiscience.org/aist.html>

Norberg, Johan (2006) 'China Paranoia Derails Free Trade', *Far Eastern Economic Review*, 169(1): 46–49

Nunn, Alex and Sophia Price (2004) 'Managing Development: EU and African Relations through the Evolution of the Lome and Cotonou Agreements', *Historical Materialism*, 12(4): 203–30

NV (2005) 'Struggle Toward a Self-Sustaining Economy: Museveni's Labour Day Speech', 5 May

Nwugo, Jude-Cyprian (1977) *African Responses to an Issue of Disputed Representation in the United Nations*, PhD dissertation, Howard University

Nyamwana, Dismas (2004) 'Cross-Cultural Adaption: African Students in China', *Ife Psychologia*, 12(2): 1–16

Nyang, Sulayman (2005) 'US–Africa Relations over the Last Century: an African Perspective', Social Research 72(4): 913–34

Nye, Joseph (2005) 'The Rise of China's Soft Power', *WSJ Asia*, 29 December

Nyerere, Julius (1974) *Freedom and Development*. Dar Es Salaam: Oxford University Press

Observer (2007) 'Red Gold: China's Quest for Oil', 7 January

OECD (2005*) The Development Effectiveness of Food Aid*. Paris: OECD

Ohio University Database (ca. 2001) 'Distribution of the Overseas Chinese Population' <http://www.library.ohiou.edu/subjects/shao/databases_ popdis.htm>

O'Neill, Mark (2007) 'A New Frontier', *SCMP*, 29 January

Pallister, David (2005) 'Alarm Bells Sound Over Massive Loans Bankrolling Oil-Rich, Graft Tainted Angola', *Guardian*, 1 June

Palmerston, Lord (1848) *Hansard's Parliamentary Debates*, 3d ser. vol. 97, col. 122, 1 March

Pan, Esther (2006) 'China, Africa and Oil', *CFR,* 12 January <www.cfr.org/publication/9557/>

Parwani, Audrey 'HK a Stop on Guangzhou Drug Route', *SCMP*, December 23: 4

Pawson, Lara (2005) 'You Let Her into the House? Reflections on the Politics of Aid in Africa', *Radical Philosophy*, May/June <www.radicalphilosophy.com/default.asp?channel_id=2187&editorial_id +17648>

PD (2000) 'Fruitful Sino-African Cooperation in Education and Culture', 2 October <http://english.people.com.cn/english/200010/02/eng20001002_51732.html>

___ (2002) 'Chinese Citizens Evacuated to Safety from Bouake', 28 September

___(2004) 'Cultural Exchanges Promote Sino-African Cooperation', 10 May

___(2006) 'China and Africa Enjoy Bright Prospect of Mutual Investment', 12 January <http://english.people.com.cn/200601/12/print20060112_234994.html>

PE (2006) 'Forward with China', 8 May

Peel, Michael (2003) 'Trade Union', *New Republic*, 7 April, 19

___(2006) 'Mining's Multicultural Mix', *Financial Times*, 22 December

Pires, Mark, et al (1999) *Investing in Return: Rates of Return of African PhDs Trained in North America*. New York: Social Science Research Council

Poston, Dudley, et al (1994) 'The Global Distribution of the Overseas Chinese Around 1990', *Population & Development Review*, 20(3): 631–4

PRCMOC (2006) 'China South Africa Education Cooperation', 26 April <www.csc.mofcom.

gov.cn/csweb/sacc/infor/Arictl.jsp?a_no+62079&col_no=626> and <www.csc.mofcom.gov.
cn/csweb/sacc/info/Article.jsp?a_no=60278&col_no=621>

PRCMOFA (2006) 'China's African Policy', *PD*, 12 January <http://english.peopledaily.com.
cn/20060112_234894.html>

PTI (2007) 'Free Trade Areas Vital for China's Foreign Trade: Minister', 22 February

Qi Jianwei (2005) 'Talking Points for Deputy Direct-General Qi Jianwei ...', 24 May <www.
focac.org/eng/hxxd/ jzgz/t196993>

Raffer, Kunibert (1987) *Unequal Exchange and the Evolution of the World System: Reconsidering
the Impact of Trade on North-South Relations*. London: Macmillan

Ramo, Joshua C. (2004a) *The Beijing Consensus: Notes on the New Physics of Chinese Power*.
London: Foreign Policy Centre

___(2004b) 'China has Discovered its own Economic Consensus', *FT*, 7 May

___(2004c) 'Beijing Gongshi' (Beijing Consensus), *Caijing Wenzhai*. no. 8: 19 <www.wiseman.
co.cn/magazine/cjwz/0408/04101.htm>

Reina, Peter (2004) 'Chinese Contractors Flex Lean Muscles in Sudan', *Engineering News-
Record*, 12 April, 18

Ren Kie (2007) 'Chinese Airline Announces First Regular China–Africa Link', *Radio France
Internationale*, 5 January

Reuters (2004) 'Bank of England Voted 9–0 for Rate Rise', 24 June

___(2005) 'China Muscles in to Africa Oil Scramble', 15 December

Rice, Andrew (2004) 'Letter from Uganda', *The Nation* (New York), 30 August, 28–30

Rieff, David (1998) 'In Defense of Afro-Pessimism', *World Policy Journal*, 15(4): 10–22

Roberts, Sam (2005) 'More Africans Entering US than in Days of Slavery', *NYT*, 21 February

RTE (Ireland) (2005) 'FDI in Africa Leans too much toward Mining', 13 September <http://
www.rte.ie/business/2005/0913/africa.html>

RW (2004) '"Beijing Consensus": a China Model', 31 May <http://bj.people.com.cn/
GB/25527/33619/33784/2534531.html>

Ryu, Alisha (2004) 'China's Expanding Political, Economic Reach Deep into East Africa',
VOA, 29 September, <www1.voanews.com/article.cfmn?objectID=D6721C6C-1CD0-42C%-
B4AEF9884859806>

Sandbrook, Richard (2005) 'Africa's Great Transformation?' *Journal of Development Studies*,
41(6): 1118–25

Sautman, Barry and Yan Hairong (2007) *East Mountain Tiger, West Mountain Tiger: China, the
West and 'Colonialism' in Africa*, Baltimore: Maryland Series in Contemporary Asian Studies,
no. 187

SCMP (2006) 'Missing Millions Reveal Ills of Africa's Aid Funding System', 2 June: A16

___ (2007) 'Gabon's Pigmies Pin Hopes on Resource Hungry China', 27 February

Segal, Hagai (2006) 'Germany's Goal: to Defeat a Dual Threat', *SCMP*, 8 June

Shambaugh, David (1993) *Beautiful Imperialist: China Perceives America, 1972–1990*. Princeton:
Princeton University Press

Shichor, Yitzhak (2005) 'Sudan: China's Outpost in Africa', CB 5(21): 9–11

___(2007) 'China's Darfur Policy', CB 7(7): 5–8

Shinn, David and Joshua Eisenman (2005) 'Dueling Priorities for Beijing in the Horn of
Africa', CB 5(21): 6–9

Shinn, David (2005) 'China's Approach to East, North and the Horn of Africa', testimony,
US–China Economic & Security Review Commission, 21 July

Simpson, Peter (2006) 'Beijing's New Street Hustlers', *SCMP*, 2 July

Singh, A. (2006) 'China and Africa: Friend and Foe', *Financial Mail*, 3 March: 41

Smith, Christopher (R-IL) (2005) Statement in 'China's Influence in Africa', hearing, House
Subcommittee on Africa, Washington: GPO, 28 July

Soderbom, Mans and Francis Teal (2004) 'How Can Policy Towards Manufacturing in Africa Reduce Poverty? A Review of the Current Evidence from Cross-Country Firm Studies', in K.A. Wolmuth et al, *African Development Perspectives Yearbook 2002/2003*. Muenster: Lit-Verlag

Srkar, P. (2001) 'The North-South Terms of Trade Debate: a Re-examination', *Progres in Development Studies*, 1(4): 309–27

ST (2006a) 'Competition from China Sharpens Minds in Sector,' 29 October: 10

___(2006b) 'Chinese Envoy to S. Africa Defends Country's Policy Toward Africa', 14 March

Sudan Tribune (2005) 'China and Sudan Reap Benefits from Marriage of Convenience', 22 March

Sutter, Robert (2005) 'China is on the Rise ...' *YG*, 22 April <http://yaleglobal.yale.edu/display.article?id=5612>

TD (2005) 'Can Nigeria be Africa's China?' 2 August

___(2006a) 'Trade with China Hits $3bn Mark', 26 February

___(2006b) '50,000 Nigerian Engineers Unemployable', 7 April

___(2007) 'Chinese Investment in Nigeria – What Motives?', 27 February

Teunissen, January and Age Akkerman (eds) (2004) *Diversity in Development: Reconsidering the Washington Consensus*. Hague: FONAD

TEA (2007) 'France Bungles Policy', 6 March

'The Twisted Triangle: America, China, and Sudan' (2006) 11 September, <http://chinamatters.blogspot.com/2006/09/twisted-triangle-america-china-and.html>

Thiong'o, Nick (2006) 'China Unveils Move to Curb Sub-Standard Exports', *Kenya Times*, 23 November

Thomas, Charles (2004) 'From Underclass to Community Leaders: the Chinese Experience in South Africa', 23 April <www.publish.gio.gov.tw/FCJ/current/04042371.html>

Thompson, Drew (2005) 'China's Soft Power in Africa: from the 'Beijing Consensus to Health Diplomacy', *CB*, 5(21): 1–4, 13 October

Thomsen, Stephen (2005) *Foreign Direct Investment in Africa: the Private-Sector Response to Improved Governance*, Chatham House IEP Briefing Paper 05/06 <www.riia.org/pdf/research/ie/BPafrica-fdi.pdf>

Thornton, Alan (2005) 'Prepared Statement ...' , hearing, Committee on International Relations, House of Representatives, China's Influence in Africa, 28 July. Washington: GPO

Tian Ye (2007) 'Doufu Lin chuang Feizhou' (Beancurd Lin Breaks a Pathway in Africa), *Banyue Tan* No. 5, <http://news3.xinhuanet.com/banyt/2007-04/27/content_6035448.htm>

Timberg, Craig (2006) 'From Competitors to Trade Partners', *WP*, 3 December

TN (2005) 'Enter the Dragon', 1 November

___(2006) 'China's Growth Debunks Capitalist Myth', 3 January

___(2007a) 'India and Africa: It's Old Friends, New Game and Rules', 9 February

___(2007b) 'Hot on China's Heels, Brazil is Coming', 2 February

TP (2005) 'Chinese Doughnuts Producers Perturb Bamileke Traders', 25 July

Tull, Denis (2005) *Die Afrikapolitik der Volksrepublik China*. Berlin: Deutsche Institut fur Internationale Politk und Sicherheit

___(2006) 'China's Engagement in Africa: Scope, Significance and Consequence', *Journal of Modern African Studies*, 44(3): 459–479, September

Turner, Jennifer and Juli Kim (2007) 'China's Filthiest Export', *Foreign Policy in Focus*, 7 February <www. fpif.org/fpifxt/3978>

TZ (2006) 'Chinese Investors Prevent Minister from Visiting Coal Mine', 25 May

UN (2003) 'China: Support for NEPAD', <www.un.org/esa/africa/support/China.htm>

___(2007) *World Economic Situation and Prospects 2007*. New York: UN, Department of Economic and Social Affairs

UNCTAD (2003) *The African Growth and Opportunity Act: a Preliminary Assessment*. New York: UN

___(2006a) 'Data Show Foreign Direct Investment Climbed Sharply in 2005', <www.unctad.org/Templates/webflyer.asp?docid+6733&intItem ID=1528 &lang =1>

___(2006b) *World Investment Report 2006*. New York: UN

UNOSAA (2005) 'Resources Flows to Africa: an Update on Statistical Trends', <www.un.org/africa/osaa>

UPI (2005a) 'Chinese Influence in Africa Raises Fears', 29 July

___(2005b) 'Africa Big Oil Supplier to China', 18 July

USACOC 2005 'State Department Issues Background Note on Angola', <http://www.us-angola.org/pressreleases/200503.htm>

USAID (2005) 'Burundi Complex Emergency Situation Report #2', <www.reliefweb.int/rw/RWB.NSF/db900SID/EGUA-6EFQGF?OpenDocument.>

USAID/OTI (2005) 'Sudan Field Report' <www.usaid.gov.our_work/cross-cutting_programs/transition_initiatives/country/sudan/rpt>

USDOC (2006) *US Africa Trade Profile*. Washington: DOC

USDOE (2004) 'US Petroleum Imports and Exports', October <www.eia.doe.gov/oil_gas/petroleum/info_glance/importexport.html>

USSD (2005) 'Africa Central to US Private Sector Oil and Gas Agenda', *States News Service*, 30 November

Vanguard (2006) 'No Economic Development without Democracy – Nnamani', 28 April

Waal, Alex (2007) 'The Wars of Sudan', *The Nation* (US), 19 March

Wainaina, Binyavanga (2006) 'How to Write About Africa', *Granta*, no. 92, <www.granta.com/extracts/2615>

Wang Haiming (ed) (2005) *Beijing gongshi* (Beijing consensus). Beijing: Shehui kexue chubanshe

Wang Hui (2003) *China's New Order: Society, Politics, and Economy in Transition*. Cambridge: Harvard University Press

Wanyeki, L. Muthoni (2006). 'Oil Wars are Coming to Africa', *East African*, 28 February

WB and IMF (2006) *Applying the Debt Sustainability Framework for Low-Income Countries Post Debt Relief*. Washington: WB & IMF

WBGAR (2004) *Patterns of Asia-Africa Trade & Investment: Potential for Ownership and Partnership*. Tokyo

WEF 2006 'Trade Winds: Chinese Investment in Africa', 26 January <www.weforum.org/site/knowledgenavigator.nsf/Content/_S16446>

Weidlich Brigitte (2006) 'Forty Thousand Chinese in Namibia', *Namibian*, 21 November

WH (2003) 'President Bush Discusses US-Africa Partnership from South Africa', Office of the Press Secretary, 9 July <www.whitehouse.gov/news/releases/2003/07/20030709-35.html>

Whi, Lyal (2006) 'A Match Made in Beijing', *M&G* (Johannesburg), 20 January

White, David (2006) 'A Spectacular Resurgence', *FT*, 21 November

WHO (2006) *2006 World Health Report*. Lusaka: WHO

Widdershoven, Cyril (2004) 'Chinese Quest for Crude Increases Focus on Africa', *Energy Security*, 15 November, <www.iags.org/n1115004>

Wilhelm, Janet (2005) 'The Chinese Communities in South Africa', in Sakhela Buhlungu, *State of the Nation 2005-2006*. Cape Town: HSRC Press

Williams, Kristen (1985) 'Is 'Unequal Exchange' a Mechanism for Perpetuating Inequality in the Modern World System?', *Studies in Comparative International Development*, 20(3): 47–73

Woods, Ngaire (2003) 'The United States and the International Financial Institutions: Power and Influence within the World Bank and the IMF', in Rosemary Foo (ed) *US Hegemony and*

127

International Organisations: the United States and Multilateral Institutions. New York: Oxford University Press

___(2006) *The Globalisers: the IMF, World Banks and their Borrowers.* Ithaca: Cornell University Press

Wortzel, Larry and Devin Stewart (2005) 'The US Formula for China', *Asia Times*, 9 November <www.cctr.ust. hk/articles/20051109_USformula.htm>

WP (2007) 'China and Sudan', 30 January

WSJ (2007) 'Africa Tops Mideast in Supply Oil to US', 22 February

Wu, Jia Huang (2005) PowerPoint presented to General Conference of UNIDO, Industrial Development Forum, 28 November, Vienna, <www.unido.org/file_storgae/download?file_id=46437>

Wu Shiqing and Cheng Enfu (2005) 'The "Washington Consensus" and "Beijing Consensus"' *PD*, <http://english.people.com.cn/200506/18/print20050618_190947.html>

WWF (2005) 'Failing the Forests: Europe's Illegal Timber Trade', 22 November <www.illegal-logging.info/textonly/papers/fo_ failingforests.pdf>

XH (1997) 'Tanzania, China Launch Joint Textile Firm', 1 April

___(2000) 'Tanzania to Establish Export Processing Zones', 15 October

___(2005) 'China has Education Cooperation Ties with 50 African Nations', 27 November

___(2006a) 'China to Promote Trade, Economic Links with African Countries in 2006', 7 January

___(2006b) 'Zambia, China Benefit from Increasing Bilateral Trade, Investment', 17 May

___(2006c) 'China's Premier Wen Gives Press Conference in Cairo', 19 June

___(2006d) 'China Trains 11,000-plus African Professionals', 19 October ___(2006e) 'S. African Diplomat say "No Organized Effort" Against Chinese in his Country', 13 February

___(2006f) 'Dam up the Nile to Benefit Poverty-Stricken Sudanese', 29 January

___(2007a) 'Africa to be more Attractive for Chinese Investors', 3 February

___(2007b) 'China–Africa Cooperation to Break "Products-for- Resources" Doctrine', 6 January

___(2007c) 'Full Text of President Hu Jintao's Speech at South Africa's Pretoria University', 7 February

Xinhuanet (2007) 'Wuganda jinfang wei zai wu huaren huaqiao juban anquan jiangzuo' (Ugandan police organises security seminar for overseas Chinese) <http://news3.xinhuanet.com/world/2007-03/17/content_5861198.htm>

Zatt, Brandon (2007) 'Trading Rhythms', *SCMP*, 3 January: 7

Zhang, Chongfang, (2007) 'Shige Zhongguoren de Feizhou guishi' (Ten Chinese African tales), *Banyue Tan*, no. 5 (2007), <http://news3.xinhuanet.com/banyt/2007-04/27/content_6035448.htm>

Zhang Weiwei (2006) 'The Allure of the Chinese Model', *IHT*, 2 November

Zhang Xiaojing (2004) 'Tansuo jinrong quanqiu shidai de fazhan daolu: qianxicong "Huasheng gongshi" dao "Beijing gongshi" (Exploring the financial global era development paths: a preliminary analysis of moving from the 'Washington consensus' to the 'Beijing consensus'), *Xueshi Shibao*, 16 August

Zhonghua Minguo (Taiwan) Qiaowu Weiyuanhui (2005) 'Overseas Ethnic Chinese Population Figures' <www.ocac.gov.tw/index.asp>

Zhu Wenwei and Xu Tian (2007) 'Bingqi pianpo yu chengjian gongying caifu yu weilai (Abandon bias and stereotypes; have wealth and a future together), Zhongguo Maoyi Xinwen Wang, 12 April <www.chinatradenews.com.cn/Article.asp?NewsID=3296>

21SJBD (2006) 'Feizhou dalu de Beijing gongshi' (The African continent's Beijing Consensus), 3 November

Glossary of abbreviations used

AC	Africa Confidential	NE	New Era (Namibia)
ACBF	Africa Capacity Building Foundation	NEPAD	New Partnership for African Development
ADB	Africa Development Bank		
AFP	Agence France Presse	NMI	Nelson Mandela Institution
AGOA	African Growth and Opportunity Act	NV	New Vision (Uganda)
		OECD	Organisation for Economic Co-operation and Development
AHD	American Heritage Dictionary		
AP	Associated Press	PD	People's Daily
APA	Angola Press Agency	PE	Petroleum Economist
BBCMIR	BBC Monitoring International Reports	PRCMOC	PRC Ministry of Commerce
		PRCMOFA	PRC Ministry of Foreign Affairs
BBCRF	BBC Radio Four	PTI	Press Trust of India
BD	Business Day (S. Africa)	RTE	Radio Television Erin
BR	Beijing Review	RW	Renmin wang
BT	Business Times (Singapore)	SAPs	structural adjustment programmes
CABC	China–Africa Business Council		
CB	China Brief	SCMP	South China Morning Post
CCS	Centre for Chinese Studies	ST	Sunday Telegraph
CD	China Daily	TD	This Day (Nigeria)
CFR	Council on Foreign Relations	TEA	The East African
CH	Current History	TN	The Nation (Kenya)
CI	China's Industries	TP	The Post (Cameroon)
CSM	Christian Science Monitor	TWQ	Third World Quarterly
DC	Daily Champion (Nigeria)	TZ	Times of Zambia
DN	Daily News (S. Africa)	UN	United Nations
DPA	Deutsche Presse Agentur	UNCTAD	United Nations Conference on Trade and Development
DTe	Daily Telegraph (UK)		
DTr	Daily Trust (Nigeria)	UNOSAA	UN Office of the Special Advisor for Africa
EAS	East African Standard		
ECA	Economic Commission on Africa	UPI	United Press International
EH	Ethiopian Herald	USACOC	US–Angola Chamber of Commerce
FDI	foreign direct investment		
FES	Friedrich Ebert Stiftung	USAID	United States Agency for International Development
FNS	Federal News Service		
FOCAC	Forum of China-Africa Cooperation	USDOC	US Dept. of Commerce
FPC	Foreign Policy Centre	USDOE	US Dept. of Energy
FT	Financial Times	USSD	US State Department
FTAs	Free trade agreement	WB	World Bank
IADB	Inter-American Development Bank	WBGAR	World Bank Group Africa Region
IEA	International Energy Agency	WEF	World Economic Forum
IHT	International Herald Tribune	WH	White House
IOM	International Organization for Migration	WHO	World Health Organisation
		WTO	World Trade Organisation
IPS	Inter Press Service	WWF	Worldwide Fund for Nature
IRIN	Integrated Regional Information Networks	WSJ	Wall Street Journal
		WP	Washington Post
M&G	Mail & Guardian	XH	Xinhua
MOE	Ministry of Education	21SJBD	21 Shiji Jingji Baodao
NA	New African (London)		

Notes

1 Queen Victoria criticised her foreign minister Lord Palmerston for sympathising with Poles seeking independence from Britain's ally Russia. He replied, 'We have no eternal allies, and we have no perpetual enemies. Our interests are eternal and perpetual, and those interests it is our duty to follow.' Palmerston (1848). Ironically, Palmerston is best known in China for prosecuting the two Opium Wars.

2 Eisenman and Kurlantzick (2006) put it that to avoid a 'Chinese victory on the continent ... Washington needs to convince Africans to work more closely with the US, EU and international financial institutions.'

3 See Kaplan (2005) on Taiwan and US support for Chad's authoritarian regime.

4 The UN, EU, Medecins sans Frontieres and leading Darfur specialists dispute US claims of genocide in Darfur (Cornwell 2005; Carroll 2004; Birchall 2006; Waal 2007). For a penetrating analysis of the politics of the claim, see Mamdani 2007. China has sought, seemingly successfully, to persuade Sudanese leaders to accept UN troops to serve alongside African Union peacekeepers in Darfur (Shichor 2007).

5 The US improved political relations with Sudan in 2001–05. In 2006, it initiated international military education and training programmes for Sudanese officers (The Twisted ... 2006; allAfrica.com, 2006).

6 Butler (2005); WWF (2005); Commey (2003); Turner and Kim (2007); Thornton (2005:65); Greenpeace (2000); Illegal Logging (2006). Three-quarter of China's imported timber comes from the Asia Pacific. Much of the remainder is from Africa and amounted, in 2003, to 42 per cent of Africa's timber exports. Many developed countries also import a high percentage of their tropical timber from Africa, e.g. 83 per cent of Spain's in 2000 and 98 per cent of Germany's in 2002.

7 The overall China–Africa Export Similarity Index is 4 per cent (IADB 2006: 8).

8 About 85 per cent of cloth used in African apparel exports to the US is made with third country, mainly Chinese, fabric (*L'Express* 2005; *EAS* 2006).

9 Both China and the US are seeking FTA's with the Southern African Customs Union. Bilateral FTAs weaken poor countries' power in multilateral trade negotiations by fragmenting their coalitions and also harm third parties (Bhagwati and Panagariya 2003; McDonald and Walmsley 2003).

10 Akinjide (2005); USDOE (2004); Jaffer (2004); USSD (2005); IEA (2004); Lee (2006); *PE* (2006); Booker and Colgan (2006); *WSJ* (2007); *Houston Chronicle* (2007).

11 Reuters 2005; Pan 2006; Konopo 2005; Shichor 2005; *DTr* 2006a; Thiong'o 2006; IRIN 2006a; Klare 2006.

12 *PD* (2006); UNOSAA (2005); UNCTAD (2006a); AMPlify Wharton (2003); Harsch (2003); Konopo (2005); Shinn and Eisenman (2005); Thomsen (2005); Thiong'o (2006); PTI (2007); Sutte (2005); USDOC (2006:4); Pan (2006); *CD* (2006a); *Economist* (2004); Dixon (2007); *EH* (2007); *CSM* (2007).

13 Shinn (2005); *DTr* (2005); *DC* (2006); interviews with scholars and officials in South Africa and Ethiopia, 2004; Ghana, 2005; Tanzania, 2006.

14 Studies of unequal and disparate exchange deem the concept empirically robust (Custers 2002).

15 In a half-dozen major African states, all or almost all US investment is in oil, yet the US officially criticises China for focusing too much investment in Africa on raw materials (Knight 2002; AFP 2006b).

16 See APA (2006a) (PRC builders used 90 per cent Angolan labour); APA (2006b) (PRC firm uses 80 per cent Angolans to build 5,000 apartments); CCS (2006: 64) (PRC firms use mainly African labour in construction); *ST* (2006a) (PRC firms use only local labour in South Africa construction).

17 Meles Zenawi, the Ethiopian president and US ally, has criticised neoliberal market reforms and praised East Asia's 'strong developmental states' (*FT* 2007).

18 See also 'imperialism' in *AHD* (2000): 'The policy of extending a nation's authority by territorial acquisition or by the establishment of economic and political hegemony over other nations.'

19 Stephen Friedman of South Africa's Centre for Policy Studies has said of China in Zimbabwe that 'the political effect so far is less than might have been imagined. The argument is that they have helped Mugabe. But they haven't much. It has been more of a symbolic gesture' (T. Leonard 2006). Since 2006, China has obviously distanced itself from Mugabe (Kleine-Ahlbrandt and Small 2007).

20 France has over 10,000 troops in five African ex-colonies (AP 2006).

21 Ni (2006) (Chinese-owned conglomerate employs 20,000 Nigerians); *TD* 2006a (PRC factories in Nigeria make 90 per cent of country's motorcycles, as well as air-conditioners, machines, consumer electronics, telecommunications equipment); Timberg 2006 (2,000-worker Chinese-owned shoe factory in Kano, Nigeria; *AFX News*, 21 Jan. 2007 (1,100 to be employed in Chinese-owned Nigerian appliance factory); XH 2006b (Chinese firms employ more than 10,000 Zambians, some as managers).

22 On neoliberalism in Africa, see Harrison (2005; 2006); Ayers (2006).

23 China has military missions in or sells major weapons to seven African states (Pan 2006). Chinese small arms are sold in many other African states (Curtis and Hickson 2006). Overall, 'China's involvement in military affairs on the continent has made little headway' and 'China's security and strategic role in Africa … pales in comparison to that of the United States' (DeLisle 2007). US military aid and major arms go to 47 African states (Hartung and Berrigan 2005).

24 On hierarchy in the IFIs and WTO, see Woods (2003: 92-114) and Milanovic (2005: 150-1)

25 Seeking FDI is itself a key neoliberal prescription for developing countries, despite its potential displacement of domestic industry (Chandra 1999).

26 See also the Wangfang Shuju database, http://scholar.ilib.cn/abstract. aspx?A=sjjjyzzlt200501016.

27 Mittelman (2006) has questioned whether there is a Chinese consensus on development. For a leading Chinese scholar's critique of the prevailing model, see Wang (2003).

28 France has held quadrennial summits with African leaders for five decades. See *TEA* (2007). Japan pioneered the Tokyo International Conference on African Development in the 1990s (*Japan Journal* 2005). In 2006, an India Africa Partnership Conference was held in New Delhi, while the presidents of Brazil, four other South American countries and 20 African states summited in Nigeria (*TN* 2007a and 2007b).

29 XH (2007c); *PD* (2000); Ministry of Education (2003:13); Ching (2005); *CD* (2006b); Qi(2005); interviews with Dr Teshome Mulatu, speaker, Ethiopian House of Federation (Beijing University PhD) and Jirma, general manager of Administration Bureau of City Transport, Addis Ababa (Fudan University one year course), Addis Ababa, July 2004.

30 By 2005, China had cancelled debt totalling $1.3b from 31 African countries. In 2007, it cancelled $1.4b more African debt. 'Chinese Investment … ,' 2007. Africa's total indebtedness to China is unclear, but as of late 2004 all developing countries together owed China $5b (WB and IMF 2006: 8).

31 China granted Angola additional loans in 2004–06. While official statements now place the total Chinese loans to Angola at $6b, 'independent estimates put the total amount at $9b (Moorcraft 2007). The interest on China's loan to Angola can be compared with that on a 2004, $2.35b loan to Angola by British banks at 2.5 per cent above the base London bank rate. The mid-2004 base bank rate was 4.5 per cent; the interest was thus around 7 per cent (Pallister 2005; Reuters 2004).

131

32 Western grants often are in the form of direct budget support, paid into government treasuries, where they are more easily pilfered (*SCMP* 2006; Dowden 2005).

33 Western analysts, in contrast, often subtly shift the focus away from the West's business and political practices in Africa by focusing on the Chinese presence. Wainaina (2006) satirically advises Western writers, 'When talking about exploitation by foreigners, mention the Chinese and Indian traders.' See Hilsum (2006) and Peel (2006) on Chinese workers' basic-level living working conditions in Africa

34 The Eight Principles were followed in 1983 by four principles, including that 'The experts and technical personnel sent by the Chinese side do not ask for any special treatment' (Ai Ping 1999).

35 The Taiwan government 2004 figure is 154,000 (Zhonghua Minguo (Taiwan) Qiaowu Weiyuanhui 2005).

36 The total number of Chinese in Africa has been estimated at perhaps 500,000 (Jeune Africque.com 2006). Another estimate puts the number as high as 2 million (*DN* 2006). A PRC source with official links has stated that 750,000 Chinese have an jia li ye (settled down and built careers) in Africa. Zhang (2007).

37 XH (2006e); Poston (1994); Chen (1996); Liu (2003); Thomas (2004); Johannesburg Star (2004); Wilhelm (2005); AFP (2006c); *ST* (2006b); Davies (2007); O'Neill (2007); Interviews with South African Chinese, Johannesburg and Cape Town, June-July 2004.

38 On Tanzania's 'Friendship Mill,' see Black Panther (1969: 3). In the mid-1990s, the mill still had 4,000 workers and received technical assistance from China. In 1997, it became a joint venture of Dieqiu Textiles of China (51 per cent) and Tanzania's government (49 per cent) and in 2000 was declared an Export Processing Zone (XH 1997; 2000; Bagachwa and Mbelle 1995).

39 More than 10,000 farmers from Baoding, Hebei have moved to Africa (*CD* 2007).

40 By 2005, the accumulated value of PRC firms' construction contracts in Africa had reached $34b, with 74,000 Chinese workers involved. PRC workers in Africa are however a small part of the 3.2m Chinese sent abroad to work (CF&F 2005).

41 Hong Kong's Customs Service estimates 80,000 Africans in Guangzhou (Parwani 2006). Interviewees in Guangzhou in January, 2007 deemed 10,000 plausible. Nigerians are the largest group of Africans in China and Guangzhou. At least 2,000-3,000 Nigerians reside in Guangdong province (Leu 2006).

42 Interviews with Africans in these cities, 2005–06. Such figures refer to longer term, legal residents. If shorter term and legallyproblematic migrants are included, the numbers are far larger.

43 Federici and Caffentzis 2004; Mazrui and Kaba 2004; Makokha 2005; MacGregor 2005; Docquier and Marfouk 2004: 9-12.

44 Remittances to sub-Saharan Africa amount to US$8b a year, i.e. about $10 per African (Dowden 2006)

45 Much higher figures are collected in a dataset of bilateral migration flows of African doctors and nurses to nine receiving countries (Clemens 2006). Only African doctors and nurses who continue to work in these professions are included in statistics. See, e.g., Hagopian (2004). The figures would be higher still if all emigrating health professional emigrants were included. See ECA (2006): 7–8

46 'Because China exempts so many of its imports from actually paying tariffs, much comes in duty free. Actual tariff collections relative to the value of imports are only 2 per cent' (Lardy 2007). From 1820 to 1945, US average tariffs on manufactures exceeded 40 per cent (Chang 2002). Applied average tariffs on manufactures in Africa are now 12 per cent (Nankani 2005).

47 One editoriallyAfrican newspaper said of SAPs: 'Economic liberalisation, deregulation

of capital movements, suppression of subsidies, privatisation of valuable public assets … fiscal austerity, high interest rates and repressed demand became the order of the day … Structural adjustment programmes … ended up transforming these countries into dumping grounds for over-subsidised Western agricultural surpluses and over-priced and obsolete manufactured goods' (*Namibian* 2006b).

48 In contrast, Hu Jintao has said 'Both China and Africa have a brilliant and colourful culture that has made important contributions to the progress of human civilisation' (BBCMIR 2006).

49 Our interviews with Africans in PRC cities indicate, however, that it is not dangerous to be African in China, at least not in the same way it is to be non-white in some European countries, such as Germany (133 racial murders from 1990 to 2006) or Russia (54 racial murders in 2006 alone) (Segal 2006; Kramer 2007).

CHINA'S STRATEGIC INFRASTRUCTURAL INVESTMENTS IN AFRICA

LUCY CORKIN

Over a remarkably short time, Chinese multinationals have begun to claim their share of the increasingly promising African market. Is their engagement primarily of benefit to Chinese commercial interests or do they also bring benefits to the countries where they work?

Introduction: Africa as a strategic partner for China

The People's Republic of China has become an important and influential player in Africa and an increasing source of political and financial support for governments across the continent, particularly countries rich in natural resources. This is a fairly recent development in diplomatic relations spanning several centuries. China's pragmatic policy shift to economic concerns has been deeply reflected in the drive behind China's foreign diplomatic relations, particularly with regard to African countries. Increased diplomatic activity has thus, by design, paved the way for the entry of Chinese companies of all sectors into Africa's economies.

By the end of 2006, there were over 800 officially registered Chinese companies active in Africa, engaged in a variety of sectors.[1] Such enthusiastic Chinese commercial interest on the Africa continent has several explanations.

Energy security

While not the only reason,[2] one of the most important motives for Chinese commercial forays into Africa is the growing need for raw materials and oil to feed China's burgeoning economy. China became a net oil importer in 1993. It was ranked as the second largest oil importer after the US in 2004.[3] China currently imports 28 per cent of its oil from Africa, primarily from Sudan, Congo, Angola and Nigeria.[4] Particularly due to its strategic importance for economic growth, the procurement of secure oil supplies are a principal national interest and form a fundamental part of China's foreign policy. Unsurprisingly, all China's oil companies are state owned, and have worked in close concert with China's Exim Bank in several key African oil acquisitions in countries such as Nigeria, Angola and Sudan.

China's interest in African oil has been encouraged by the established US presence in the Middle East, consolidated by the invasion of Afghanistan in 2001 and Iraq in 2003. In addition, despite affirmations of cooperation with China, Russia has decided to direct the proposed East Siberian-Pacific oil pipeline to Japan and not China.[5] While a dog-leg tributary to China has not been ruled out, the oil supply that China will receive from Russia is considerably less than originally expected, further prompting China to look elsewhere to procure oil supplies.

These developments in global oil dynamics have spurred China's state-owned oil monoliths to court Africa's petro-states with increased ardour.

Political consolidation

While China's oil companies negotiate oil agreements in Africa, other no less strategic deals are worked out in other sectors. The state-directed nature of Chinese investment in Africa, channelled through the larger state-owned enterprises, lends itself to being used as a political tool. In previous years, this was aimed at achieving recognition of China by African states, at the expense of Taiwan. With only five African countries continuing diplomatic relations with the latter,[6] this political goal has been all but achieved. China's most recent political convert is Chad, which severed diplomatic relations with Taiwan to recognise the People's Republic of China in August 2006. Shortly thereafter Chad received a packet of debt relief, economic cooperation agreements and medical donations worth US$80 million.[7]

As the largest group of developing countries in the world, the 'African bloc' is also being courted by China as the largest collective voice in the United Nations General Assembly, to block Japan's possible ascension to the United Nations Security Council (UNSC) in favour of an African candidate. Despite healthy trade relations, there is little love lost between China and Japan,[8] with historical colonial tensions too fresh to be forgotten. Having usurped Japan's role as the growth engine of Southeast Asia, China is eager to consolidate its position as the emerging Asian power.

A commercial launch pad

Aspirant Chinese multinationals which are not yet confident enough to attempt penetration into developed countries have adopted the approach of entering less competitive developing countries' markets. In the wake of increased diplomatic and commercial traffic between China and Africa, the latter has become a favoured 'testing ground' in which aspirant Chinese multinationals can cut their teeth.

In addition, Africa consumers are more likely to be swayed by the price tag than the brand name of products on the shelves. Chinese companies are extremely price competitive, but weak in terms of branding. This has led to Chinese companies manufacturing under licence for European markets, in order to get an (unacknowledged) foothold in the fiercely competitive European markets.[9] In African markets, branding is not as much of an issue, allowing Chinese firms to expand market share in several sectors, under their own names, thus promoting their own brand recognition.

The need for new markets

Decades of an industrially-led command economy have resulted in gross oversupply in many sectors in China's domestic market, driving down prices. In addition, regional competition between companies is consequently so fierce that products sold but not made in any given province are heavily taxed. Expansion into international markets provides more scope for a product to attain greater market distribution with fewer tax obligations.[10] It also stimulates foreign demand for products substantially cheaper than the global average, due to Chinese domestic market saturation. The need to find new markets for products that are in oversupply has become a matter of survival for many Chinese companies.

African countries, for their part, have been experiencing the highest rates of economic growth in several decades, fuelled in no small part by China's appetite for African oil and raw materials.[11] Consequently, African markets are promising ones for Chinese firms, as there is a growing market of African consumers. While far from wealthy, they are nevertheless now more able to afford the kinds of products that Chinese companies can produce. As market entry into developed countries' markets has been particularly challenging, Africa's markets are being targeted.

Chinese companies have made large commercial strides into several sectors across the African continent.

Telecommunications

An industry traditionally dominated by British Vodafone, France Telecom[12] and South Africa's Vodacom and MTN, African telecommunications have recently seen the arrival of Chinese companies such as state-owned Zhong Xing Telecommunication Equipments Company Limited (ZTE) and the private Chinese multinational Huawei.

Mundo Startel, the Angolan fixed line telecommunications utility, has signed a framework agreement with ZTE for the purchase of telecommunications equipment worth US$69 million.[13] ZTE is to put US$400 million into the Angolan telecommunications industry. This investment will be used for the construction of Angola's telecom network, improvement in military telecommunications system, construction of a mobile phone factory, the creation of a telecommunications institute for the training of Angolan staff, and the establishment of a telecommunications research laboratory. The company's products are also used in 15 other African countries.[14]

Although Huawei and ZTE are actually equipment manufacturers, in Africa they have been bidding for telecoms operation tenders. ZTE is part of the consortium that won the tender for Sonitel in Niger[15] and is also reportedly near to acquiring Zambia's Zamtel.[16] Huawei meanwhile has, in partnership with Canadian Nortel, won a US$100 million contract as the leading code

---

The procurement of secure oil supplies is a principal national interest and forms a fundamental part of China's foreign policy

---

division multiple access (CDMA) provider for Nigeria's fixed wireless phone operator, Multilinks.[17] State-owned enterprise China Mobile has also tendered a US$4 million bid for Nasdaq-listed Millicom International, a global mobile operator with African subsidiaries in Chad, Democratic Republic of Congo (DRC), Ghana, Mauritius, Senegal, Sierra Leone and Tanzania.[18]

Energy sector

The energy sector is possibly where Chinese multinationals have left their most high-profile footprint in Africa. Chinese multinationals involved in the energy sector have received particular support from the Chinese government in overseas acquisitions. Especially since China National Offshore Oil Corporation's (CNOOC) failed bid for American Unocal in August 2005, Chinese oil companies have increasingly been looking for African assets.

In January 2006, CNOOC bought a 45 per cent stake in Nigeria's OML 130 oil area, also known as the Akpo field, for US$2.27 billion from privately owned Nigerian company South Atlantic Petroleum Ltd. In March 2006 the company announced a further purchase of a 35 per cent stake in the Nigeria OPL 229 oil contract to explore oil in Nigeria for US$60 million.[19] CNOOC's subsidiary, CNOOC Africa Ltd, has also signed oil production sharing contracts in Kenya.[20]

In March 2006 Chinese state-owned enterprise Sinopec and Angolan state-owned Sonangol announced the formation of Sonangol-Sinopec International (SSI). The joint venture involves the development of a new refinery at Lobito in Angola (Sonaref), requiring a total investment of US$3 billion. According to reports in May 2006, Sonangol held 45 per cent and Sinopec 55 per cent.[21] Work on the oil refinery, Angola's second, will begin before the end of 2007 and is estimated to have a total capacity of approximately 240,000 barrels per day; 80 per cent of which will be for the general export market. Through the joint-venture SSI, Sinopec thus acquired the stakes of 27.5 per cent, 40 per cent and 20 per cent in the off-shore blocks 17, 18 and 15 respectively.

China National Petroleum Corporation (CNPC) has begun operations at two oil blocks in Sudan with annual output estimated at 10 million metric tons of crude in total, equivalent to 200,820 barrels a day.[22]

Construction

This is possibly the sector in which China has made the largest inroads, as many Chinese companies have become heavily involved in road and railway rehabilitation in Africa, as well as several other large infrastructural projects. These projects are usually undertaken by Chinese state-owned enterprises. Following the 'going global' strategy and dove-tailing with the Chinese government's foreign aid programmes to African countries, these projects are often financed by Chinese government loans. Listed below are several examples of this kind of engagement.

In Angola, the China Road and Bridge Corporation (CRBC) is rebuilding a 371km stretch of road between the capital Luanda and the northern agricultural and mining province of Uige, connecting the Angolan localities of Kifangondo (Luanda), Caxito (Bengo), Uije and Negage (Uije); as well as a 172km stretch of road between the towns of Ondjiva and Huambo.

African countries, for their part, have been experiencing the highest rates of economic growth in several decades, fuelled in no small part by China's appetite for African oil and raw materials

---

These projects are being financed by a US$211 million loan from the Chinese government to Angola to assist with post-war reconstruction.[23] CRBC also has permanent representation in Burundi and Rwanda, while in the latter the company has been contracted to undertake all major road refurbishments.[24]

In addition, in January 2006 Hong Kong-based China International Fund Ltd began a US$300 million refurbishment of the Benguela railway line, which was almost completely destroyed during the civil war. The railway line, on restoration, will run 1,300km from Benguela to Luau, on the border with the DRC. The railway also has a link to Lobito, 700km south of Luanda. This is significant as there is a strong possibility that extensions to Uige and Zambia maybe be envisaged, providing a direct line of transport from the Zambian copper mines to the Angolan ports.

In May 2006, China National Electronics Import and Export Corporation (CEIEC) won the tender for the renovation and widening of the water distribution network in Caxito, Bengo province in Angola. The work, which began in February 2006, will take approximately 18 months to complete at a cost of US$4 million. An additional US$3 million is to be used to upgrade the Dande district by the same company. In Tanzania, China Civil Engineering Construction Corporation has been involved in water infrastructure projects in the Shinyanga (2004) and Chalinze (2001) areas, collectively worth nearly US$90 million.[25]

China's edge in the infrastructure sector

China's increasing activities particularly in Africa's telecommunications and energy sectors has facilitated the entry of Chinese construction companies into African markets due to the extensive infrastructure upgrades required for investment in these sectors. Chinese construction firms have since branched out into housing and civil engineering projects across the continent, illustrating the competitiveness of these relative newcomers.

One of Chinese construction companies' biggest advantages is the facilitation of their access to capital, often through Chinese government concessional loans. Chinese companies can secure the necessary funds for advance payment and performance bonds from their head offices in China.

The quality of work by Chinese construction companies is widely perceived to be inferior, but in some cases, very little distinguishes the quality and standards of Chinese construction companies from the other firms, whether local or foreign

---

They and other smaller private companies can also secure loans at flexible rates from Chinese banks such as the Bank of China, the China Development Bank and the China Exim Bank.[26]

This has significant implications for the companies' overheads. Thus, while local and foreign construction companies operate on profit margins of 15–25 per cent, Chinese companies usually operate on margins of under 10 per cent, thereby making them extremely competitive. There have also been reports of a large Chinese state-owned enterprise in Ethiopia slicing projected profit margins to as low as 3 per cent.[27] Chinese companies may occasionally undercut competitors by up to 50 per cent on the price of the overall bid.[28] While this may not be a hard and fast rule, it is clear that Chinese companies' entry into African country's construction sectors has intensified market competition.

Quality and standards

The quality of work by Chinese construction companies is widely perceived to be inferior, but in some cases, very little distinguishes the quality and standards of Chinese construction companies from the other firms, whether local or foreign. As with the price of the overall bid, the level of standards among Chinese companies varies. Therefore supervision is of critical importance. Non-compliance or irregularities in the procurement of materials and problems in workmanship can only be the result of poor supervision and/or collusion between the contractor and the consultant. This is true of both Chinese and Western firms.

Thus, while there are instances of Chinese companies completing work of substandard quality, they have clearly proved themselves capable of achieving extremely high quality work, as demonstrated in Zambia.[29] This underlines the importance of supervision with regards to quality and standards. In countries such as Sierra Leone and Angola, where the government authorities lack the capacity or political will to enforce building codes, structures of sub-standard quality are more common than in countries where the authorities effectively enforce the law.

Procurement of materials

There is a general trend of construction companies increasingly buying materials imported from China due to the cheaper prices.[30] Although opinions on the quality of these Chinese materials vary, the majority of construction contractors in African markets agree that quality is improving.[31] In smaller markets such as Sierra Leone only lower quality materials are available. This has led to a situation where lower-end quality Chinese goods have pushed out many foreign competitors while high quality Chinese products are simply not readily available. Although several knowledgeable respondents insisted that a market for better quality materials exists, albeit at higher prices, the market appears to judge otherwise.

Chinese companies in each of the countries surveyed have been granted tax breaks on the importation of construction materials. Yet there were widespread reports that these tax breaks are being abused. For example consumer goods such as clothes and electrical items for local distribution are being smuggled in along with construction materials. Such allegations remain difficult to verify.

Labour

Labour has been an extremely contentious issue in all the countries where Chinese companies have a presence. The general perception is that Chinese companies not only bring in their own labour, but also underpay the local labour they do employ. On closer examination, this is not necessarily the case. While predominantly employed as unskilled casual labourers, there were many instances of locals employed in administration and managerial positions. This is a phenomenon that was more common in companies with a longer in-country presence such as Tanzania and Zambia as opposed to Sierra Leone, and more especially Angola, that had very few local employees.

Chinese worksites are usually highly organised and all the personnel, from the executive down, invariably live and work on the site full time. This 'hands on' style of management saves considerable time and provides management with a profound understanding of the project and the ability to handle challenges as they occur.[32]

Chinese workers often live on-site in very simple accommodation. Chinese managers, engineers and labourers usually live together with little visible difference between them. This facilitates understanding and communication, drastically reducing costs. A good number of Chinese managers have suggested that the low cost of labour was the main advantage they had over other foreign companies that paid expatriate engineers exorbitant salaries and provided them each with their own housing and transport.[33] Without exception, all the Chinese construction companies commented on the lack of skills and extremely high turn-over of local workers.

Chinese workers are well trained and considered skilled; their skill levels are recognised across the industry. They usually undergo an intensive training programme, prior to expatriation. In addition, they are multiskilled and will be involved in each section of construction. Whereas it is normal practice to employ tiered hierarchies of workers, it has been found that Chinese artisans can also double up as site diggers and participate in manual labour as well as the more skilled undertakings of an artisan. Thus one Chinese worker will dig the foundations, lay the cables and orchestrate the electrics of a construction site. Such a modus operandi drastically reduces the number of workers required on a site.

In addition, the 'hot bed' shift strategy employed by some Chinese companies ensures that workers can be on site around the clock. In some compounds, there is a 'one bed, two workers' policy whereby a night-shift worker and a day-shift worker share the same bed, ensuring 24-hour productivity.

The rate of absenteeism of Chinese construction workers is very low. The majority of contractors using local labour reported that absenteeism is rarely less than 20 per cent. This effectively increases labour costs by one-fifth. Chinese workers by contrast have absentee rates of practically nil.[34] Aside from countries like Angola and Gabon, where the price of local labour is already relatively high, Chinese companies in the other three countries surveyed appear to be gradually increasing salaries to retain 'good' employees.

The labour dynamic that exists within China must, however, be examined in order to understand current trends as regards Chinese construction firms operating in Africa. Salaries for unskilled labourers in China vary enormously,

---

Chinese managers have suggested that the low cost of labour was the main advantage they had over other foreign companies that paid expatriate engineers exorbitant salaries and provided them each with their own housing and transport

---

generally ranging between US$1–3 a day depending on location, ownership of the company and the legal status of the workers. There are over 100 million migrant workers from rural areas in Chinese cities without work permits supplying approximately 80 per cent of China's construction labour.[35] The conditions are usually poor and underpaid by global labour standards.

Chinese workers can expect a salary increase of between 30 and 400 per cent as an incentive to work overseas. Chinese employees interviewed also explained that working in their company's overseas operations provides an opportunity to broaden the scope of their responsibilities, such as the management or supervision of local employees, enabling them to work on a single project from beginning to end. Several respondents also pointed out that working overseas enables them to look for opportunities to establish their own business as traders or restaurateurs. There are, however, exceptions to this kind of enthusiasm: one senior manager of a prominent state-owned enterprise suggested that working overseas was detrimental to his career development because in his company's Africa operations, he was not exposed to the cutting-edge technology used in China.

Since Chinese companies compete on price they will continue to push down the price of labour, although they will have to contend with wage increases to retain competent workers. With regard to Chinese companies' employment of skilled local labour, Chinese companies rely more heavily on certificates and professional papers to evaluate the capability of potential employees. Few construction workers in Africa possess formal training and qualifications, thereby putting them at a disadvantage for recruitment. It has been suggested that due to their longer presence and better knowledge of the market, European companies are more thorough and able to identify capable local personnel.

There are widespread rumours of Chinese construction companies in all countries surveyed using Chinese prison labour. We found no evidence to support these rumours. It must also be borne in mind that the respondents who provided the information were not independent observers, having been put at a disadvantage due to Chinese companies' entry into both the market and the political arena concerning Angola.

African economic and trade cooperation zones

In late 2006, the Chinese government announced its intention to develop between three and five special economic zones within Africa, in order to encourage investment in the continent by Chinese companies. This is in line with a pledge made by China's President Hu Jintao during the November 2006 FOCAC Summit in Beijing. It ostensibly forms part of the 'China-Africa development fund',[36] with a value of US$5 billion, being set up for this purpose. The Chambishi Copper belt in Zambia, where the China Non-ferrous Metal Corporation own the Chambishi Copper mine, was confirmed as the location of the first such economic and trade cooperation zone during President Hu Jintao's visit to Zambia in February 2007. This formed part of the US$800 million investment package offered to Zambia during the Chinese president's visit.

Within these special economic zones, it is anticipated that China will negotiate bilaterally with the special economic zone host government for Chinese companies to operate free from the tax and labour law restrictions that normally apply to commercial operations in other parts of the country, thus promoting an improved investment climate. In return, the heightened productivity of the area is expected to render high foreign direct investment returns and promote economic growth. This arrangement leaves Chinese companies operating within the special economic zones with a decided advantage over other market competitors.

Coalition investment projects

The Chinese government adopts a long-term view of its business forays in Africa. This longer term vision of commercial engagement also quantifies risk in a different manner to traditional investors. Chinese companies are often perceived to be less cognisant of risk when investing in Africa compared to other foreign investors. However, this is not necessarily true: Chinese state-supported investors are simply afforded a longer time-period in order to allow their investment to be realised. China's 'state capital' approach to engagement through the likes of China Exim Bank is answerable to political stakeholders, not private or institutional shareholders.

The state-directed nature of Chinese engagement in Africa results in 'coalition investment' across various sectors. This is very evident in several African countries where Chinese companies work on projects spanning construction and extractive industries, such as in Angola, Gabon and Zambia. This endows China Inc. with a competitive advantage that its traditional competitors do not enjoy, particularly if financed by Chinese government concessional loans.

The development of transport infrastructure will also assist with a wider market distribution of Chinese imported goods. Thus, Chinese investment in road and railway systems such as the Benguela, Tazara and Belinga railways is of strategic importance in providing Chinese products market access. In addition, heavy investment by Chinese companies in the telecommunications infrastructure in countries such as Angola and Uganda, oil pipelines from southern Sudan to Port Sudan on the Red Sea coast, electric power lines, massive irrigation and hydroelectric power systems, along with procurement, supply and distribution networks across the continent can be expected to have a significant impact in reducing the cost of producing and transporting products.

The competitive landscape of Africa is thus being transformed by China's commercial engagement. African economies are clear beneficiaries of this emerging trend, but this is likely to come at the expense of traditional investors and donors on the continent.

Chinese firms have essentially redefined Africa's risk profile. Although investment in Africa is traditionally seen as a commercially risky venture, given the often inhospitable business environment and political instability, Chinese companies appear to adapt to the African environment more readily and quickly find their feet, providing them with a strong competitive edge.

China's rise as a development partner for Africa

May 2007 saw substantial developments in China–Africa relations on foreign aid and assistance. From 16 to 17 May 2007, the African Development Bank (AfDB) held its 42nd annual board meeting in Shanghai. The meeting brought together more than 2,500 participants: top government officials, business leaders, representatives of NGOs, civil society, as well as members of the academic community and the media. A ministerial round-table discussion dealt with the development of partnerships between Africa and Asia as well

Chinese companies are often perceived to be less cognisant of risk when investing in Africa. However, this is not necessarily true: Chinese state-supported investors are simply afforded a longer time-period in order to allow their investment to be realised

as trade and capital flows between the two continents. Entrepreneurship, private sector development in Africa, Asian lessons on human capital and technology in development as well as regional cooperation and trans-boundary challenges were discussed. In-depth discussions on Sino-Africa economic cooperation were held.

This choice of venue is significant because it is only the second time that AfDB has convened outside of the African continent and the first time an Asian venue was selected. In Shanghai, the AfDB clearly acknowledged China and Africa's burgeoning relations and the substantial role foreseen for China as a donor for Africa.

Shortly after the conclusion of the meeting the Chinese State Council approved the creation of US$5 billion China-Africa Development Fund, to be administered by the China Development Bank. Chi Jianxin, president of the fund, has said that the China Development Bank Investments Bureau will analyse proposed projects from each branch and recommend the most promising programmes to fund managers. However, the China Development Bank has denied itself controlling stakes since shares from a single investment will not exceed 40 per cent of a given enterprise's total equity.[37] The investments of the fund will be targeted at providing capital for Chinese enterprises engaged in development, investment, economic and trade activities in Africa. The fund will also provide support for African countries' agricultural, manufacturing and energy sectors, as well as support for urban infrastructure and the extractive industries.[38]

This is a noteworthy development in China-Africa relations as it is a further gesture of China's intention to play a major role in Africa's development. It is interesting that China has chosen to establish its own vehicle for assistance in promoting Chinese companies' investment in Africa, rather than work within the existing framework of international institutions. Nevertheless, it is possible that China feels that this structure will be more effective and easier to manage as a bilateral partnership between China and Africa.

Implications for Africa

In a remarkably short space of time, Chinese multinationals are emerging to claim their share of the increasingly promising African market. Such expansion is not without its challenges. Despite the lack of affluence amongst African consumers, some still shun the cheaper Chinese products under the misconception that they are always of inferior quality. In fact, the quality among Chinese companies is variable. Many Chinese firms, however, have shown their mettle and are overcoming the stigma attached to the label 'made in China'.

Chinese multinationals' engagement in Africa has the potential to benefit both African countries and Chinese commercial interests. Africa will benefit by receiving cheaper goods and services than it would from traditional market players, as well as the possibility of technology transfer. Chinese companies will benefit from the opportunity to realise their global aspirations in Africa, having been less successful in the American and European markets.

However, there are several issues that must be resolved in order for this potential to be realised. The influx of Chinese workers and businessmen into Africa is a potentially serious social issue in the context of a continent ravaged by high levels of unemployment. Michael Sata, the opponent to President Levy Mwanawasa in Zambia's September 2006 presidential elections, achieved great popularity with his anti-Chinese rhetoric and campaign promises to expel Chinese nationals living in Zambia. Although unsuccessful in the presidential election, Sata's popularity is indicative of the rising anti-Chinese sentiment in some African countries, where Chinese workers are perceived to be taking jobs away from locals.

In addition, there is a concern that the lack of institutional regulatory frameworks and government capacity to monitor and encourage direct investment, in terms of local skills development and technology transfer, will limit the positive knock-on effect of Chinese activity in African economies. If left unaddressed, these issues will needlessly tarnish the reputations of China's multinationals and African economies will miss out on much needed infrastructural development.

This article draws on the report China's Interest and Activity in Africa's Construction and Infrastructure Sectors, *Centre for Chinese Studies, Stellenbosch University <http://www.dfid.gov.uk/countries/asia/China/partners.asp>, which the author of this article co-authored, as well as the working draft of research conducted for a scoping exercise of China's engagement with Africa, commissioned by the Rockefeller Foundation.*

Notes

1 Wenping He (2006) 'China-Africa relations moving into an era of rapid development', *Inside ASIA*, numbers 3 & 4, October–December, pp. 6.
2 Ian Taylor (2006) 'China's oil diplomacy in Africa', *International Affairs*, 82(5), pp. 940.
3 Gal Luft (2004) 'Fuelling the dragon: China's race into the oil market', *Institute for the Analysis of Global Security* <http://www.iags.org/china.htm>.
4 Adam Wolfe (2006) 'The increasing importance of African oil', *Power and Interest News Report*, 20 March <http://www.pinr.com/report.php?ac=view_report&report_id=460>.
5 Sergei Blagov, (2005) 'Russia's confusing Pacific oil game', *Jamestown Foundation Eurasia Daily Monitor*, 2(27), 8 February <http://www.jamestown.org/publications_details. php?volume_id=407&issue_id=3224&article_id=2369225>.
6 These are Gambia, Sao Tomé and Principe, Swaziland, Malawi and Burkina Faso.
7 Betel Miarom (2007) 'China signs deal worth $80 mil with ally Chad', *Reuters*, 5 January <http://today.reuters.com/news/articleinvesting.aspx?type=bondsNews&storyID=2007-01-05T111653Z_01_L05578532_RTRIDST_0_CHINA-CHAD-UPDATE-2.XML&pageNumber=0&i mageid=&cap=&sz=13&WTModLoc=InvArt-C1-ArticlePage2>.
8 Willy Lam (2006) 'Beijing enlists Washington to "reign in" Tokyo', *The Jamestown Foundation China Brief*, 6(4), 15 February <http://www.jamestown.org/publications_details.php?volume_ id=415&&issue_id=3621>.

up at China's door were not qualified for any assistance by moral, ethical, humanitarian or any other acceptable standards. It is, therefore, no accident that China finds itself at the centre of worldwide campaigns organised by African as well as international civil society organisations.

China's second policy states that there should be no interference in internal affairs. However, while this policy guideline looks attractive in terms of the recognition it gives to the sovereignty and political affairs of the recipient states, it does not make much difference in practice, nor does it make sense given the magnitude of China's lending to different African states. China's lending to African countries currently runs into billions of dollars. Indeed, such huge amounts of money will inevitably have far reaching consequences for the receiving states. Without a doubt, the money will strengthen the position of the communities or the groups that control the government and other state institutions. Given the fact that the majority of African states are neither democratic nor representative, plus the spread of tribalism and ethnic conflicts, these amounts of money – as we have witnessed – are utilised, in most cases, to settle historical accounts between these rival tribal groups. The situation in Sudan is a good example. It is not surprising then, that the Chinese policy makers, despite their proclaimed developmental objectives, find their assistance fuelling ethnic conflicts and forced displacement of millions of people around the continent. Indeed, when the magnitude of lending reaches this level, which no doubt affects the internal power balance and wealth distribution within and between communities, China wittingly or unwittingly becomes part of these internal affairs. This is the inevitable corollary that Chinese policy makers should take into account when dealing with Africa.

China's image and reputation have suffered greatly over the last five years due to its unconditional lending to some abhorrent African governments. While China's quest for natural resources and its desire to widen international trade links are legitimate and understandable, some projects and investment have cost China dearly in terms of its reputation and respectability. Standards and conditions are therefore needed, not to make it difficult for African states to receive lending, but to protect China's own reputation and interests. In fact, while the 'no conditions' policy has won China the support of a few African governments, China has equally lost respect among many African communities and groups that were affected by projects supported by China. Chinese policy makers have yet to examine these drawbacks and whether siding with governments against communities is a feasible long-term policy that China will pursue.

The case of the Merowe dam

The Merowe dam project in Sudan is the largest hydropower project currently under construction in Africa. The dam is located on the River Nile fourth cataracts in northern Sudan. According to the dam authority the project is expected to add 1250MW to the country's national electrical grid.

The two main Chinese companies constructing the dam are the China International Water and Electric Company (CWE) and the China National Water Resources and Hydropower Engineering Corporation (CWHEC), which set up a joint venture known as CCMD. The CCMD contract amounts to $555 million. The second one is Harpin-Jilin, another Chinese joint venture which is building the power towers network. The Harpin-Jilin contract amounts to $460 million. The total cost of the Merowe project is not known, but it is estimated to be $1.966 billion. China Export Import Bank is the main foreign funder of the project, with a contribution of $520 million.

The dam will displace more than 75,000 people, mainly small farmers living on the banks of the River Nile. The affected communities are the Hamdab, representing 8 per cent of the total number of the affected people, Amri, representing 25 per cent and the Manasir, representing 67 per cent. Generally speaking, the affected communities are not opposed to the project.

Since its start the project has been marred by massive human rights violations. To date, it has major unresolved social and environmental problems. As it currently stands, the project violates Sudanese law, and a series of internationally recognised social and environmental standards. Internationally renowned experts who visited the project in 2005 reported that it violates World Bank guidelines on at least 63 counts. As with regard to the rights of the affected communities, repression and violence have been the norm.

On 30 September 2003 a group of men, women and children from Korgheli village organised a demonstration around the dam site, protesting their displacement. The police ruthlessly attacked them, using live bullets, tear gas and plastic rods. Three men were shot and severely injured. A number of women were injured in the scuffles with the police.[1]

In November 2005, the Chinese contractors building the power towers network occupied water wells in the Bayouda desert and prevented the Manasir nomads from accessing the water. The Chinese contractors said they want water for the project building components and for their own domestic uses.

On 22 April 2006, the dam militia armed with machine guns and heavy artillery attacked Amri people who were meeting in the local school courtyard. The attacking militia opened fire on the people without warning, killing three on the spot and injuring more than 40. In August 2006, the houses and properties of more than 2,000 families in Amri were flooded without warning. The dam authority cordoned the area, refusing access to the media and relief aid. The aim was to force these families to go to the desert where the dam authority has built few houses.

Journalists who managed to visit the resettlement projects reported that an average of five families live in a two bedroom house. An estimated 800 families have no houses and no farms and are living in the open air. Some families are building their own houses

Despite the fact that the affected communities and international non-governmental organisations (INGOs) have written to the China Exim Bank and other authorities since 2004 regarding the plight of the communities, to date no reply has been received. Last year the chief executive of China Exim Bank promised to send a team from the bank to investigate the shooting incident in Amri, but there is nothing to show that that promise has been

Last year the chief executive of China Exim Bank promised to send a team from the bank to investigate the shooting incident in Amri, but there is nothing to show that that promise has been fulfilled

fulfilled. To date, there has been no report from the Exim Bank to show their position on the shooting and killings of affected communities. Indeed, such an uncooperative position makes dialogue with Chinese institutions impossible. It also hints that Chinese institutions and officials are not interested in dialogue.

International standards, safeguarding policies and measures are available and widely known and used. China can either follow the available standards or work out its own standards, which ensure China's adherence to international good practices.

China must seek ways and means to open channels of communication with African civil society. Chinese policy makers should consider going

beyond official government channels and create forums and links with Africa's civil society. To achieve this the Chinese government should support and encourage the establishment of a meaningful platform for Chinese non-governmental organisations and other civil society groups to work with their counterparts in Africa and elsewhere.

Conclusion

The Merowe dam and other similar projects financed by China Exim Bank are counterproductive to China's effort to help Africa develop. Evidently, the lack of standards has led China Exim Bank and Chinese contractors to get involved in this project, which is ill-prepared and lacks basic background research. When lending money to African states, China policy makers must take into account the historical path through which African nation states have come into being. The fragile internal unity of many African states must be sensibly considered and China must ensure that its money will not be used by one community against another given the widespread tribalism and regionalism in Africa.

This can only be achieved if China subjected the projects under consideration to scrutiny, on political, social, economic and environmental grounds.

Note
1 See <http://www.sudaneseonline.com/cgibin/sdb/2bb.cgi?seq=msg&board=2&msg=10713 47981&rn=1>.

CHINA'S INTEREST IN ANGOLA'S CONSTRUCTION AND INFRASTRUCTURE SECTORS

LUCY CORKIN

Using Angola as a case study, Lucy Corkin examines the factors driving China's recent and rapid commercial engagement in Africa, the competitiveness of these companies and the Chinese government's efforts to build and nurture political relationships in Africa. In evaluating the market entry models of Chinese state-owned enterprises in Africa, she also addresses concerns over China's politically determined business models, and perceived reluctance to build local capacity and collaborate with local and foreign companies.

Introduction

The People's Republic of China has become an important and influential player in Africa. It is increasingly a source of political and financial support for many African governments, particularly economies that are resource endowed. Chinese state-owned and private companies are making strategic inroads into African economies' construction and infrastructure sectors, sectors which have traditionally been dominated by European and South African companies. China's state-owned enterprises (SOEs) in the construction sector are active in almost every African economy.

The field research on which this paper is based was conducted in mid-2006 for the UK Department for International Development (DFID) and had several objectives:

- To examine the key investments and commercial arrangements of

Chinese SOEs in Africa's construction and infrastructure sectors
- To understand the market entry strategies employed by Chinese SOEs in these sectors when planning investments in specific African states
- To derive the drivers of competitiveness of Chinese SOEs
- To evaluate the Chinese SOEs' market entry impact on local and traditional players in the construction industry
- To uncover market entry experiences of Chinese SOEs
- To distinguish cross-cutting market trends amongst all case studies in terms of Chinese SOE engagement
- To explore Chinese SOEs views on collaboration and evaluate possible examples of cooperation with Africa private sector companies
- To detail recommendations for greater cooperation between China's SOEs with local partner firms in the construction sector.

Profile of Angola

Angola, a former Portuguese colony, has a population of approximately 14 million, almost half of whom live in the capital city of Luanda. Between 80 and 90 per cent of all economic activity in the country is concentrated in Luanda. The country has recently emerged from a civil war which lasted 27 years. Following the signing of a peace accord in April 2002 and subsequent political stabilisation, the potential for Angola's economic growth is high.

Angola is a country rich in natural resources. Oil production accounts for 52 per cent of the country's US$24 billion economy and oil accounts for over 80 per cent of fiscal receipts in 2005.[1] While this figure is expected to increase year-on-year according to the Ministry of Finance figures, the oil industry itself can provide only a fraction of the jobs in a country where unemployment is widespread. Sociedade Nacional de Combustiveis de Angola (Sonangol), the state-owned oil company, employs approximately 7,000 Angolans out of a total labour force of 5.1 million people. The unemployment rate is estimated to be approximately 30.6 per cent of the economically active population. The primary sector accounts for 85 per cent of the employed workforce, with the remaining 15 per cent in the service industry; agriculture represents no more than 8 per cent of the country's GDP. Extractive industries, diamonds and oil, account for 95 per cent of Angolan exports and 57 per cent of GDP, but employs only 1 per cent of the Angolan workforce.[2]

Angola's growth rate in 2007 was reportedly the highest in the world at 21.4 per cent,[3] driven principally by high commodity prices. Angola's non-oil economy is expected to grow 19.5 per cent in 2008, reflecting Angola's efforts to diversify away from oil related activities.

Public spending for the year 2006 was initially budgeted at US$7.9 billion, five times the figure for 2005. According to the National Agency for Private Investment (ANIP), however, a revision of the state budget indicates that US$7 billion has been set aside for public investment in the road, railway and marine sector alone. Significantly, Angola's main export markets after the United States are the People's Republic of China (30 per cent of Angola's total exports) and Taiwan (8 per cent of total Angola's exports). Private investment in Angola from 2003–06 reached a value of US$2.8 billion, 76 per cent of which was in the civil construction sector.[4]

Between the 2002 peace accord and mid-2006, Angola had received loans totalling US$5.5 billion, of which China has contributed 58 per cent. In the specific case of Angola, China seems to continue to dominate aid despite several aid packages that have been granted by countries such as Japan, Russia, Brazil and Portugal The trade volume between the two countries in 2002 was US$1.148 billion, of which China's exports to Angola were US$61.30 million, while Angola exported US$1.087 billion to China.

The two countries' bilateral trade has recently seen a significant increase

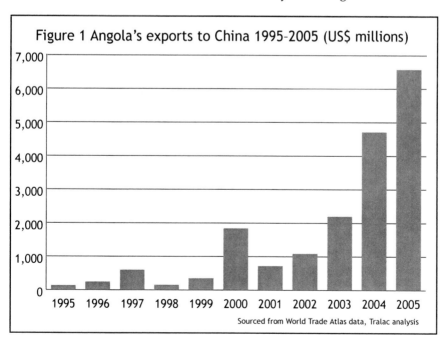

Figure 1 Angola's exports to China 1995-2005 (US$ millions)

Sourced from World Trade Atlas data, Tralac analysis

(see Figures 1 and 2): up 41.6 per cent to US$6.95 billion in 2005, with China's exports to Angola reaching US$372 million in 2005, representing an increase of 91.18 per cent from 2004 to 2005 alone. Angolan exports to China, however, primarily oil, totalled US$6.58 billion, making Angola China's largest African trading partner. Despite a leap in Chinese imports to Angola, however, China has continued to run a considerable trade deficit with Angola due to the rapidly rising rate of oil importation from the African country.

Historical links

Although the People's Republic of China and the Republic of Angola established official diplomatic ties on 12 January 1983, China and Angola have historically had a long political association. In addition to the ideological solidarity expressed in the anti-colonialist movements of the early 20th century, the socialist tendencies of the ruling party Movimento Popular para a Liberação de Angola (MPLA) have provided the basis for a natural alliance with the Chinese Communist Party, despite the latter's stint supporting Jonas Savimbi's opposing União Nacional para a Independência Total de

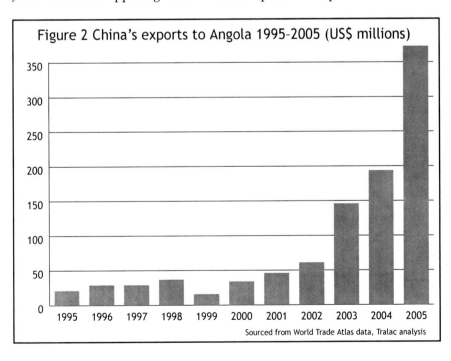

Figure 2 China's exports to Angola 1995-2005 (US$ millions)

Sourced from World Trade Atlas data, Tralac analysis

It is expected that Angola will soon house the largest expatriate Chinese community in Africa In exchange for the loan, payable at 1.7 per cent over 17 years, Angola is to provide China with 10,000 barrels of oil per day

Angola (UNITA) during the civil war. This was due to tensions between Beijing and Moscow, as the latter was supporting MPLA. Many now see renewed relations between Angola and China as 'the resuscitation of an old relationship, both moral and material, that has now come to fruition'.[5]

The governments of China and Angola signed a trade agreement in 1984 and set up a Mixed Economic and Trade Commission in 1988. The Angolan government flirted with establishing diplomatic relations with Taiwan in the early 1990s, sending several ministers to the island, but this did not materialise. With increased commercial cooperation between Angola and China, Taiwanese diplomatic efforts have disappeared from Angolan soil.

Official bilateral agreements

Nine new cooperation agreements were signed by China and Angola as a result of a visit to Angola by the Chinese vice-premier, Zeng Peiyang, in 2004. They included the following:

- Two agreements covering cooperation in the fields of energy, mineral resources and infrastructures
- An agreement on economic and technical cooperation
- An agreement involving a loan for funding Angolan projects by the Chinese, amounting to approximately US$6.3 million, free of interest
- An agreement covering cooperation between the Angolan Ministries of Oil and of Geology and Mining and the National Commission for China's Development and Reform
- A business-related agreement covering the supply of oil by Sonangol to Sinopec
- Two memoranda of understanding concerning a joint study of oil concession Block 3 to be done by Sonangol and Sinopec

- A phone networking agreement between Chinese Group ZTE Corporation International and the Angolan Mundostartel, worth US$69 million.[6]

US$1 billion of the credit has already been spent on various projects, such as:[7]

- Acquisition of lorries to be given to Angolans who lost their vehicles during the civil war
- Acquisition of construction equipment for use in projects embarked upon by Chinese construction companies
- Expansion of the electricity network in Luanda province
- Road repairs
- Construction and refurbishment of schools
- Rehabilitation of hospitals and health centres
- Rehabilitation and modernisation of irrigation areas
- Rehabilitation of energy and water infrastructure.

The most importance of these projects will be expanded upon in this paper.

US$100 million credit from China was spent on the health sector in Huambo province. The money went towards rehabilitating and equipping the regional hospital in Huambo city, as well as constructing two district hospitals. The Angolan government and China Export Import Bank (China

---

China was regarded as a welcome alternative loan source to a country desperately in need of the financial means with which to rebuild a war-torn economy

---

Exim Bank) have signed 12 individual accords of credit, with regard to a US$2 billion loan. The agreements, destined to support the projects in the fields of agriculture, energy and water, education and mass media, were signed by the Angolan minister of finance, Jose Pedro de Morais, and by the China Exim Bank's deputy chairperson, Su Zohong. The signed protocols represent a significant step for the implementation of the economic and commercial cooperation agreement that the Angolan Executive signed in 2003.

The government of China has also donated 46 containers of 960 tonnes of mainly agricultural products such as hoes and handles, axes, scythes, ploughs and machetes to Malanje province. The value of this donation is estimated to be in the region of US$1 million.

Mundo Startel, the Angolan fixed line telecommunications utility in which Telecom Namibia holds a controlling interest, has signed a framework agreement with the Chinese company ZTE Corporation International for the purchase of telecommunications equipment. The agreement signalled the start of Telecom's new business operations in Angola, as Mundo Startel began constructing the physical infrastructure for its network, which was launched in 2006. ZTE Corporation is to put US$400 million into the Angolan telecommunications industry. At least US$300 million is to be used in the construction of Angola Telecom's network while the remainder will go to: the military telecommunications system; the construction of a mobile phone factory; the creation of a telecommunications institute for the training of Angolan staff; and the creation of a telecommunications research laboratory.

As a direct result of China's involvement in the reconstruction and rehabilitation of Angolan infrastructure, Chinese nationals are the largest immigrant group in Cabinda province, Angolan's richest province in terms of natural resource deposits and it is expected that Angola will soon house the largest expatriate Chinese community in Africa.[8]

According to Huang Zequan, a lecturer in African studies at Peking University and adviser to Chinese companies entering the Angolan market, 10,000 Chinese businessmen have visited Angola.[9] Actual figures in terms of the number of Chinese living in Angola are inconclusive.[10] It is estimated that between 20,000 and 30,000 Chinese nationals reside in Angola. There are expectations that this number will increase as relations between China and Angola continue to strengthen, with the result that the Chinese community in Angola may rival the resident Portuguese population in Angola, currently numbering 47,000.[11]

China and Angola's oil cooperation

China's rapid rise as a global power, leading to an increased demand for natural resources, has been well documented. Especially in the context of energy security, China has increasingly sought to improve relations with African oil producers as strategic partners. Bilateral cooperation between Angola and China in the oil sector is pivotal to China's strategic interests in the country.

China became a net importer of oil in 1992, the following year a net importer of refined oil products, and in 1996 China became a net importer of crude oil. By 2005, China consumed 25 per cent of Angola' crude oil exports, accounting for 99.91 per cent of all exports to China. Indeed, oil has accounted for more than 99 per cent of Angola's total exports to China for more than 10 years. This surpassed even the United States, although Angolan exports covered just 13 per cent of China's oil needs. Angola's oil reserves are estimated at around 12 billion barrels and the Angolan offshore area is divided into 74 blocs, in shallow, deep and ultra-deep waters. Based on a price of $75 dollars a day, and an expected increase in capacity to 2 million barrels a day in terms of production, experts predict that Angola will be generating US$55 billion a year by 2010.

Official estimates are that in 2008, daily oil production will stand at around 2 million barrels, but this value could be reached in the next year as new wells go into operation.

The oil-backed loan agreement

On 21 March 2004, during Vice-premier Zeng Peiyang's visit to Angola, China's Exim Bank extended an oil-backed US$2-billion credit line to the Angolan government; the first tranche was payable in September 2004 and the second tranche in March 2005.[12] This loan was later increased by US$1 billion in March 2006 rendering China the biggest player in Angola's post-war reconstruction process.

In May 2007, an additional US$500 million was negotiated to assist with 'complementary actions'. This, according to a representative of the Angolan Ministry of Finance, encompasses further incidental expenditures that will facilitate the integration of the newly built infrastructural projects into the national economy. For example, the purchase of school buses to transport schoolchildren to the newly constructed schools is planned for the interior provinces. [13]

The loan has placed China in a particularly favourable position with the Angolan government. This agreement is significant, particularly because Angola had recently been experiencing difficulties in securing capital from the international financial institutions, such as the Paris Club and the International Monetary Fund (IMF). China was regarded as a welcome alternative loan source to a country desperately in need of the financial means with which to rebuild a war-torn economy. For China's part, cultivating relations with Angola, the second-largest African oil producing country after Nigeria, was particularly important in terms of potential oil exploration contracts.

China Exim Bank has increased the amount for the oil-backed loan to Angola several times and the Angolan Ministry of Finance is currently managing US$4 billion. According to the OECD,[14] US$1.8 billion of the original US$2 billion loan from China Exim Bank had been spent by April 2006. Additional loans from China International Fund Ltd, a Hong Kong-based fund management company, have been placed under the auspices

Following three to four years of peace and relative political stability, Angola became the number one source of crude oil imports to China in March 2006

of GRN, headed by General Helder Vieira Dias 'Kopelipa'. Kopelipa is also minister in chief of the presidency. The GRN was created specially to manage the Chinese credit line and the large construction projects it was to finance. It is an instrument of the executive, as are the various other *gabinetes* created by the executive. The loans managed by GRN are estimated to be in excess of US$ 9 billion.[15] The result of such a structure is that the money from the PRC loan is centrally controlled by the Angolan government executive. The NGO Global Witness has raised concerns about the transparency of the procurement process of construction tenders managed by the Office for National Reconstruction.[16]

Tied to the China Exim Bank loan is the agreement that the public tenders for the construction and civil engineering contracts tabled for Angola's reconstruction will be awarded primarily to Chinese enterprises approved by the Chinese government. China Exim Bank has compiled a list of 35 Chinese companies approved by both the bank and the Chinese government to tender in Angola. Of the tenders, 30 per cent (in value) have been allocated to the Angolan private sector, to encourage Angolan participation in the tender process.

Thus, following three to four years of peace and relative political stability, Angola became the number one source of crude oil imports to China in March 2006, having shipped 2.12 million tons of crude to China

165

> *Chinese state-owned companies will pay state-determined salaries that are sometimes not in line with the market-determined price for labour in the Angolan construction industry*

in February, surpassing Saudi Arabia, the global leader in crude oil exports. Angola returned to its position as China's main oil producer after its exports increased 40 per cent in May 2006. Forty-five per cent of Angola's oil exports are destined for China, supplying 15 per cent of Chinese total imports.

On 21 June 2006, during an official state visit by Chinese Premier Wen Jiabao to Angola, the two countries further cemented political and economic relations by issuing a joint communiqué[17] detailing the signing of further agreements and legal documents on bilateral cooperation in the economic, technological, judicial, health and agricultural fields.[18] Premier Wen was accompanied by the president of China Exim Bank, Li Ruogu, in order to discuss the allocation of the loaned funds to review the infrastructural projects already completed by the Chinese companies. It is reported that the official loan figures have already been spent and a refinancing of the current loan by the Chinese government is in the offing.

Key Chinese investments

According to consultant Huang Zuquan, the selection criteria for the Chinese Ministry of Commerce's list of 35 approved Chinese construction companies include 'a positive track record in finalising contracts within the deadline and on budget ... whether they in fact have the machines, personnel and financial capacity to carry the project through'.[19] When the Angolan government wishes to put out a tender for a construction project, this is communicated to the Chinese government, which then launches the tender in China. According to regulations stipulated by the Angolan government, the Chinese government, although it only releases the tender to the 35 pre-approved Chinese companies, must allow at least three different companies to tender for the same bid. The Angolan government then selects the winning tender from those submitted.

Between the end of 2004 and mid-2006, Chinese enterprises secured more than US$3 billion worth of construction contracts. Tied to the Chinese oil-backed credit line, the majority of these contracts are for government buildings and general national infrastructure. Angola's desperate need for infrastructure is being satisfied by the speed with which Chinese companies can deliver upon their projects.

Lobito Oil Refinery (Sonaref)

The most important and tangible form of cooperation and investment is a joint venture between the Chinese oil company China Petroleum and Chemical Corporation (Sinopec) and the Angolan company Sonangol to form Sonangol-Sinopec International (SSI). The joint venture, announced in March 2006, involves the development of a new refinery at Lobito, Sonaref, requiring a total investment of US$3 billion.

Work on the refinery, Angola's second, was to begin before the end of 2007. It was estimated that the refinery will have a total capacity of approx. 240,000 barrels per day, 80 per cent of which was planned for the general export market. SSI planned to take on the entire capital of each of the new concessions, and proposes to drill 10 test wells. The initial phase was supposed to produce 120,000 barrels a day, which is still almost double the capacity of the existing refinery in Luanda, which has a current capacity of 65,000 barrels per day.

The announcement in March 2007 that the negotiations around the construction of Sonaref – SSI joint-venture had collapsed pose some interesting questions regarding the developing dynamics surrounding Angola's oil reserves, and particularly Angola's burgeoning relationship with China.

Nevertheless, the joint venture also tenders for oil exploration and already owns 20 per cent of Angola's block 15 (estimated reserves of 200,000 barrels). SSI made the largest bid in May 2006 to develop Angola's oil blocks 17 and 18, with collective reserves of approximately 4 billion barrels, totalling at least $2.4 billion, including $1.1 billion in bonuses for each block and US$100 million in 'social projects'. The joint venture holding, following its announcement in March, was reported as Sonangol holding from 70 per cent shares and Sinopec 30 per cent. By May 2006, a report stated that Sonangol held 45 per cent and Sinopec 55 per cent.[20]

The joint venture seeks to capture a 50 per cent stake in both blocks 17 and 18 and is being financed by a consortium of banks which include

Agricultural Bank of China, Bank of China, China Construction Bank and China Exim Bank, Bayerische Landesbank, BNP Paribas, Calyon, ING Groep, KBC Groep, Natexis, Banques Populaires, Societe Generale and Standard Chartered. In June 2006, it was announced that SSI had secured stakes in blocks 17 and 18, with expectations that oil production will be boosted 100,000 barrels a day after they come on stream. Through the joint venture SSI, Sinopec thus acquired the stakes of 27.5 per cent, 40 per cent and 20 per cent in the off-shore blocks 17,18 and 15 respectively through its joint venture with Sonangol. It was reported in June 2006 that Sinopec holds a 75 per cent stake in SSI, indicating that Sinopec had increased its share of the joint venture by 20 per cent in one month.

Road and bridge infrastructure

China has granted Angola a US$211 million loan to finance the first stage of a project to rebuild roads destroyed in the 1975–2002 civil war. The first such project is a 371km stretch between the capital Luanda and the northern agricultural and mining province of Uige connecting the Angolan localities of Kifangondo (Luanda), Caxito (Bengo), Uije and Negage (Uije).

The China Road and Bridge Corporation (CRBC), contracted to undertake the project, has invested at least US$30 million in the purchase of equipment for the construction of a national road and bridges in Bengo province. The rehabilitation project is estimated to cost US$212 million and to take two years to complete. The works include the repair of 12 bridges on the road. Ten of the bridges are new, with the project involving the repair and construction of 200 aqueducts. More than 3,000 Angolan and Chinese workers will be involved in the project according to ANIP. The project, commissioned by the National Road Institute (INEA), is being supervised by the German firm Galf Engineering.

CRBC is also rebuilding a 172km stretch of road between the towns of Ondjiva and Humbe. The project includes relaying the road's surface, widening the embankments, drainage works and protection against erosion, road signage, building of new aqueducts and small bridges; it represents an investment of US$47 million. The rebuilding of the road, which is part of the government's national reconstruction programme, is considered important as it provides a link between Luanda and the provinces of Kwanza Sul, Huíla, Benguela, Huambo and Cunene as far as Namibe.

CRBC also won the tender to build a concrete bridge over the River Dande

Figure 3 Map of Chinese railway and road construction projects

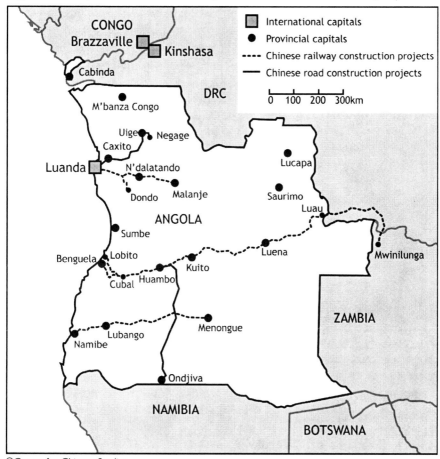

©Centre for Chinese Studies

in Angola. The bridge, which will be over 100m long, will be built alongside the current metal bridge and will have a capacity of over 60 tons and be 12m wide.

Other Chinese SOE infrastructure projects

A new international airport, Bom Jesus, has been planned as an alternative to the existing 4 de Fevereiro airport. The first stage of the new airport, to be situated 40km north-east of Luanda, is estimated to cost US$450 million, and will be led by the National Reconstruction Office, under the supervision of the Presidency.[21] The work is reported to be contracted to the Brazilian construction firm Oderbrecht and a consortium of Chinese companies.

At the end of January 2006, repairs to a railway line nearly destroyed in Angola's civil war began, which will reconnect the east with the west in a US$300-million project funded by the China International Fund Ltd, a Hong Kong-based construction firm. The railway line, on restoration, will run 1,300km from Benguela to Luau, on the border with the Democratic Republic

---

Whereas it is normal practice to employ tiered hierarchies of workers, it has been found that Chinese artisans also double up as site diggers ... Thus one Chinese worker will dig the foundations, lay the cables and orchestrate the electrics of a construction site

---

of Congo. The railway also has a link to Lobito, 700km south of Luanda. The project was to take 20 months, and was scheduled to be completed in August 2007. Due to logistical and financing complications inherent in a project of this size, however, as of the beginning of 2008, work was yet to be concluded. There is a strong possibility that there will be extensions to Uige and Zambia, providing a direct line of transport from Zambian copper mines to the Angolan ports.

Up to US$2 billion is also to be spent rehabilitating and modernising the Moçamedes railway, which stretches from the southern Angolan port of Namibe some 856km to Menongue, more than halfway to the Zambian border. This four-year project began in March 2006.

In February 2006, the Luanda General Hospital was completed by the Chinese Overseas Engineering Company (COVEC). The hospital, located in Luanda's Kilamba Kiaxi district, occupies 800,000m^2 inside five acres of land and has the capacity to hospitalise 100 patients and tend to 800 patients per day. COVEC completed the $8 million dollar project within 15 months, reportedly using a workforce comprising 90 per cent Angolans, according to statements by the Angolan government. The money used to build this hospital was reportedly an interest-free loan from the Chinese government.[22]

In March 2006, in a major housing project, China International Fund Ltd was contracted to build 44 15-floor buildings, with 5,000 apartments in total, in Cabinda City, Cabinda province. This is reportedly part of a drive by the Angolan government to provide 200,000 residences countrywide by 2008. Funded by the Chinese government, the operations are to be coordinated by the Angolan National Reconstruction Department. The Cabinda urbanisation project is to employ 4,000 Angolans and 1,000 Chinese workers over a period of 30 months.

In May 2006, China National Electronics Import and Export Corp. (CEIEC) won the tender for renovation and widening of the water distribution network Caxito, Bengo province. The work, which began the previous month, will take approximately 18 months and cost US$4 million. An additional $3 million is to be used to upgrade the Dande district.

Chinese company China Jiangsu International has been contracted to finish construction work on the Palace of Justice building in Luanda. The contract, reportedly valued at US$41 million, was tendered by the Angolan Ministry of Public Works and was ratified by the Angolan cabinet. China Jiangsu is also completing renovations on the provincial government buildings in Luanda.

Golden Nest International Group was contracted to build the Ministry of Finance building in Luanda. The building has been completed and has been commended for the quality of the work by the South African consulting firm which oversaw the project, Africon.

Profiles of the Chinese SOEs involved in the above projects can be found in Appendix 1.

Investment trends in the infrastructure sector

Chinese investment, especially in the case of Angola, is primarily concerned with transport infrastructure and the extractive industries, primarily oil. In Angola, this is seen principally through the joint venture partnership SSI in building the oil refinery in Lobito. This joint venture is the largest and clearest example of direct foreign investment as most of the Chinese construction companies that win tenders have yet to carry out their expressed intentions to establish joint ventures with local partners. It is possible that the current Angolan skills base is too low for joint ventures with Chinese firms to be a viable proposal over the short term. Aside from the refinery, the largest projects involved road and rail rehabilitation. Such basic infrastructure is urgently needed in Angola in order for it to recover from the ravages of the civil war, during which most of the country's infrastructure was destroyed.

As the China–Angola financial agreement is in the form of an oil-backed loan, the Chinese involvement in the Angolan economy is not direct investment in the traditional sense. It should also not necessarily be regarded as an indicator of long-term confidence by the Chinese in the Angolan economy. It does, however, provide the means and momentum for Angola to finance the rebuilding of its infrastructure, which can be seen as a long-term investment in terms of business facilitation, especially where improvement in transport networks are concerned. A representative from the Angolan Chamber of Commerce and Industry cited the view that the oil-backed loan extended by China Exim Bank still involves capital risk, as it is a sizeable sum that is being invested in a developing African country. China is also the only country to make such amounts of money available to the Angolan government.

Due to the nature of the loan, and the fact that the money received from the Chinese government is administered by the government bodies of the Ministry of Finances and the Cabinet for National Reconstruction, Chinese investment is also concentrated in the public sector.

Only two Chinese firms are officially registered with the National Agency for Private Investment (ANIP). This suggests that while there are numerous Chinese construction companies active in China, they are mostly state-owned or state-invested with few private Chinese companies operating in Angola. A possible reason for this is that the majority of the contracts undertaken by the Chinese construction companies in Angola are being financed by the Chinese government loan. As the Chinese government must approve the Chinese companies allowed to tender in Angola, SOEs have a natural comparative advantage.

Market entry strategies

Prior to the entry of Chinese companies in Angola toward the end of 2004, the industry was dominated by the larger Portuguese construction firms, whose presence is still marked in private contracts. The work of the Brazilian and Portuguese firms had traditionally been supported and secured by oil-backed loans of approximately US$300–500 million, but nothing of the magnitude of the China Exim Bank approved loan. China's entry into the Angolan construction market has somewhat displaced traditional commercial interests.

According to a prominent South African construction firm,[23] construction firms usually need an incubation period of about 10 years in Angola due to the civil war having interrupted normal commercial relations. This notwithstanding, within 18 months of entry from the end of 2004, Chinese firms had established a considerable presence in the Angolan market.

In March 2006, following the rapid increase of Chinese commercial presence in Angola, a Chamber of Commerce for Chinese Companies in Angola (CCCCA) was established. Based in Luanda, the chamber currently has 26 members. Its leading members include the China National Machinery & Equipment Import & Export Corporation (CMEC), Jiangsu International and China International Water & Electric Corp, ZTE Corporation, Huawei, Sinosteel Corporation, China Petroleum & Chemical Corporation (Sinopec), China National Overseas Engineering Corporation (COVEC) and China State Shipbuilding Corporation (CSSC). According to a representative[24] from the Chinese embassy economic councillor's desk, the CCCCA was established to facilitate an interchange of ideas between Chinese and local companies.

Drivers of competitiveness

Government-backed support has been instrumental in establishing market entry for Chinese SOEs in the Angolan construction industry, spearheaded by the oil-backed line of credit extended by China Exim Bank. The loan, primarily intended for use in the reconstruction and rebuilding of Angola's infrastructure, is monitored and managed by the Ministry of Finance and the Office of National Reconstruction. Thus, heavily aided by the Chinese government through political cooperation in the form of a bilateral agreement between the Angolan and Chinese governments, Chinese companies – especially in the civil construction industry – have secured 70 per cent of all contracts financed by the Chinese credit line as under the terms of the lending agreement.

As mentioned earlier, following the agreement whereby the China Exim Bank extended a US$2 billion loan to the Angolan government, the Chinese government declared a list of 35 selected companies that were pre-approved by the Chinese government. These companies were able to tender for contracts in the Angolan construction industry so inclusion in the list resulted in entry into the Angolan construction market. Interestingly, however, this list does not only include state-owned enterprises. Guangsha Group, the largest non-state-owned construction company in China,[25] was on the list. The group has several member companies and is the holding company for several more, one of which, Guangsha Chongqing First Construction (Group) Company Ltd (CGS International Co Ltd), has a presence in Angola. Once a presence has been established in the market, it is anticipated by the Chinese firms interviewed that they will secure further contracts.[26]

The Chinese loan is the most attractive financial package offered to the Angolan government, principally because of the extremely low interest rates offered by the state-owned banks. Offers by other foreign banks and governments offer higher cost of capital rates by comparison on much smaller amounts. The traditional source of loans, the World Bank and the International Monetary Fund (IMF), have been less than forthcoming with large-scale long-term loans as the Angolan government has not fulfilled the prerequisites in terms of transparency and practice of good governance. Angola is still struggling to implement the governance practices that are deemed necessary by the Western donors before such loans are granted. The emergence of China as an alternative source of funding has been particularly welcome considering the paucity of options available to the Angolan government[27] and the urgency with which such funds are required.

A factor which has played considerably to the advantage of the Chinese SOEs has also been Angola's urgent need to secure the loans which would allow the government to embark upon the reconstruction of the economy and the country's infrastructure. Chinese preferential loans are allocated without conditionality. This is well received by the Angolan government. It seems however that the Chinese companies receive rapid project approval from the Angolan government. The Angolan government has reportedly been easing the way for approval and inspection of the work carried out by the Chinese companies.[28] This is due to the contractual advantages being offered in financing the work via the Chinese credit line for rebuilding the country and the pressure the government is under to rebuild the country.

A Chinese or an Angolan labour force?

Chinese firms are often engaged in importing Chinese labour to work on a contractual basis for infrastructure projects. When questioned as to the desirability of Chinese contractors employing Chinese nationals as opposed to the local labour force, a representative of the Angolan Chamber for

Commerce and Industry pointed out that China, as a populous country, also struggled with unemployment problems and it was natural that this trend would develop, especially as other foreign-based companies also employed such practices.

Chinese state-owned companies will pay state-determined salaries that are sometimes not in line with the market-determined price for labour in the Angolan construction industry. As wages are a large expense in the labour-intensive construction industry, Chinese companies typically provide food and housing compounds for their workers as well as providing a daily stipend of US$1 per Chinese worker. This means they will compete favourably with companies that must pay US$3–4 per day for local Angolan labourers.

> *The problem of the language*
> *barrier appears to have been*
> *underestimated by the SOEs*

The average wage for an Angolan construction worker is US$120–150 per month. Similarly, Chinese engineers are paid approximately US$ 130 per month, one-sixth of what European construction firms would pay Angolan engineers.[29] This is also in contrast with the expatriate salaries that are paid by other foreign-based companies to their skilled employees.

The cost of labour, however, is not the only determinant of competitiveness. Industry competition is complementary of the quality of human capital employed by the Chinese firms. There are three factors that contribute to the productivity of the Chinese workers employed by the Chinese SOEs. First, the shift strategy employed by some Chinese companies ensures that workers are on site around the clock. In some compounds, there is a 'one bed, two workers' policy whereby a night-shift worker and a day-shift worker share the same bed, ensuring extended working times. Second, the rate of absenteeism at the Chinese construction sites is very low. According to other contractors who use local labour, the absentee rate is never less than 20 per cent.[30] This effectively increases labour costs by one-fifth. Chinese companies in contrast have absentee rates of practically nil.[31] Third, Chinese workers are relatively well trained. The level of skill of the Chinese workers is recognised across the industry, each worker having undergone an intensive training programme prior to expatriation. In addition, workers on Chinese sites are multiskilled and will be involved in each section of construction. Whereas it is normal practice to employ tiered hierarchies of workers, it has been found that Chinese artisans also double up as site diggers, participating in the manual labour as well as the more skilled undertakings of an artisan. Thus one Chinese worker will dig the foundations, lay the cables and orchestrate the electrics of a construction site. Such a modus operandi drastically reduces the number of workers required on a site.

Due to the speed with which the projects are completed, a number of Chinese companies have not seen it as a necessary step to establish a permanent office in Angola, unless they have secured several large and extended contracts. CGS International Company Limited, for instance, although contracted to a project spanning 11 provinces in Angola, have only

---

There is a perception among China's competitors that Chinese companies have an unfair advantage due to the extensive support offered by China's government

---

been in Angola since the beginning of 2005 and estimate that their project involvement will be completed by 2007, whereafter they will leave, unless they secure another contract. At the moment they only have six administrative overseers in Luanda, all operating on working visas.

According to one representative from Guangdong Xinguang International Group, Chinese firms from the south of China have a distinct advantage over northern Chinese companies due to their proximity to Hong Kong and the speed with which they may mobilise their procurement strategies. Procurement strategies are particularly important for Chinese companies that choose to import all their materials and equipment from China. In terms of material procurement, the Chinese companies enjoy a substantial advantage. According to a report in the *Boston Globe* (24 December 2005) by John Donnelly, a 50kg bag of Angolan-made cement would cost US$10, while China's imported cement costs US$4. Chinese companies' cost per square metre of construction is reportedly a fourth of that of European companies.

176

The experience of key Chinese companies

According to the majority of Chinese companies canvassed in this respect, one of the biggest challenges in operating in the Angolan market is that of the language barrier. Few Chinese speak Portuguese and Angolan knowledge of Mandarin is almost nonexistent. Some companies have tried to remedy this by recruiting from the Chinese diaspora. There has also been a natural inclination to recruit Chinese from Macau, a former Portuguese colony where people have a knowledge of Portuguese. This may have facilitated Chinese firms' entry into the Angolan market.

Chinese international workers, however, are more likely to have chosen English as their second language. While it is found that the more educated Angolans may speak French and some English, this is not widespread enough to remedy the language problem, which remains an obstacle to on-site communication and thus productivity. The problem of the language barrier appears to have been underestimated by the SOEs. According to a report in the local newspaper,[32] Angolans, who are often employed as the site workers, are not provided with a translator and have overseers that cannot speak Portuguese.

In addition, lack of education manifests itself as a problem, especially in terms of specialised skills. This is the rationale offered by most of the Chinese companies when questioned about their lack of local recruitment. It was agreed across the board by the Chinese companies interviewed that local labour was substandard. In addition, as much of the technology and equipment used by Chinese construction companies is in fact imported from China, Chinese engineers and operators familiar with such technology are also required.

A private Chinese firm complained that on assessing the bids, government departments tend to only consider the bottom line and do not pay enough attention to the quality of the workmanship, materials and technology implicit in a slightly higher price.

From such a complaint, it can be inferred that, while other local and foreign-based firms may compete for the same bid, the only major competition faced by a Chinese firm is another Chinese firm. It seems indeed that this competition is encouraged by the Angolan government, which has made a prerequisite that at least three Chinese companies from the list of 35 pre-approved companies bid for the same tender contract. Consulting companies nevertheless maintain that Chinese SOEs do not yet compete enough amongst each other.

According to the experience of the Chinese companies in Luanda, the project cycle is the most challenging aspect of construction in Angola. There are only three operational ports in Angola: Luanda, Benguela and Cabinda. This contributes to project concentration in and around these three areas, although all three also have other strategic importance: Luanda is the political capital and consequently the location of the majority of the national government contracts. As Chinese companies import most of their equipment, materials and labour from China, these ports play an integral role in the Chinese supply chain. Materials and equipment can be retained in these ports for as long as two to three months after arrival.

Mobilisation time for Chinese companies is, however, relatively slow. Goods procured often arrive after the prescribed 30-day mobilisation period. As many of the projects undertaken by Chinese companies are still ongoing, it remains to be seen whether they will be completed on time. Some Chinese companies claim that their projects would be completed in a matter of months without such delays, but are now forced to take one to two years, although this still seems to be quicker than the traditional players.

Some Chinese contractors have also had problems with their payments. One Chinese company said that this was countered by demanding payment up front. Where this was not possible, i.e. with government contracts, the experience was that payment from the National Cabinet for Reconstruction was eventually delivered, although it was often delayed.

Competition with traditional players

At the beginning of 2004, Angola, after two years of peace, was slowly beginning the process of reconstruction. The construction contractors which had had a presence in the country for several decades, for example Portuguese firms such as Texeira Duartes, Mota Engil and Soares da Costa, as well as Brazilian firms such as Oderbecht and South African firms such as Grinaker Lta, Group 5 and Murray and Roberts, were the traditional recipients of the construction contracts and tenders available in Angola.

The more well-established Portuguese firms continue to receive contracts, but many of the South African firms have lost market share to the Chinese companies. It is suspected, however, that the Angolan government still owes other privately owned foreign-based firms such as Soares da Costa considerable amounts of money and will therefore still award contracts to these companies to keep their creditors at bay.[33]

Portugal and Brazil, whose companies have been long-time players in the Angolan construction industry, have historically always extended oil-backed loans to the Angolan government with the understanding that the loaned money would be used to contract the respective Portuguese or Brazilian construction firms. In order to compete with the Chinese, the larger construction firms have had to provide even more investment. Oderbrecht, the Brazilian construction giant that has been operating in the country for almost 25 years, announced in June 2006 that it would be investing US$400 million in property development. The company would invest in the diamond industry, water infrastructure, energy sector and urbanisation, particularly in the newly developing, up-market suburb of the Luanda-Sul (Presidencia) Futunga.

It was found that Angolan government officials and investment agencies generally view Chinese commercial engagement in a very favourable light when compared to the traditional foreign investors. They welcome the fact that China is willing to inject large amounts of capital into the Angolan

South African investors are also perceived to be arrogant and there have been several instances of bad corporate practice involving South African construction firms

economy, albeit as a loan and not necessarily as direct investment, whereas other investors were not willing to run the risk of investing such capital. It was found that there is a particular negativity towards the South African corporate investor.

There is a perception among China's competitors that Chinese companies have an unfair advantage due to the extensive support offered by China's government. According to some traditional construction players, contracts have in some instances been dissolved and re-awarded to Chinese companies. Contract dissolution was due to an inability to comply with contractual specifications. An example is a South African company, which was contracted to build corporate headquarters for an Angolan firm, a US$126 million contract. When it could not source the components and finishes specified by the Chinese-based design firm, which had been appointed by the Angolan

179

client, the contract was re-awarded to a Chinese company, which was able to source the materials in China.

South African investors are also perceived to be arrogant and there have been several instances of bad corporate practice involving South African construction firms. Group 5, for instance was forced to issue a cautionary announcement on 8 June 2006, declaring that 'at least some basis appeared to exist for reasonable suspicion that irregular activities had taken place' concerning their operations in Angola, the first of which was the Nova Vida housing project undertaken by government contract in 2001 and worth US$135 million.

In addition, according to Africon,[34] a South African construction consulting firm with experience in the Angolan market, South African construction companies are currently some of the most expensive in the industry, due in part to the strength of the South African rand. With current market

---

Most of the Chinese companies are relative newcomers to the Angolan construction market and must compete with engineering firms who have been established in the Angolan construction industry for decades and have detailed market knowledge

---

conditions, it was estimated that South African firms could only hope to be competitive if the currency rate dropped to R8 to the US$.[35] This must be seen against the ability of Chinese firms to undercut the closest competitor by approximately 20 per cent in terms of overall bid value, with much shorter completion times.

It seems that both Chinese firms and their competition agree that there is a degree of variability in the quality of workmanship displayed by Chinese companies. A representative from Africon stated that Chinese firms, although known to cut corners on cost, were consistent in adhering to the level of quality if clearly stipulated by the civil engineering consultancy firm working on the project.

Examples of collaboration

In terms of collaboration, in February 2006, China National Overseas Engineering Corporation (COVEC) publicly expressed interest in entering into joint venture initiatives with the Angolan government. The company's deputy director general Shi Ping has stated the company's willingness to finance some projects in a bid to compete on an international level for entry into the Angolan construction industry in public-private sector partnerships.[36]

The company has also approached Portuguese construction companies working in Angola with a view to partnerships or joint ventures, admitting that the challenges posed by the language barrier are considerable. Shi Ping stated that, 'the Angolan market is also important because COVEC is already on the EXIM Bank list, which qualifies us automatically for developing projects that benefit from the bank's credit line, both in Angola and in other Portuguese-language countries'.[37] Such joint ventures are to be encouraged.

The potential opportunity for cooperation between South African companies and Chinese companies in Angola's construction sector is great. It is becoming evident that many foreign-based companies that used to dominate the Angolan market, such as those from Brazil, Portugal and South Africa, are rapidly losing market share to Chinese companies. Subcontracting, however, is still an option. For Chinese firms, there is an added advantage that South African companies speak English, a language generally more accessible than Portuguese. There are also several instances where the Angolan government appoints civil engineering firms to projects to ensure construction quality control. An example is the ministry of finance building, built by a Chinese construction firm and managed by South African consultants.

The challenge seems to be that Chinese companies prefer not to subcontract once the tender has been won, but import their labour, equipment and materials wholesale from China. 'When a country launches a tender, it thus has the certainty that the company that has won it is the one that carries out the project, that does not subcontract it out to other companies, as do, for example, Western companies in Africa, such as the Spanish,' according to Huang Zequan, a consultant for Chinese companies that wish to move into African markets and an academic at Beijing University.[38] Huang explained that the financial sector and the state work together on the internationalisation of Chinese companies in Africa.

Key strategies used by the Chinese

Within the context of Angola, Chinese state-owned enterprises have a very clearly defined market entry strategy. The Chinese government and China Exim Bank, through the extension of the oil-backed loan, have guaranteed market access for the Chinese companies as at least 70 per cent of all construction contracts is paid for with this credit facility.

Then there is the list of 35 pre-approved construction companies which have been selected to enter the Angolan market. Only the Chinese companies which have been subjected to inspection tests by the PRC government and form part of this list may bid for public tenders offered by the Angolan government, which will be financed by the oil supply-backed loan. This ensures that bidding companies are able to carry out the construction work effectively. Chinese officials maintain that the importance of this list lies in the fact that all companies appearing on it have been evaluated for quality by both the Chinese government and the financial institution underwriting the loan, China Exim Bank, as a precondition for financing the project.

The arrangement is touted as a way of the Chinese government making a positive contribution to ensuring that bidding firms are capable of carrying out the task. Most of the Chinese companies are relative newcomers to the Angolan construction market and must compete with engineering firms who have been established in the Angolan construction industry for decades and have detailed market knowledge, such as Portuguese firms Soares de Costa, Texeira Duarte and Motengil, or Brazilian Oderbecht.

Headline research findings

The Chinese interaction with the Angolan government while considerable is not in any way different from the commercial arrangements entered into by the Angolan government with other stakeholders in the construction industry, such as Brazil and Portugal.

Both have oil-backed credit extensions to the Angolan government, who are contractually obligated to award tenders to companies who have their origins in the creditor country. Tenders are announced and offered to qualifying companies, provided they submit pre-qualifications to the consulting firm overseeing the tender. The Chinese credit line is only distinguished by its size and the fact that the companies eligible for the Chinese-financed tenders are pre-approved by the Chinese government.

Nevertheless there is a growing concern by NGOs that what little leverage they have to influence the Angolan government in terms of transparency and good governance is being eroded as the Angolan government turns more to the Chinese for financial assistance to rebuild the economy.

Emerging trends

Currently, Chinese construction companies import all their required materials, technology and labour directly from China, rendering little direct investment in the local economy. China's credit lines are extended to pay for the supply chain, and are not designed to support local procurement. This absence of local procurement is compounded by the lack of local industry that is able to supply the construction sector: poor quality and comparatively high cost of local materials as well as a lack of local skilled-labour. Improvements in the production of local building materials or materials sourced from the surrounding sub-Saharan African countries would realise a direct benefit to these economies as well as increasing the potential for joint venture cooperation between Chinese and African businesses.

Indeed, even Angolan companies are now sourcing Chinese construction materials because they are more freely available and at lower cost. The only regional economy that has the capacity to supply the construction supply chain is South Africa. However, Chinese firms are unfamiliar with building materials procurement strategies from South Africa. A Chinese firm stated that it did not have the local know-how or inroads to approach South African suppliers.[39] The ability of South African industry to supply Chinese construction firms is a strategic consideration that deserves more research.

There are exceptions, however. Guangdong Xinguang International Group, which has recently won a tender to construct large cold-storage facilities in all of Angola's provinces, has approached the South African Embassy in Luanda for assistance in securing South African materials for their project supply chain.

Chinese companies in Angola are involved predominantly with government tenders and work for the public sector. This is primarily because the money used to finance their projects is a bilateral loan from the Chinese to the Angolan government, specifically to fund large-scale-infrastructure rehabilitation projects. Currently, many of the projects that are contracted to Chinese firms are managed by the Sigma Group, an Angolan state-owned consultancy.

*Currently, little evidence exists to suggest
that Chinese companies will enter into joint
venture partnerships with Angolan firms beyond
contracting Angolan site-workers*

Although the majority of the contracts are awarded to SOEs, private Chinese companies have also been given a window of opportunity and have also submitted proposals according to the National Agency for Private Investment in Angola (ANIP).

The most important and tangible form of cooperation, announced in March 2006, is the joint venture between Chinese oil company China Petroleum and Chemical Corporation (Sinopec) with Angolan company Sonangol to form Sonangol-Sinopec International (SSI) to build and develop a new refinery at Lobito, Sonaref, requiring a total investment of US$3 billion.

Currently, little evidence exists to suggest that Chinese companies will enter into joint venture partnerships with Angolan firms beyond contracting Angolan site-workers. Not only is there a very low local skills base, but the language barrier is seen as the biggest in-market obstacle for Chinese companies. Chinese companies such as COVEC have, however, shown interest in forming joint ventures with Portuguese companies, and others, such as Guangdong Xinguang International Group, are looking to procure materials from South African sources.

Currently there is little in the way of local capacity building or skills transferral as the majority of the Chinese companies import all their requirements in terms of materials and labour directly from China. This is due to the lack of local skills base, according to the Chinese companies, as well as the inexperience of local engineers with the imported Chinese technology and equipment.

The Angolan economy needs capacity development. The current practice of Chinese SOEs importing all necessaries from China – equipment, labour, and materials – needs to be addressed to ensure that Angola can develop the capacity to sustain the infrastructural development and benefit from technology transfer. It has been pointed out by ANIP that the other foreign-based companies also initially used expatriate employees, but gradually employed the local labour force. They expect this trend will also emerge with

184

Chinese companies. For example, it was widely reported by government sources that the Luanda General Hospital, built by COVEC, was built with a labour force comprising 90 per cent Angolans.

There is also a need to encourage a culture of social development parallel to the infrastructural development in which the Chinese firms are engaged. Initiatives such as educational programmes for local workers are necessary. While other firms do engage in such projects, these additional costs are an aggravating factor in pricing the companies that compete with Chinese companies out of the market place. It is recommended that the donor community consider the possibility of supporting capacity building programmes and skills workshops around the local construction sector in Angola. While the projects themselves, however, once completed, will improve the functioning of the economy due to infrastructural improvement, there are no current cases of skills development or social investment.

Recommendations for increased collaboration

While it seems that there is gradual movement towards the establishment of joint ventures and collaborative projects, this trend is not developing particularly strongly, and local companies have voiced concern over the guarantee of 70 per cent of the national reconstruction projects going to (foreign) Chinese companies. Despite the argument for a rapid infrastructural development to facilitate national growth, the stimulation of local business and entrepreneurship is essential for sustainable economic growth. Consequently, the following recommendations are made.

The outsourcing of quality control management could also lead to increased collaboration. Currently, most of the projects contracted to Chinese firms do not have independent quality control management, which compromises the accountability of the project workers. Establishing requirements for an independent firm which manages project quality would not only increase the accountability of the project, but also provide another reason to form joint partnerships and collaborations.

What is also important, however, is that these stipulations are clear and well circulated and enforced. The development of a social 'scorecard' which accredits construction companies for skills development and social upliftment programmes would be beneficial. ANIP could perhaps undertake this initiative when assessing commercial tax break qualifications.

The Angolan government should take advantage of the leverage provided

by the Angolan-Chinese loan agreement to negotiate the selection criteria of the Chinese companies to include skills transferral and local capacity building projects. The donor community could participate in the organisation and coordination of such projects.

The government should also create further contract stipulations that a fixed percentage of materials be sourced from local suppliers. In order to be able to do this however, the local availability must be addressed and improved. Currently the local capacity to produce construction materials is very low, with most of the construction companies having to import their own materials.

Conclusion

The entry of the Chinese construction industries into Angola, albeit controversial, has marked a period of rapid infrastructural regeneration. For Angola, as a country only recently emerging from civil war, the rehabilitation of vital roads and railways and the development of infrastructure in general is recognised as a national priority to sustain economic growth and encourage investment. Chinese companies have made a broadly positive contribution to such important development.

Of concern are the challenges posed by a lack of institutional framework and government capacity to monitor and encourage direct investment in terms of local skills development and technology transfer. The National Office for Reconstruction, the Chamber of Commerce and Industry and ANIP need to reinforce the promotion of joint ventures and the development of corporate responsibility among firms active in Angola to ensure that the positive contribution of the rapidly increasing construction industry has sustained socio-economic benefits.

Appendix 1 Companies already engaged in major projects in Angola

The China Road and Bridge Corporation

Initially established in 1979 as the China Highways and Bridges Engineering Company, the present corporation was established in 2005 after China's State Department of state-owned assets supervision and management committee assumed control of what was then one of China's largest SOEs. Primarily engaged in project contracting, construction, design, supervision, counselling and international trade operations, the company has five categories of affiliates and 31 overseas branches.

Chinese Overseas Engineering Corporation (COVEC)

Formerly an enterprise under China's Ministry of Foreign Trade and Economic Cooperation

(MOFTEC), China National Overseas Engineering Corporation (COVEC) joined China Railway Engineering Corporation (CREC) to consolidate its international project contracting. COVEC specialises in China-financed foreign-aid projects, investment in overseas businesses, leasing business of large engineering equipment and machinery, overseas labour service and import/export business.

One of the first SOEs to enter the global market, over 30 years ago, COVEC has undertaken over 1,000 large and medium-sized international projects. The corporation has won a cumulative total of US$2.6 billion worth of contracts, with US$2.2 billion in turnover. COVEC has been listed by the US magazine *Engineering News Records* as one of the top 225 international contractors for years, starting from the mid-1990s, and has operations in West Africa, southeast Africa, South Pacific and Southeast Asia. COVEC is one of the 167 SOEs selected for preferential support by China's state-owned Assets Supervision and Administration Commission to be a flagship enterprise.

Jiangsu International

China Jiangsu International Group is a comprehensive transnational group of enterprises. Its principal businesses cover overseas and domestic contracted engineering projects, overseas labour service, import and export trading, investment in industries, exploitation of high-grade science and technology and development of real estate. It has over 50 member companies, of which 30 are based abroad.

The core of the group is China Jiangsu International Economic-Technical Cooperation Corporation (CJIETCC). Approved by the State Council, CJIETCC has undertaken projects linked to China's overseas economic aid as well as other private overseas projects. CJIETCC is present in over 80 countries and regions and has established 30 branches and offices abroad, with annual contract value and turnover exceeding US$100 million. The corporation has received such accolades as one of '500 All-China Giant Service Firms' by the State Council, one of 'Top 100 Firms in International Economic Cooperation & Trade' by the State Statistics Bureau, one of 'Top 30 Firms in the Line of Foreign Economy' and a 'Key Enterprise Earning Foreign Exchange under Special Care' by the Ministry of Foreign Trade and Economic Cooperation.

China National Electronics Import and Export Corporation (CEIEC)

China National Electronics Import and Export Corporation, the largest foreign trader of electronics in China, is a comprehensive foreign trade enterprise with import and export of electronic technology and products as well as other services. The company, established in 1980, now has 56 solely-funded and proprietary subsidiaries both at home and abroad, five offices abroad and more than 200 joint ventures. By the end of 2000, CEIEC, with its total assets reaching RMB8.4 billion, had a total sales income of RMB7.5 billion and a gross profit of RMB68.65 million yuan. CEIEC, at present, has a staff of 4,500.

The company's primary concern is importing and exporting electronic technology, equipment, elements and products, as well as undertaking government trade, contracting international engineering projects, labour service, co-production, joint venture operations, processing with supplied materials, samples and blueprints, setting up maintenance and after-sale service centres by foreign electronics manufacturers, sales agents, consignment sale of spare parts; software development and financial leasing, packaging and transportation, exhibition and advertising, market information and legal consultation service in the foreign trade, etc.

Since its establishment, CEIEC has concentrated on foreign-based contracts. The company's trade volume from 1980 to 2000 totalled $24.2 billion. Since 1992, CEIEC has been ranked in the top ten among the 500 largest Chinese importers and exporters, with an annual export volume of US$1 billion for several consecutive years. The company has established trade relations with

more than 140 countries and regions in the world.

Guangdong Xinguang International Group

This company, based in Canton province, is a state-owned enterprise that has recently been granted a contract to build cold-storage vessels for the Angolan government in all the provinces. The company operated not only in Angola, but also in Nigeria, where it has just been granted a US$2 billion project. The company also works in USA and Macau. Its presence in Macau, of course, gives it a distinct advantage in terms of the language barrier – cited as one of the most challenging aspects of working in Angola.

As one of the companies on the approved list, the Guangdong Xinguang international group company was encouraged to come to Angola by the Chinese government, and succeeded in winning the contract against all competitors, including the two other mandatory Chinese companies that participated in the bidding process. While complaints were heard about the nature of competition against other Chinese firms,[40] a representative from the South African-based consulting firm Africon voiced the opinion that the level of competition between Chinese companies for contracts could and should be higher.

According to this company, the Angolan government awards the tender according to the overall price, the length of time the contract will take, the professionalism of the company and the historical record of its projects.[41]

Guangsha Group

Headquartered in Hangzhou, capital of east China's Zhejiang province, the Guangsha Group is one of the first of 49 large group trial units approved by the Ministry of Construction and one of five key backbone enterprises in Zhejiang province. The group has expanded from a small company to a multi-trade group covering the fields of culture, film and television, tourism, finance and trade over the past decade. Its output value climbed to US$670 million last year and its net profits totalled US$19 million.

CGC Overseas Engineering Company

CGC entered Angola in November 2003, when it established an Angola Management Division, registering as CGC Overseas Construction Angola LTA, one of only two registered Chinese companies in Angola. CGC has three divisions: Developing, Engineering, and Material and Resource.

CGC Overseas Construction Angola LTA (known as CGCOC) has registered capital of US$26 million and investors which include Sinopec Star Petroleum Co Ltd, China Geo-Engineering Corporation, Sichuan Tianchen Group, the Chinese Ministry of Land and Resource/Shanxi Geological Mineral Prospecting Development Agency, China National Chemical Engineering No.13 Construction Company and individual investors.

As a result of its outstanding performance in overseas markets, CGCOC has become one of China's key external trading companies. CGCOC's management was selected to nominate the standing committee director of Beijing and Business Association and the vice-president of the Foreign Economic and Technological Cooperating Association in Beijing.

Golden Nest International Group

The Golden Nest International Group (Pty) Ltd is a company which is owned by Chinese investors and registered in South Africa. Since its establishment in 1997 the company has evolved into a large multinational group with its business interests ranging from construction, property development, mining and smelting, light industry, medicine, finance, culture, education, tourism and trading.

The headquarters of the group is in Johannesburg, South Africa, and its branches are located in Cape Town, Bloemfontein, Ermelo, Bethal, and Standerton in South Africa and Luanda in

Angola. The group also has offices in the Chinese cities of Beijing, Shanghai, Xia Men, Xi An and Hong Kong. The core business of the group is property development and construction. There is a research institute within the group and over 20 companies that are fully or partially owned by the group. The total work force of the group is about 3,000, of whom about 300 are technical and managerial personnel.

The total turnover of the group for 2002 was $40 million. The group has completed approximately 25 engineering and property development projects in China, South Africa and Angola, among them six projects have an investment value of over US$13 million. The Angolan Penguila new town project, which has an investment value of US$150 million and occupies an area of 100 ha, was completed in February 2003.

China Complant

Since its foundation, China Complant has been authorised by the Chinese government to implement economic aid to foreign countries by undertaking turn-key projects and offering technical assistance when needed. China Complant also plays an important role in international civil engineering contracting and providing labour services.

Notes

1 Christopher Thompson (2006) 'Angola gets $2.6 bln non-oil FDI in 2005', Reuters, 11 April.
2 Angolan Chamber of Commerce and Industry (2005) *Mensageiro económico*. 1(6).
3 Macauhub (2007) 'Economic activity during 2008 will increase in all Lusophone states, especially Angola', 31 December, <http://www.macauhub.com.mo/en/news.php?ID=4608>
4 Macauhub (2006) 'Increased private investment registered in Angola', 20 July.
5 Interview with the South African ambassador to Angola, Themba Kubeka.
6 Mbendi, 'Profile of China in Angola'.
7 Ibid.
8 François Lafargue (2005) 'China's presence in Africa', *China Perspectives,* no. 61, September–October, pp. 2.
9 H. Botequilla (2006) *Visão*, no. 286, p. 8.
10 This may be partly due to the fact that Angolans seem not to be able to distinguish between the different oriental nationalities conducting business in Angola, such as Japanese, South Koreans and Phillipinos among others, resulting in a large variance in reported numbers.
11 J. Reed (2006) 'China on track to win many friends in oil-rich Angola', *Financial Times,* 4 March; H. Botequilla (2006) *Visão*, no. 286, p. 8.
12 Alex Vines (2006) 'The scramble for resources: African case studies', *South African Journal of International Affairs*, 13(1), Summer/Autumn, p. 71.
13 According to *Agora* (6 May 2007), Chinese companies have been contracted to construct a total of 53 schools across Angola.
14 Renato Aguilar and Andrea Goldstein (2007) 'The Asian Driveres and Angola', draft paper, OECD Development Centre, p. 13.
15 Interview with a director of a foreign-invested bank in Luanda, 7 June 2006.
16 Integrated Regional Information Network (2005) 'Angola: Oil-backed loan will finance recover projects', 21 February, available: <http://www.irinnews.org/report.aspx?reportid=53112>.
17 'The Joint Communique between the Government of the People's Republic of China and the Government of the Republic of Angola'.
18 MOFA (2006).
19 Macauhub (2006) 'Chinese companies in Africa have government "seal of quality", says

Chinese consultant', 27 February.

20 Macauhub (2006) 12 May.

21 General Helder Vieira Dias 'Kopelipa', who heads up the National Reconstruction Office, is also minister in chief of the presidency.

22 *People's Daily* (2001) 'Chinese economic trade delegation ends visit to Angola', 24 May.

23 Interview with representative from Grinaker LTA. It was stated that Grinaker entered Angola in 1995 and have only recently secured their first significantly sized construction contracts.

24 Su Ming Sheng.

25 Although not considered a state-owned enterprise, this does not necessarily preclude the Chinese government or a related body from having a shareholding in the company.

26 Interview with representatives from Guangsha group and from Guangdong Xinguang International Group; interview with representative from the Chinese economic counsellor's office.

27 This statement refers to the fact that the World Bank and the international Monetary Fund (IMF) have been reluctant donors to Angola, as the Angolan government failed to comply with the necessary preconditions of good governance and transparency.

28 This may be through the consulting firm Sigma, owned by Sonangol, the state-owned oil company.

29 H. Botequilla (2006) *Visão*, no. 286. p. 8.

30 Interview with a representative from Murray and Roberts.

31 The comparative Aids rates amongst workers, both local and Chinese, may have a significant impact on their respective absentee rates.

32 *Capital* (2006) 3–10 June.

33 Interview with a director from Standard Bank.

34 A South-African-based multinational with extensive experience in the construction industry on the African continent. Africon has overseen several high-profile projects, such as the Ministry of Finance building contracted by Golden Nest, a Chinese firm.

35 At the time of writing, the rand exchange rate had been fluctuating between R6.50 and R6.85 to the US$.

36 *Radio Nacional de Angola – Canal A* (2006) 'COVEC propõe parcerias público-privadas', 21 February.

37 Macauhub (2006) 'Chinese builder COVEC interested in state-private partnerships in Angola', 20 February.

38 Macauhub (2006) 'Chinese companies in Africa have government "seal of quality", says Chinese consultant', 27 February.

39 Interview with a representative from CGS First Construction Company.

40 Interview with a representative from Guangsha group.

41 This assertion came from a representative of Guangdong Xinguang International Group.

CHINA'S RISE AND INCREASING ROLE IN ASIA

DOROTHY-GRACE GUERRERO

Since it joined the World Trade Organisation in 2001, China has increased its involvement in East Asian regional economic cooperation in order to enhance its global competitiveness. The Chinese government has shifted its diplomatic strategy from that of a developing country focused on domestic concerns to one taking regional and global leadership. What is the nature of China's rise and what are its implications?

China is rapidly becoming the predominant power in Asia Pacific and is starting to challenge the role of both the United States and Japan in the region. The question is: Will China's increasing importance in the region make the Association of Southeast Asian Nations (ASEAN) countries more prosperous, more stable, and equitable? To address this, one must understand the current importance of China and the many challenges that come with China's new role in the region.

ASEAN–China relations

The countries within ASEAN started to strengthen their bilateral relationships with China in recognition of China's growing role as a source of investment. ASEAN–China relations began in 1991 when China first expressed its interest for closer cooperation with ASEAN, but it was only during the 29th ASEAN ministerial meeting in Jakarta in 1996 that China gained full dialogue status with ASEAN.

All mechanisms at the working level were coordinated through the ASEAN–China Joint Cooperation Committee. During this meeting China also agreed to the establishment of the ASEAN–China Cooperation Fund. The ASEAN–China Senior Officials Political Consultation was also set up as a forum for political and security issues. A Code of Conduct for the use of

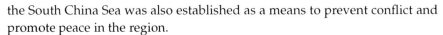

the South China Sea was also established as a means to prevent conflict and promote peace in the region.

The financial crisis that hit Asian countries in 1997 brought together the region's north and south to discuss common responses during the ASEAN meeting that year in Kuala Lumpur. The evolution of the ASEAN Plus Three (Japan, China and South Korea) came as a result of a recommendation of the East Asian Vision Group that was formed to propose possible substantive areas of cooperation. ASEAN adopted the ASEAN Plus Three (APT) Framework during the 2004 ASEAN summit in Vientiane, Laos. This resulted in the historic First East Asian summit (EAS) in Kuala Lumpur in 2005.

Two giants on one mountain

The summit, which was held despite tensions that emerged during the later stages of its formation, was China's floating balloon for the realisation of an East Asia Community, inspired by the European Union. China saw an opportunity to steer East Asian multilateralism along the lines of the Shanghai Cooperation Organisation so as to serve Beijing's strategic goals and further weaken the US influence in East Asia.[1] Japan and ASEAN members that were wary of an East Asia Co-Prosperity Sphere under China's leadership responded to Beijing's diplomatic offensive by proposing the inclusion of India, Australia and New Zealand. In effect the debate over which countries would be part of the 2005 East Asian summit was a proxy battle between China and Japan.

The rift in the first EAS was the tip of the iceberg that is the Sino–Japanese conflict. Scholars and diplomats in the region are in agreement that the future of an East Asia Community will remain bleak if the two giants will not settle their historical differences. The feud is continually reignited by a number of sparks, which include: Beijing's blockage of the possibility of Japan having a permanent seat on the UN Security Council; their competing claims to petroleum deposits and islands in the East China Sea; and China's irritation at the visits of former Prime Minister Koizumi to the Yasukuni Shrine, where Japan's war dead, 14 of whom are regardeded as war criminals by China and South Korea, were buried.

There is a saying that two giants cannot live on the same mountain. It seems that this will be true for China and Japan for now, particularly since the 'mountain' is becoming more and more important in geostrategic considerations.

ASEAN–China Free Trade Agreements

The ASEAN–China Free Trade Agreements (ACFTA) are a crucial component of East Asian regional economic integration. In 2002, Chinese and ASEAN leaders signed the Framework Agreement on Comprehensive Economic Cooperation and decided that an ASEAN–China FTA would be set up in ten years. When realised, the ASEAN–China FTA will be the largest FTA in Asia. It will also be the biggest FTA between developing countries and biggest in terms of population covered, representing a market of 1.85 billion consumers and a combined gross domestic product of almost US$2.5 trillion. The ACFTA will be fully implemented for the ASEAN-6 in 2010, and will integrate Vietnam, Laos, Myanmar and Cambodia by 2015.

On 1 January 2004 the two parties began implementing what China called an 'early harvest plan' or EHP. This plan grants three-year duty-free entry for ASEAN goods into the Chinese markets. After this, China's manufactured goods will have full free tariff access to Southeast Asian markets. This secures China's

There is a saying that two giants cannot live on the same mountain. It seems that this will be true for China and Japan for now

access to the region's raw materials and at the same time removes barriers to China's exports. The EHP cut tariffs on more than 500 products as part of the efforts to facilitate the FTA. The ACFTA will strengthen China's clout by making it the centre of gravity in Asia and surpassing the influence of Japan and the US.

The 8th China–ASEAN Summit on 29 November 2004 in Vientiane resulted in a package of agreements on trade in goods and dispute settlement. China and ASEAN began to cut tariffs on more than 7,000 products, a move indicating the start of the substantial tariff reduction phase between the two parties. Trade between China and ASEAN has been on the rise, growing at an annual average of 19 per cent between 1995 and 2002. The 2002 trade record is US$54.8 billion.[2] This leapt to more than US$100 billion for the first time in 2004 and further increased to US$130.37 billion in 2005.[3] ASEAN trade with Japan and the US remained higher at US$136 billion each in 2004, but this is expected soon to be overtaken by ASEAN–China trade.

Supporters of ACFTA argue that the Chinese and ASEAN economies complement one another. But China's expansion is not being welcomed by everyone. In fact, reaction to China's growing economic presence is becoming more negative, especially from small farmers and manufacturers in the region. Those in electronics, furniture, motorcycles, and fruits and vegetables, increasingly see China as a threat. In Thailand, farmers despair

> *As China continues with its charm offensive through government assistance and regional investment, it must also take increasing responsibility for its actions*

of selling their own produce anymore because of the low-priced Chinese vegetables that invade the markets in both rural towns and cities.[4] Malaysian and Indonesian workers are also complaining about jobs being lost to Chinese workers because of the closing of enterprises that are losing orders to China. Increased Chinese textile exports since 2005 to Cambodia and Vietnam have started to supplant local producers in the two countries.[5]

The strong drive and interest by the ASEAN elite to deepen economic ties with China is not shared by farmers and small businesses that fear the competitive advantage of China in churning out low-priced goods. Environmental interest groups also worry about the impacts of Chinese demand on natural resources in the region.

Development cooperation

In recent years, the flow of Chinese development assistance to Southeast Asia, especially to Laos, Burma and Cambodia, has been increasing. In the Greater Mekong region, China is actively pursuing cooperation for the construction of power plants and regional grid interconnection. China also finances projects in Vietnam (Kon Giang 2 and Bao Loc) and the rest of Southeast Asia.[6] In Malaysia, it supports an ongoing project for the rehabilitation of Tenompangi hydropower plant in Sabah. Laos' Nam Tha and Tha Som and Myanmar's Kun are also benefiting from China's external development assistance.

China is balancing its deepening trade partnership with ASEAN with development support and is now trying to match Japan's role in development assistance, which remains dominant. Clearly, the current swirl of Chinese money to development projects within ASEAN is intended to warm the relationship between China and its neighbours.

However, there are hard edges to Beijing's soft-power economic push into Southeast Asia. China is perceived as a source of many environmental problems. Its development of the Mekong river within its border negatively affects the countries downstream, which include Thailand, Laos, Cambodia and Vietnam. Last year, the Cambodian case of a pinewood plantation operated by Wuzhishan in Mondolkiri area covering 199,999 hectares of land and leased to China for 99 years showed a disregard for the concerns of the local population. As China continues with its charm offensive through government assistance and regional investment, it must also take increasing responsibility for its actions.

From Pax Americana to Pax Asia Pacifica?

China's diplomatic offensive in Southeast Asia has raised concerns about the impact of China's rise on the balance of power in the Asia Pacific region. Those fearing a China threat see China's increasing influence and political muscle flexing as signals of its interest in attaining regional hegemony. The US, for instance, has reasons to be threatened as China's rise could disrupt its pre-eminent role in Asia, including its ability to shape regional politics to serve its interests.

China sceptics argue that as China's economic power grows, it may seek to expand its political power because it wants to protect and affirm its interests. They fear that over time China might use its growing military capability to control politics in Asia in the same manner as the US. China on the other hand continually takes pains to ensure that its rise is perceived as non-threatening. Chinese officials always point out that China is expanding its political influence through the institutional approach, that is through international cooperation. It has established itself as an Asian and world power through increased integration into the international community. China's peaceful rise is being pursued through trade, confidence-building measures, development cooperation and assistance. There is also a growing perception that China is not challenging the US but is rather 'filling-up' the space vacated by the US as it becomes pre-occupied elsewhere.

With ASEAN, China has never been aggressive. In October 2003 it signed the Treaty of Amity and Cooperation,[7] which indicates China's commitment to respect the ideals long held by ASEAN – sovereignty and non-interference in each other's internal affairs, and the settling of disputes in a peaceful manner. In terms of military cooperation, China initiated security policy conferences in the Asian Regional Forum (ARF), which were held in Beijing in 2004 and in Vientiane in 2005. There are now joint military exercises with Australia, the Philippines and Thailand, the training of ASEAN officers and the provision of language training to military personnel from ASEAN countries. All this is done to show that China identifies with the regional security ideals of ASEAN.

China's initiative on the Code of Conduct, which will come up with plans for joint development in the South China Sea, also pacifies, at least for the time being, ASEAN member claimants of the disputed territories. In the past, conflicts between the Philippines, China and Vietnam have erupted over control of islands in the South China Sea. In March 2005, state-owned

> *Despite growing anti-American sentiment in the region, the US is still considered by many as a more democratic country and a better supporter of human rights*

oil companies from the three countries signed a three-year agreement for joint exploration for oil and gas in the disputed area.[8]

However, there remain security issues involving China that pose a challenge to ASEAN and to Asia generally. The issue of Taiwan is key. China's insistence on the one-China policy may not always match the economic imperatives of ASEAN. The visit of Singaporean Deputy Prime Minister Lee Hsien Loong (son of former leader Lee Kuan Yew) to Taiwan in July 2004 displeased Beijing and caused the cancellation of the visit by Chinese Central Bank Governor Zhou Xiaochuan to Singapore.[9]

It will still take some time to see whether China's gestures of non-interference and cooperative security and 'filling-in' moves will indeed eat at the role of the US in the region. The US Pentagon's Quadrennial Defence Review released in February 2006 reaffirms that the US will not allow the rise of a competing superpower.[10] Indeed, the US has taken steps to re-establish relationships with ASEAN countries. However, the Bush administration's blinkered focus on a military response to the challenge of terrorism increased anti-American sentiments among Muslims in Asia.

China as model?

While China has yet to gain the status of an alternative to US leadership in the region, ASEAN could always use China's potential as a possible alternative in its balancing act with the US and Japan in various political, economic and security negotiations. There are also some lessons that other developing countries could learn from China: China demonstrated the importance and effectiveness of state ownership of key sectors and of the banking system, of strong state control over capital allocation, powerful regulation of investment (foreign and domestic) and international trade.

It is important that we take a more careful look at the nature of the growth process in East Asia. The dynamic growth of the tiger economies in the 1980s that followed the newly industrialised country model of development did produce improvements in the living conditions and resulted in dramatic development of the formal sector of employment in South Korea, Taiwan, etc. However, such gains came at a very high cost.

China's growth under the current globalisation of capital accumulation is accompanied by much harsher conditions for working people. The hype about such growth merely paints a false picture of what capitalist success means. The interest of those that are promoting such a one-sided picture is to encourage the view that adopting the policies of the East Asian countries (growth before democracy and equality) can produce economic miracles like China. Not only is that a big lie, it also hides the more alarming situation that even the gains that were achieved at the cost of social and environmental injustice are fast disappearing.

The way ahead … will people matter?

ASEAN is the 'mother of all regional formations' in Asia. It has gone through a long history, many challenges and rebirths. The presence of China in the evolving regional community and its role in the governance of the region's economic, political and security relations have potential benefits to member countries. China's leadership in combating drug trafficking in its border could contribute to the solution of transnational crimes. Its initiatives for deeper cooperation on health issues such as the spread of severe acute respiratory syndrome (SARS) and HIV/Aids will certainly give a big push to efforts to address these problems.

If successful, China's efforts to solve its internal problems through its new social policies for the countryside may provide a good model for a redefined activist state's role in economic governance. However, China's growing influence does not necessarily ensure human security, deeper democracy, political transparency and protection of the environment and human rights in the region. Despite growing anti-American sentiment in the region, the US is still considered by many as a more democratic country and a better supporter of human rights.

The China–Africa Summit held in Beijing in November 2006 showed the level of China's appreciation for the participation of civil society organisations in geopolitical events. NGOs were not part of the big meeting, which was attended by 43 African heads of state. Stronger civil society participation in ASEAN affairs will most certainly not be championed by China. Asian movements, NGOs and campaign groups are increasingly recognising the importance of engaging China. To do so, they need to understand China better and get to know their counterparts and like-minded organisations within the mainland. It is crucial to engage China and work with the increasing number of people and organisations there that are working to make China more responsive to social concerns.

Notes
1 Mohan Malik (2005) 'The East Asia Summit: More Discord then Accord', YaleGlobal, 20 December.
2 Bian Shen (2003) 'New opportunity for ASEAN–China trade', *Beijing Review*, 1 May.
3 Li Guanghui (2006) 'China–ASEAN FTA both necessary and beneficial', *China Daily*, 6 November.
4 Supara Janchitfah (2006) 'Lost in statistics', *Bangkok Post*, 13 August.
5 Denis Gray (2004) 'Anxiety and opportunities mount as Chinese colossus exerts influence on Southeast Asia', Associated Press, 30 March.
6 Please see details of these projects at the Rivers Watch East and Southeast Asia webpage <www.rwesa.org>.
7 *People's Daily* (2003) 'China joins Treaty of Amity and Cooperation in Southeast Asia', 9 October.
8 ASEAN (2002) Declaration on the Conduct of Parties in the South China Seas, 4 November <www.aseansec.org/13163htm>.

EXPEDIENCY AND INTERESTS IN CONTEMPORARY CHINA–MYANMAR RELATIONS

YUZA MAW HTOON AND KHIN ZAW WIN

As to be expected with neighbours, relations between China and Myanmar have had their ups and downs. What marks the present age is that economic and population growth, the return of peace to Myanmar's border areas, its difficult political transition and globalisation itself have all intensified relations between the two countries to a degree not seen before. Whether this results in good or ill depends on the governments and citizens of both countries, write Yuza Maw Htoon and Khin Zaw Win.

At the United Nations Security Council on 12 January 2007 a draft resolution titled 'The Situation in Myanmar' and jointly tabled by the US and UK was defeated by a double veto from China and Russia. This was perhaps the culmination of two opposing currents that had been gathering steam for some years. A point worthy of note here is that none of Myanmar's neighbours have complained that a threat is being posed to them.

On the matter of the overarching relations between the two countries, a long-time scholar of Myanmar, Andrew Selth,[1] has put it elegantly and convincingly:

It is possible to identify three schools of thought regarding China's relations with Burma. The 'domination' school believes that Burma has become a pawn in China's strategic designs in the Asia–Pacific region, and is host to several Chinese military facilities. The 'partnership' school sees a more balanced relationship developing between Beijing and Rangoon, but accepts that China has acquired bases in Burma as part of a long term strategy to establish a permanent military presence in the Indian Ocean. The 'rejectionist' school, however, emphasises

Burma's strong tradition of independence and Rangoon's continuing suspicions of Beijing. This school claims that, despite the conventional wisdom, Burma has been able to resist the enormous strategic weight of its larger, more powerful neighbour. Some members of this school argue that Burma has the whip hand in its relations with China, and has been able successfully to manipulate Burma's sensitive geostrategic position to considerable advantage.

Widespread protests and disturbances had engulfed the country in 1988, and in September of that year the Burma Socialist Programme Party (BSPP) party-state was dismantled and a military regime was installed. Political parties were allowed to register and a general election was held in May 1990. There was no provision for a transfer of power, and differing interpretations of this on both sides of the political divide led to further protests, unrest and repression.

The democratic opposition, many of whose members are now abroad, found support among Western governments, which had been appalled by the military government's clampdown. Various methods were used, such as isolation, ostracism and economic sanctions, with the intention of forcing the regime to relent and come to terms with the opposition, but without much success. Recourse to the UN Security Council was seen by most of the democrats and some Western governments – notably the United States – as the ultimate means of reining in the Myanmar military regime.

On the other side, the military council – the State Peace and Development Council – had adamantly refused to accede to the demands of the opposition and the West. When efforts gathered momentum to take Myanmar's case to the UN Security Council, the protection provided by a veto-wielding permanent member – China – assumed critical importance.

The Saffron Revolution

There had been sporadic small-scale demonstrations in Yangon earlier in 2007, calling for stabilisation of the rising costs of basic necessities. Some protesters had been detained but were later released. Then on 15 August, without any public announcement, the government raised the prices of petrol, diesel and CNG (by two-thirds, 100 per cent and 500 per cent respectively). As a result, public transport fares went up (except for trains), causing great hardship for the public, especially those from low-income groups who have to travel to work everyday.

The '88 Generation' Students Group staged two marches in Yangon, and members of the public joined in. The authorities did not interfere with the marches but on 21 August, 13 members off the 88 Generation group were arrested. The government media said they were receiving support from abroad and were attempting to create disturbances. Consequently, they would be charged.

On 9 September at Pakokku in central Myanmar, a number of monks began a pattern of clerical protest that spread subsequently to many towns over the country. They would march peacefully in a procession chanting Buddhist scriptures, particularly the *metta sutta* (discourse on loving-kindness). The local authorities at Pakokku broke up the monks' protest march, using

---

When efforts gathered momentum to take Myanmar's case to the UN Security Council, the protection provided by a veto-wielding permanent member – China – assumed critical importance

---

violence in which the government's mass organisation, the USDA, and its vigilantes were implicated. Although no one was killed, a number of monks were hurt and/or arrested. In retaliation the next day, monks held a number of government officials hostage and set their vehicles on fire.

This incident sparked off a larger wave of revulsion and dissent; existing and emergent monks' organisations issued four demands, calling for a government apology, the release of political prisoners and negotiations with the opposition. The deadline set for the government to accede to the demands was 17 September, failing which a nationwide act of excommunication would be held. Senior military officers held ceremonies at which offerings were donated to high monks, as a kind of propitiatory-cum-pre-emptive gesture, but the government did not respond to the demands. At midday, on 17 September, the first of many acts of *pattanikujjana* (excommunication from the faith) for the junta was held. And the next day, 18 September, a procession of around a hundred monks walked in downtown Yangon. This was repeated daily, with increasing numbers, up to tens of thousands. Similar *pattanikujjana* rituals and protest marches were held in about a dozen other towns.

The monk-centred demonstrations, which continued till 26 September, caught the world's attention and came to be known as the 'Saffron Revolution'. On that day, the government started to violently suppress the movement, leading to shootings, killings, severe beatings and arrests of demonstrators. This later spread to the monasteries themselves. There was an international outcry and many foreign governments undertook action against the Myanmar regime.

On 11 October the UN Security Council came up with a presidential statement – a step below a council resolution – that 'strongly deplores the use of violence against peaceful demonstrations in Myanmar and welcomes the Human Rights Council resolution s-5/1 of 2 October 2007'. It was the first time that China had acceded to a consensus on Myanmar at the Security Council, and showed a slight shift in the 'protection' that it offers to the military regime.

With the situation being the way it is, Myanmar will continue to be dependent on China's support. Political change will come about slowly, and both the pace and the result are likely to be contentious. If there is no substantial improvement in dealings with the West, the present relationship with China can only grow stronger and deeper. China's role in this partnership is cursorily viewed and criticised in some quarters as 'coddling dictators'.

And the next day ... a procession of around a hundred monks walked in downtown Yangon. This was repeated daily, with increasing numbers, up to tens of thousands

But even after discounting China's stand on intervening in internal affairs, a closer look reveals that detailed and forceful advice is being delivered to the top leaders in the Myanmar military council. Member of China's State Council Tang Jiaxuan visited Myanmar in late February this year and advised Myanmar leaders to settle thorny issues with the International Labour Organisation (ILO) as well as bring about better cooperation with the UN. An amicable outcome with the ILO followed not long after. Mr Tang is also reported to have warned the military council against any precipitous move to disarm the ethnic paramilitaries with whom peace agreements had been reached. This is real leverage, being applied with finesse upon a withdrawn, recalcitrant regime. This is the kind of thing that the West would love to bring about, yet cannot.

After September there was added pressure from the Myanmar opposition abroad and also from Western governments to persuade and even pressurise China to exert more of its influence on the Myanmar regime. A special envoy from China in the person of deputy foreign minister Wang Yi was in Myanmar from 14 to 16 November 2007. Amongst other goals that his country wished for its neighbour, he hoped that the facilitation of Myanmar democratisation could be promoted through appropriate discussions.

Security

As one would expect, given its close proximity, on at least three occasions (one of them global) in the 20th century, turmoil, war and revolution in China have had an impact upon Myanmar

- Following Japan's invasion of China in 1937, the 'Burma Road' connecting the port of Yangon to southwest China was built to transport much-needed war materiel and other supplies to the beleaguered Chinese government. One could say that the World War II campaign in Myanmar was in large part fought over control of this strategic road.
- At the end of the civil war in China, Kuomintang units entered Myanmar and gained a foothold. They were supplied by air and offensives were launched against the People's Republic of China, only to be defeated. It took military operations and diplomatic efforts at the UN over many years to evict them from Myanmar.
- The Cultural Revolution affected Myanmar from 1967 and strained relations till 1985.

There was an about-turn in relations over security affairs following 1988 and the advent of the military government. Observers estimate that Myanmar's acquisition since then of arms and security-related materiel from China is in the order of $1.4 billion. A large part of the hardware (as well as the software) in the Myanmar armed forces originates in China. However there have been problems over the standard of workmanship and capabilities of the materiel.

Recently a scholar studying China used an impressive set of figures on China-in-Myanmar – on trade, investment, oil and gas, arms transfers, etc

– to illustrate how minimal they were compared to similar figures for other countries. His point was that China's major concern vis-à-vis Myanmar was over sovereignty – particularly its sovereignty over Taiwan. China is standing fast on Myanmar's sovereignty because it is aware that the very same issue could rear its head at any time – at the Security Council and elsewhere – with regard to Taiwan. Nonetheless, the 'induction' of Myanmar into China's 'sphere of influence' – politically, economically and what have you – remains a telling development.

Economic relations

Economic stagnation and chronic shortages were pervasive during the days of socialist autarky in Myanmar. As a result, Myanmar's borders became conduits for essential goods. It was this parallel market or unofficial trade, first with Thailand, then with other countries, that provided the Myanmar people with what their government could not or would not deliver. China's turn came in the mid-1980s when textiles, medicines and even items like toothpaste started coming in. With the legalisation of border trade in 1988, things have not looked back. In a recent paper, Toshihiro Kudo[2] writes: :

> Against the background of closer diplomatic, political and security ties between Myanmar and China since 1988, their economic relations have also grown stronger throughout the 1990s and up to the present. China is now a major supplier of consumer goods, durables, machinery and equipment, and intermediate products to Myanmar. China also offers markets for Myanmar's exports such as wood, agricultural produce, marine products, minerals, and recently oil and gas. Border trade provides a direct route connecting the centre of Upper Myanmar to Yunnan Province in China. Both physical infrastructure developments such as roads and bridges and institutionalisation of cross-border transactions, including 'one-stop services', promote border trade. Without the massive influx of Chinese products, the Myanmar economy may have suffered severer shortages of commodities. Without the opening up of China's export markets, Myanmar may have suffered severer shortages of foreign currencies.

As to deeper regional cooperation, the Greater Mekong Subregion (GMS) and ASEAN+3 both include Myanmar and are currently underway. The ASEAN Free Trade Area and East Asian Community are being established. Myanmar's political problems are making it difficult for it to participate fully in ASEAN. Taken together, Myanmar is among the weakest partners and is

---

Even in a globalised world, African failed states are far removed, whereas an imploding Myanmar is right next door, with all the manifold implications, threats and consequences

---

perhaps the weakest link in all of this. The GMS – which also includes Yunnan province – is in a way the shape of things to come. There are provisions for the free flow of not only trade but also technology, capital and people across borders but this is getting off to a rather slow start. An important question for economically weaker countries like Myanmar has to be what are the implications of a very open but uneven regional grouping.

Comparisons with the African experience

Taylor[3] and Tull[4] rightly debunk China's claims of non-interference in African politics. Its loans do have strings, in the form of ties to the use of Chinese companies, guarantees of access to future oil production and, internationally, to African states toeing the Chinese line not only on Taiwan, but also in the forums of global governance institutions. But most importantly, it also has an impact on governance in the African states in which it invests, an argument long held by those critical of China's investments in Myanmar and elsewhere. Supplying arms to Sudan during the conflict in Darfur, with guaranteed access to oil in the disputed area, is interference. Another scholar, Howard French[5] states that:

> For China to establish a meaningful difference from its European and American predecessors on African soil, it will have to overcome its insistence on a policy that raises 'non-interference' to a first principle and see no evil wherever it goes. In the longer term, after the flush

of excitement from the rush of new investment and attention from the East has passed, more and more Africans will come to see this stance for what it is, a shirking of responsibility and an excuse for doing whatever suits Beijing. In the African context, where poverty is the norm, where institutions are weak, and where the temptation for corruption is as powerful as it is anywhere on earth, preaching non-interference equals moral abdication.

It does Africans no good for China to insist on Western hypocrisy, given the West's long and shameful record of moral failure in Africa. China has a great deal to offer Africa, and if it is to become a true partner to the peoples of the continent, it will have to find its voice quickly on the development challenges they face and the scourges that ravage them.

Christopher Clapham[6] adds that:

At this point, the narrowness of China's engagement in Africa is likely to prove damaging. At one level, certainly, the fact that China seeks to impose no ideological agenda of its own on Africa – in contrast to ideological concomitants of Western capitalism – means that it poses less of a 'threat' than its often overbearing Western counterparts. But 'ideology', no matter how great the arrogance with which external powers seek to promote it, is not merely an alien imposition on unwilling Africans. It also strikes a local resonance, and serves to build moral linkages that extend beyond mere economic interests. For Africans who have been subjected to sometimes appallingly brutal domestic regimes, the demand for 'human rights' strikes a deep and legitimate chord. Equally, no matter how great the difficulties of instituting multiparty democracies in many parts of Africa, there is a significant part of the continent in which considerably more accountable regimes have been installed since the end of the Cold War, and despite the enduring problems of converting new political forms into economic welfare, still represent a very substantial improvement for local populations on military dictatorship or single-party rule. In cutting itself off from changes in African governance over the past two decades, China runs the risk of presenting itself merely as an interloper bent on short-term economic gain.

One would be hard pressed to find a reason why China *should not* jump in with regard to Myanmar. It is not merely the economic opportunities. One major reason that differs from engagement with Africa is the prospect of having a failed state on China's southwestern border. Even in a globalised world, African failed states are far removed, whereas an imploding Myanmar is right next door, with all the manifold implications, threats and consequences.

Discussion

Whichever way one views it, interchanges between the two countries are far more likely to grow than wane. It happens to be the natural order of things. How does any state system seek to contend with a 2,200km long border that becomes more porous with each passing day? The critical thing is to ensure that the interchanges, the diffusion, the two-way traffic, are beneficial, sustainable and equitable. As befits a relationship that stretches back a thousand years or more, the orientation towards the future should encompass centuries and not just decades to come.

China does have an influence in Myanmar, but it cannot be said to be a strong influence, much less a dominant or pervasive one. The leaders of the present Myanmar government see China primarily in terms of expediency – of providing critical support to tide over the difficulties they are faced with. And for this, they give in return what is in China's interests – economic

The leaders of the present Myanmar government see China primarily in terms of expediency – of providing critical support to tide over the difficulties they are faced with

interests mostly. Myanmar's present leaders have had to 'embrace' China – but warily. All of them have experienced the Chinese-supported Communist Party of Burma insurgency at first hand and memories are still fresh. It is hard to envision Myanmar becoming a client state in the present period. The non-approval of the Irrawaddy Waterway reflects these concerns.

Both countries have embarked upon political transitions, however slowly or reluctantly, but with important differences. The opposition in Myanmar is aiming for as full a liberal democracy as can be achieved. And even the military-sponsored constitution that is to be drafted soon allows for a multi-party system and devolution of power. One thing that could be constructively emulated from the contemporary Chinese scene is the political reforms at grassroots level.

It is sometimes said that the incumbent establishment in Myanmar inclines towards the Chinese 'model' whereby a transition to a booming market economy is achieved without letting loose the reins of political power. However, given both internal capabilities and external circumstances, this does not appear to be possible. Myanmar is staggering through a market transition that has to fend for itself most of the time while being encumbered by heavy and incompetent state interference.

It is in the consequences that commonalities are seen – the corruption, the in-equalities, the environmental costs, the social disruption and unrest. Perhaps it is wishful thinking to envisage the two countries working together on these issues and learning from each other. If carefully handled, civil society could take the lead in this far-reaching process. The 'narrowness' of engagement mentioned above could be broadened fruitfully – in Myanmar as in Africa – by cooperation and assistance in battling diseases like Aids and malaria for instance. Expediency and economic interests by themselves are poor justification in light of the immense stakes involved, especially for future generations.

Notes
1 Andrew Selth (2007) *Chinese Military Bases in Burma: The Explosion of a Myth*, Griffith Asia Institute Regional Outlook Paper no.10, Griffith University.
2 Toshihiro Kudo (2006) *Myanmar's Economic Relations with China: Can China Support the Myanmar Economy?* Discussion Paper no. 66. Chiba: Institute of Developing Economies (IDE).
3 Ian Taylor (2005) 'China's oil diplomacy in Africa', *International Affairs* 82(5): p. 949.
4 Denis Tull (2006) 'China's engagement in Africa: scope, significance and consequences', *Journal of Modern African Studies*, 44(3): p. 474.
5 Howard W. French (2006) 'China and Africa', *African Affairs*.
6 Christopher Clapham (2006) *Fitting China in Brenthurst*, Discussion Paper 8/2006, The Brenthurst Foundation.
Additional source
Burma Project Earth Rights International (2007) 'China in Burma: The increasing investment of Chinese multinational corporations in Burma's hydropower, oil and gas, and mining sectors', September <http://www.earthrights.org/files/Reports/BACKGROUNDER%20 China%20in%20Burma.pdf>. This publication contains a list of projects that Chinese multinational corporations have in Burma/Myanmar.

CHINA AND LATIN AMERICA: STRATEGIC PARTNERING OR LATTER-DAY IMPERIALISM?

ALEXANDRE DE FREITAS BARBOSA

Looking at the main features of the recent economic and geopolitical relations between China and the countries of Latin America, Alexandre de Freitas Barbosa paints a varied picture. He argues that the adverse effects of the relationship are partly due to Latin American countries' inability to come up with effective development policies of their own and that social movements in the region could act to change their government's attitudes in order to face the Chinese challenge.

The first part of this article looks at the development styles of China and Latin American countries in the 1990s. Contrasting their two approaches to foreign markets helps explain essential features of the relations between China and Latin America, which took on a new cast at the turn of the century. Then – taking Latin America as a whole – the article traces an overview of trade relations between the two regions. The third section discusses more specifically China's economic relations with Mexico/Central America, Argentina/Chile/Peru and Brazil.

The fourth part of the article summarises China's foreign policy, highlighting what this new world power seeks in Latin America. In the light of that description, it discusses the challenges posed for Latin America by China's rise. It also examines the China–Latin America 'partnership' from the viewpoint of Latin American social movements, which for the time being have not discussed the 'China phenomenon' in depth, while governments and businesses position themselves – and even then on an approach that is topic-specific, bilateral and focussed on the short term – to respond to China's economic and geopolitical advance in Latin America.

Distinct macroeconomic trajectories in the 1990s

During the 1990s, Latin America and China followed quite divergent macroeconomic trajectories. While on the one hand, both regions interacted increasingly with the international economy, they pursued their roles as players in globalisation according to sets of diverse, if not opposing, assumptions and policies.

What first stands out when their two economies are compared is the pace of expansion. From 1990 to 2002, per capita income expanded about ten times faster in China than in Latin America (at 8.8 per cent against 0.9 per cent per year), according to UN Economic Commission for Latin America and the Caribbean (ECLAC) and UNDP data.

China's vigorous GDP rests on high rates of investment, which can be explained by its booming exports, high levels of public spending and a domestic market that is burgeoning – from low plateaus and with unprecedented growth potential – in a context of extreme caution towards relaxing controls on the capitals market. In parallel with this, trade liberalisation has come gradually, so much so that trade surpluses grew substantially after China entered the World Trade Organisation (WTO). In 2006, according to WTO figures, China already accounted for 10 per cent of total manufactured exports, against a Latin American total of 4 per cent or so.

This is because China has been upgrading its exports, 91 per cent of which are of manufactured goods, while Latin America is rationalising production by de-verticalisation and by boosting imported content, especially in the most dynamic trade sectors and wherever productivity is highest. The result has been a dual process in which exports have concentrated in natural resource-intensive products, while *maquiladoras* – exporting manufactured goods with little value added on the domestic market – have proliferated.[1]

Latin American industrial exports are insignificant in terms of world trade. The exceptions are commodities and fuels, which account, respectively, for 11.5 per cent and 9 per cent of global foreign sales. In manufactured goods, Latin America's position is marginal: it contributes from 4 per cent to 5 per cent of natural resource-intensive and low-to-medium-technology manufactures and only 3.4 per cent of world sales in high-tech exports, using UNCTAD trade methodology.

In addition, China's policy model for attracting multinationals favours joint ventures with local firms, rather than the simple privatisation that predominated in Latin America in the 1990s. Although such companies do play a strategic role, they contribute only 5 per cent of gross capital formation in China and 30 per cent of manufactured output, 60 per cent of which is earmarked for the domestic market.[2] That is, the external market and foreign investments are strategic especially because they feed back into an endogenously-driven process of capital accumulation.

In other words, the essential difference between the two economic regions seems to lie in the nexus between exportation and investment, which has enabled China to expand its industrial capacity and has even helped strengthen the domestic market. In Latin America, meanwhile, exchange

---

From 1990 to 2002, per capita income expanded about ten times faster in China than in Latin America

---

volatility – due to the rapid and automatic deregulation of trade and finance – prevented that nexus from forming, instead bringing abrupt shifts in the pace of growth and investment and forcing its countries to resort to rigid monetary policies.

According to the categories set out by UNCTAD,[3] China could be classed as a rapidly industrialising country, transforming the structure of its industrial base toward sectors of greater productivity. Latin America, meanwhile, forms part of the capitalist periphery in the process of early de-industrialisation. This is because its industrial market share is declining not because the structure of industry changed to incorporate value-adding services, as in the developed countries, but because the industrial base inherited from the import-substitution model of industrialisation is shrinking.

While it is true that this downward trend in industrial market share was also seen in the first-generation Asian tigers, it was far less pronounced because it was associated with a more complex industry mix. China's industry, meanwhile, besides being increasingly diversified, accounts for 35 per cent of GDP and is leveraging expansion in the service and agricultural sectors, although the latter comprises a vast body of extremely low-productivity activities.

In summary, the differences between Latin American countries and Asian countries, especially China, stem largely from their particular conceptions of industrial policy and the strategic options of integration in the international economy.[4] Asian countries such as South Korea and Taiwan applied policies

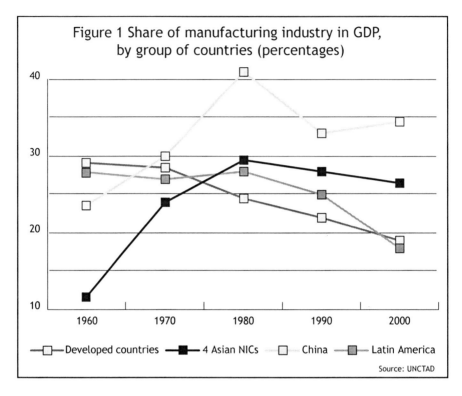

Figure 1 Share of manufacturing industry in GDP, by group of countries (percentages)

Source: UNCTAD

directed to developing domestic high-technology capabilities, while the model adopted by the other Asian tigers – Malaysia, Thailand and Philippines – hinged on attracting multinational corporations to become export platforms in high-tech sectors.[5]

In the countries of Latin America, from the 1990s onwards, horizontal industrial policies predominated, assimilating the so-called 'good policies' recommended by the developed countries. Alternatively free-trade agreements were signed between some Latin American countries and advanced economies, which tended to subordinate trade flows to the decisions of multinational corporations.

Nonetheless, industrial restructuring – pursued in this context of trade and financial deregulation, with exchange rates appreciating in several countries and economic instability resulting from substantial current account deficits – came in various styles: in Chile, de-industrialisation with reorientation outwards; in Mexico, radical integration northwards; in Argentina, export de-sophistication; and in Brazil, defensive restructuring.[6] These styles resulted

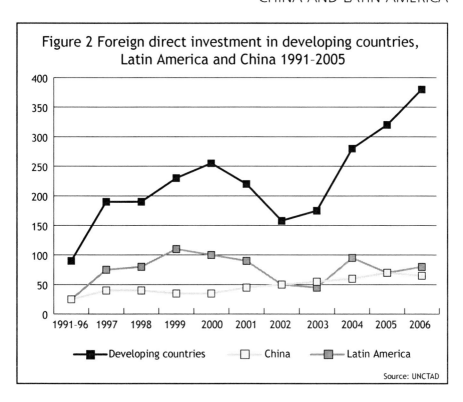

Figure 2 Foreign direct investment in developing countries, Latin America and China 1991-2005

Source: UNCTAD

from varying combinations of macroeconomic, structural and institutional factors. In parallel with this, the multinationals' decisions varied according to the nature of the adjustment, the dimensions of the respective domestic markets and the options in terms of trade agreements.

The differences in terms of macroeconomic and industrial dynamics can be summarised from how foreign direct investment (FDI) behaved in these two economic regions. In China, investments rose continuously, buoyed up by the development and diversification in the country's industrial and service base, while in Latin America, their behaviour is exogenous; that is, they rise when total investment to developing countries rises, and fall when the world economy is hit by crisis, as in the period 2001–03.

The rate of new FDI projects seems little affected by the degree of economic liberalisation or state regulation. Multinational corporations have expanded their projects in economically dynamic countries, such as China, while reducing them in Latin America, whose economies offer less diversity and domestic markets with less potential for expansion.

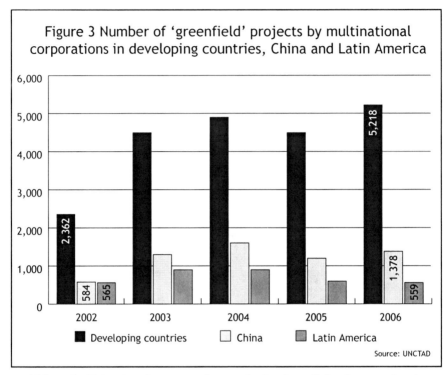

Figure 3 Number of 'greenfield' projects by multinational corporations in developing countries, China and Latin America

Developing countries ☐ China ▨ Latin America

Source: UNCTAD

Although China is a long way from substituting all foreign production – and such a situation seems hardly feasible in view of its own contradictions and the regionalised dynamics of the global economy – it does host more than a quarter of all new investment projects by multinational corporations in developing countries, while Latin America accounts for only 10 per cent.

These contrasts between the industrial, macroeconomic and international integration policies of China and Latin American countries are helpful for explaining the type of economic interaction that has developed between the two regions in recent times, as will now be examined in greater detail.

An overview of trade relations

Let us start this bilateral analysis with how important Latin America is to China's trade transactions. WTO figures for 2005 show that only 2.3 per cent of China's exports are destined for Latin America. Between them, Latin America and Africa – two regions where Chinese foreign policy has made vigorous inroads (accompanied by intensive coverage in the Western press)

Table 1 China's imports from Latin America, by product category – 2005*

	US$ bn	% total China imports from LA	% China imports of these goods
Agricultural products	8.6	35.1	20.3
Fuel and mining products	12.3	50.2	10.3
Manufactures	3.6	14.7	0.7

Source: WTO.
*Latin America excluding Mexico and the Caribbean countries.

– account for only 5 per cent of Chinese exports. Brazil ranks 14th among China's suppliers in aggregate terms, while no other Latin American country even makes it onto the list of the 20 main exporters to China.[7]

These two regions of the South thus appear marginal to China's export performance, which prioritises access to developed country markets (more than 50 per cent of its exports go to the USA, EU and Japan), besides the nearly 30 per cent destined for Southeast Asia, according to WTO data.

Meanwhile, these two regions of the South are the source of 7 per cent of China's imports. An analysis of trade distribution reveals that South and Central America account for 20 per cent of the agricultural products consumed by China and for 10 per cent of the mining products, including fuels (Table 1). The percentages for Africa, according to WTO figures, are 3.9 per cent and 38.2 per cent, respectively. In other words, a quarter of the agricultural goods imported by China come from these two regions, and the percentage rises to 50 per cent for fuels and mining products, the former predominantly from Latin America and the latter from Africa.

To this concentrated array of exports from Latin American countries, add China's thirst for foods, agricultural raw materials, mining products and fuels, and the formidable growth experienced by the region's exports to China is understandable.

Figure 4 shows how Latin American exports to China have expanded, with foreign sales to China growing around eight times from 1995 to 2005. By the end of the period, in 2005, the trade balance in Latin America's favour was US$6.6 billion.

The bulk of the export surge (80 per cent of 1995–2005 growth) is concentrated in the post-2002 period, which can be explained both by

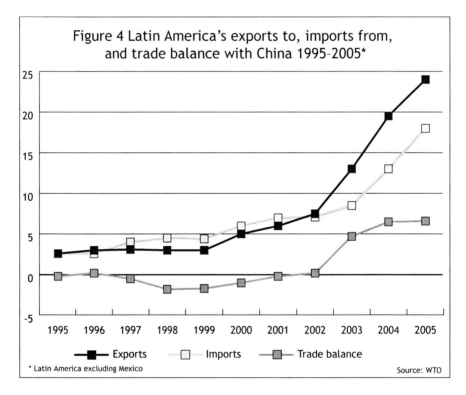

Figure 4 Latin America's exports to, imports from, and trade balance with China 1995–2005*

Exports — Imports — Trade balance

* Latin America excluding Mexico

Source: WTO

continuing growth in the Chinese economy and by higher commodity prices, factors that bear some relation to each other. Indeed, China's growth accelerated in this period, especially in the energy, metallurgy and infrastructure sectors. Yin[8] argues that part of this expansion was due also to the reduction in China's average import tariff after it entered the WTO. From 1998 to 2005, it fell from 17 per cent to 9.4 per cent. In any case, it is as well to remember that China's tariff structure continues to feature peaks, especially in the agricultural sector where tariffs stand above the mean.[9]

No less important is the upturn in Latin American demand for Chinese imports after 2002. In fact, from 2002 to 2005, the gap between exports to and imports from China narrowed, the former increasing 3.4 times and the latter 2.7 times. In 2005, compared with the prior year, China's exports to Latin America grew even more rapidly than its imports, stabilising Latin America's favourable trade surplus.

However, 93 per cent of imports to South and Central America from China are manufactured goods. In 2005, textiles and garments represented 25 per

216

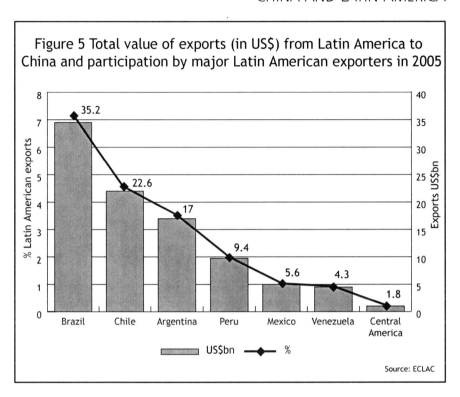

Figure 5 Total value of exports (in US$) from Latin America to China and participation by major Latin American exporters in 2005

Source: ECLAC

cent of the total, and machinery and equipment, 44 per cent.[10] It is not to Latin America alone that China is selling a larger proportion of more technology-intensive products. The changing structure of its domestic industry led to a shift in the export mix in the late 1990s. From 2002 to 2004, China's total labour-intensive exports expanded by 67 per cent, against a 100 per cent surge by medium- and high-technology products.[11] This was especially true of standardised products like PCs, mobile phones and DVD players.

The figures above have invited some hasty assumptions. Is the volatility of primary material-based economies a thing of the past? Will China prop up the world economy, leaving Latin American countries' foreign accounts less vulnerable by virtue of the improved terms of trade? These questions have to be approached with caution, because they lead to generalisations with little empirical foundation, besides disregarding specific features of the various countries in the region.

Figures 5 and 6 show the position of several Latin American countries in terms of their trade relations with China. Firstly, some 80 per cent of the

217

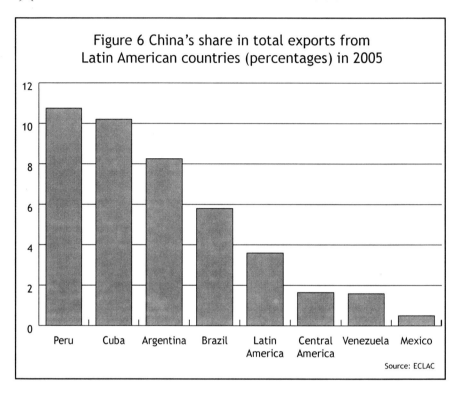

Figure 6 China's share in total exports from Latin American countries (percentages) in 2005

Source: ECLAC

region's exports to China – here including figures for Mexico – originate from only four countries: in decreasing order, Brazil, Chile, Argentina and Peru. Secondly, while on average less than 4 per cent of Latin American countries' total exports go to China, in these four countries the figure is 6 per cent or more. In particular Chile, Cuba and Peru now export to China something in the order of 10 per cent of their total foreign sales. From 1999 to 2004, China accounted for about 20 per cent of export growth in Argentina and Chile, 16 per cent in Peru and 10 per cent in Brazil. Even more striking was Costa Rica, where China contributed 35 per cent of foreign sales growth.[12]

Latin American exports are extremely concentrated not only by country, but also by product. Brazil has the least concentrated portfolio, nonetheless iron ore and soy alone represent two-thirds of its exports. Around 80 per cent of what Chile and Argentina export to China comprises a single product, as can be seen in Table 2.

218

Various regional patterns of economic relations

We now turn our attention to the patterns of trade and investment between China and the various sub-areas of the Latin American region.

The first pattern of economic relations involves Chile, Argentina and Peru. These countries' trade balances are clearly favourable as a result of their industrial specialisation and export portfolios. In this case, Chinese investment tends to be concentrated in export activities – such as Peru's iron ore and the oil reserves discovered recently in the north of the country – and in infrastructure activities, such as highways and ports in Chile and Argentina.

Chile has even opted for a free trade agreement with China, signed in November 2005. That agreement can be explained, on the one hand, by the complementarity and proximity of their two economies, and on the other, by Chile's foreign policy of expanding and diversifying its trade relations on the basis of bilateral negotiations.

This pattern is, however, not immune to protectionist policies designed to contain the Chinese 'threat'. In this regard, Argentina stands at the opposite extreme. In August 2007, the country adopted a set of restrictive measures aimed especially at China. These are automatic import licences, additional safety regulations and the requirement that importers submit 'certificates of origin' to combat under-invoicing. Interestingly in this case, the demand to introduce these measures came from the metalworkers' union, Unión Obrera Metalúrgica (UOM).[13]

The second pattern of trade can be seen between Brazil and China. Its specific features derive from the more diversified structure of Brazil's exports, the greater scale and integration of its production chains, especially

Table 2 Percentage of leading products in some Latin American countries' exports to China 2004

	% main products	first	second	third
Argentina	78.5	soy		
Brazil	67.7	iron ore	soy	
Chile	76.2	copper		
Peru	85.2	copper	fish flour	iron ore

Source: ECLAC.

industry, and the fact that Brazil's exports, at least to other Latin American countries, partly coincide with what these import from China.

True – just as in the first case described above – there is also a high degree of specialisation in Brazil's exports to China, given that more than 80 per cent of these foreign sales are grouped in primary and semi-manufactured goods. Other factors must be added, however, in order to understand their bilateral relations in all their complexity. In the first place, Brazil seems more affected by industrial imports from China than the other Southern Cone countries. This can be seen in Figure 7.

The period from 2003 to 2006, when Brazil's trade surplus slumped from US$2.4 billion to around US$400 million, coincides with a resurgence in its industrial GDP combined, at the end of the period, with strong exchange

---

Multinational corporations have expanded their projects in economically dynamic countries, such as China, while reducing them in Latin America, whose economies offer less diversity and domestic markets with less potential for expansion

---

appreciation. In the first half of 2007, Brazil even went into a trade deficit with China. Everything indicates that in 2007 China will rank as Brazil's second most important trading partner.[14] President Lula summed up this complex situation by saying that 'just as China can help, it can also hinder'.[15]

There is incomparably less concentration to Brazil's imports from China than vice versa. The ten main products that Brazil imports from China account for 26 per cent of its foreign purchases.[16] If the present macroeconomic situation continues, the combination between China and foreign exchange appreciation may open up a number of 'holes' in Brazil's industrial structure. For the moment, industrial imports from China equal only 1 per cent of Brazil's industrial output, even though this percentage increased threefold from 2000 to 2005.[17] Note, however, that the Brazilian manufacturing sector's trade deficit with China rose by a factor of 3.6 between 2004 and 2006, jumping from US$1.583 billion to US$5.681 billion.[18]

Up to 2004, industrial purchases from China had no destructive effect

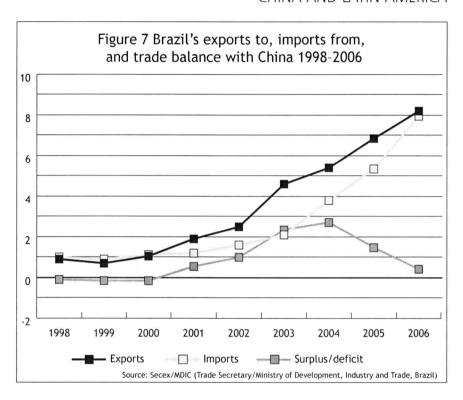

Figure 7 Brazil's exports to, imports from, and trade balance with China 1998–2006

Source: Secex/MDIC (Trade Secretary/Ministry of Development, Industry and Trade, Brazil)

on the domestic market, because in many cases, especially in goods with high added value, they were replacing goods from other foreign suppliers.[19] However, everything seems to indicate that more serious effects on the domestic market are appearing.

On the other hand, Brazil – unlike its Latin American neighbours – manages to be a prominent exporter of certain industrial goods. There is thus some room for integrating into Chinese production chains intermediate technology sectors, such as leathers, paper and cellulose; industrial components, such as auto-parts, chemical, iron and steel and electronic products; and machinery and mechanical appliances.[20]

All the same, it is as well to remember that China tends to import, at most, the production chain links with least added value, thus prioritising cellulose over paper, alumina over aluminium, and iron over steel.[21] Nor should one forget that Brazil, and also the other countries of Latin America, face competition from the ASEAN countries, with which China maintains

221

an intensive network of intra-industry trade. In the natural resource-based manufactures segment, 15.6 per cent of China's imports come from ASEAN and only 7.8 per cent from LAIA countries.[22] This disparity in shares of the Chinese market is even greater in the more technology-intensive sectors.

Other issues characterise the pattern of economic relations between Brazil and China. Brazil tends increasingly to be squeezed out of the markets it exports to in its region, where its sales of high added value industrial products are concentrated.

Figure 8 shows that this is not yet happening in the Mercosur overall, where in 2004 Brazil's share in total industrial imports was about three times larger than China's. However, everything indicates that the situation is changing rapidly, especially in certain segments. In the case of the metal-machining industry, Argentina's imports from China outstripped those from Brazil in the first half of 2007.[23] The same trend is emerging in trade with Chile and the Andean Community (CAN), where Brazil and China accounted for very similar shares in 2004 (Inter-American Development Bank (IDB) figures). Overall, under the influence of imports by Mexico, China surpassed Brazil in the region in 2004, accounting for 7.8 per cent of industrial imports to Latin America, against 6.5 per cent from Brazil.

This displacement effect is occurring not only on Latin American markets, however. More than 40 per cent of Brazil's market losses to China in the United States are concentrated in two products: footwear and mobile phones.[24]

Another feature specific to the Brazilian case is the growing presence of Brazilian multinationals operating in China – by way of joint ventures – which has contributed to driving goods and service trade flows, although at magnitudes well below the available potential. Corporations such as Embraco (compressors), Embraer (aircraft), Weg (electric motors), Sabo (auto-parts) and Marcopolo (buses) have paved the way, and others should take the same road. This is not from choice, but the only way to penetrate the medium- and high-technology sectors of the Chinese market.

The pattern of Chinese direct investments in Brazil is also more diversified. Besides forestry products and iron ore, they focus on machinery (tractors), energy and telecommunications.[25] More recently, a partnership was announced between the Chinese state enterprise, BBCA Biochemicals, and the Brazilian firm, Grupo Farias, to build two major ethanol plants in Maranhão State between 2009 and 2010.[26]

However, Chinese investments are still insignificant in terms of domestic production and employment, especially when compared with investments

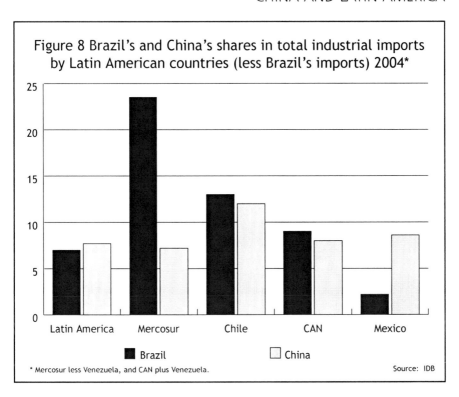

Figure 8 Brazil's and China's shares in total industrial imports by Latin American countries (less Brazil's imports) 2004*

■ Brazil   ☐ China

* Mercosur less Venezuela, and CAN plus Venezuela.   Source: IDB

possibly postponed in Brazil as a result of various multinationals having opted to concentrate their plants in China. Of course the regional operations of several of those corporations are based in Brazil, but their expansion plans for occupying world markets are all affected to some extent by the dynamism of the Chinese market and the levels of competitiveness China manages to achieve on foreign markets.

To conclude, note that some Brazilian multinational corporations, especially in the civil construction sector, now fear the advance of Chinese capital in other regions, especially on the African continent.[27] It was no coincidence that, on a visit to Africa in October, President Lula announced that the credit facility from Brazil's development bank, BNDES, for Brazilian companies exporting goods and services to Angola is to increase to US$1 billion.[28]

Mexico and the Central American countries represent the antithesis of the pattern found in South American countries, at least those where China participates significantly in trade, such as Argentina, Chile and Peru.

Especially for Mexico, the effects of foreign entry and displacement on external markets loom quite large. In 2003, China ousted Mexico from its position as the second largest exporter to the United States. Of Mexico's 20 main exporting sectors, 12 are in open competition with Chinese products. Evidence of pressure on the domestic market is provided by the fact that, up to September 2005, 40 per cent of the antidumping complaints brought against China were filed by Mexico,[29] which had also come out in open opposition to China's entry to the WTO.

Something similar is happening with most of the Central American countries, but here the adverse effects are being felt as displacement, especially on the United States market, and largely in the textiles and

China hosts more than a quarter of all new investment projects by multinational corporations in developing countries, while Latin America accounts for only 10 per cent

garment sectors. Neither can these countries supply agricultural or mining products – with the possible exception of Mexico's minerals – on a sufficient scale or competitively enough to serve as suppliers to China.

The only exception is Costa Rica, which maintains a trade surplus, thanks to the fact that 92 per cent of its exports to China are microprocessors.[30] This is a case of intra-industry trade, which can be explained by the presence of an Intel plant in Costa Rica. Mexico too is conspicuous for having supplied some electronic goods and auto-parts to China, again as part of trade conducted essentially among multinational corporations. Note also that around 50 per cent of Chinese foreign investments in Mexico are concentrated in companies in the garment sector,[31] with an eye to boosting access to the United States market.

What has happened more commonly, however, is that a number of the multinationals operating as *maquiladoras* in Mexico have transferred to China. That is to say, especially in the case of Mexico, what is involved is a pattern of trade that leads to sizeable trade deficits with China, bringing more pressure to domestic competition, in addition to displacing exports on the US market. Offsetting factors include gains by intra-multinational industrial exports from Mexico to China – although in smaller volumes than in the opposite direction – and an increase in Chinese foreign investment, as in the garment sector.

The cases of Cuba and Venezuela constitute only limited exceptions to the first pattern of trade described above. This is because both Venezuela's oil and Cuba's nickel reproduce the pattern of offering the Chinese market essentially primary products. Some differences do exist, however. With regard to Cuba, despite the increasing pragmatism of China's foreign policy, the ideological factor plays an important role. It is accompanied by narrower economic relations, to the point where, among Cuba's trading partners in 2005, China ranked ahead of Spain and second only to Venezuela.[32]

Venezuela, meanwhile, is a country seeking to ideologise relations with China, which knows how to demarcate its role in the United States' area of influence. This means that China turns a deaf ear to Chavez's anti-imperialist discourse and pursues its plans for investment in Venezuela, although without any intention of displacing the US as the prime consumer of its oil. It is worth remembering that China – whether as trade partner or investor – is not yet as conspicuous a presence here as in the other Southern Cone countries or Mexico.

Lastly, certain sectors are starting to emerge as potentially the most susceptible to Chinese expansion. Moreira[33] regards labour-intensive activities as the most affected, followed by technology-intensive activities. His calculations indicate that, from 1990 to 2004, foreign markets lost to China were worth the equivalent of 1.7 per cent of Latin America's 2004 industrial exports, a figure that rises to 2.7 per cent when low-technology products are considered. The two sectors that epitomise labour-intensive activities (textiles and garments) and technology-intensive activities (electrical and electronic appliances) are the worst affected. Remember that these calculations do not reflect domestic production displaced as a result of increasing imports.

Relations between Latin America and China have been relatively centred on trade, which is especially important to Argentina, Brazil, Chile, Costa Rica, Peru and Venezuela, all of which have trade surpluses with China. These six countries, moreover, represent 90 per cent of Latin America's exports to China.[34] Nonetheless, more recently, Chinese foreign direct investments have been growing, generally mirroring the trade pattern established in each subregion.

In 2003, 35 per cent of China's foreign direct investments targeted Latin America, and in 2004 the percentage reached around 50 per cent.[35] From 2004 to 2006, total Chinese foreign direct investment increased threefold,[36] probably with some decline in Latin America's share. This recent rise in Chinese foreign direct investment can be explained by a series of factors: surplus international reserves, overheated economy, trade tensions with a number of countries, and political/diplomatic goals connected with winning new markets. The great differential is the support they enjoy from the state apparatus and the major public banks.

In Table 3, Peru, Mexico and Brazil stand out as the main recipients of China's stock of capital. Even so, here there can be said to be three patterns of investment by Chinese multinationals. One is more directed to the export and infrastructure sectors (Peru). Another is more concerned with the export potential of certain commodities, but without neglecting the domestic market (Brazil). In the case of Mexico, the interest derives from Mexican firms' entry points to the markets in the United States, which is increasingly inclined to apply protectionist measures against China.

However, while on the one hand Chinese foreign investment tends to accompany the established pattern of trade with each country, on the other hand, foreign investment received by China may displace multinationals' investments, and thus trade, away from Latin America. As pointed out in the first section of this article, China has been an important host for multinationals' greenfield investment projects, while Latin America has lost terrain.

Overall summary

From this analysis of the patterns of trade and investment between Latin America and China, it is possible to 'estimate' the possible economic effects resulting from Chinese expansion. These comprise macroeconomic effects, impact on domestic industry, displacement on foreign markets, and net effect in terms of foreign investments, which combine in various ways in each country or region. This attempt at synthesis is set out in Chart 1.

Note that the countries have not been divided into economic blocs or geographical areas, but according to their patterns of economic relations with China. No attempt has been made to forecast, but to point up trends from what is currently happening. The actions of governments, business, workers and civil society can and should influence the process and alter the direction of the trends sketched above.

It should be remembered also that the division between favourable and adverse impacts reflects the potential opened up in terms of economic

Table 3 Stock of Chinese foreign direct investments – total in US$ and main Latin American recipients' position in the world ranking 2002

Country	Ranking as hoster of Chinese FDI	US$ millions
Peru	7	201.2
Mexico	9	183.7
Brazil	11	119.7

Source: UNCTAD

relations between these two areas, which – depending on how they are conducted – may entail losses for the environment and for considerable portions of working people, which we will discuss in the conclusion.

The chart does not mention the indirect macroeconomic effects of China's expansion. It is important to note that by financing the United States' current account deficit – and thus at least temporarily offsetting a structural imbalance – the Chinese economy has, up to this point, assured growth in the world economy and in Latin American countries indistinctively, and is even helping drive intra-regional trade in the region.

Notwithstanding that, China can be said to aggravate certain tendencies towards regressive specialisation in some economies, such as Argentina, Chile and Peru, even though these countries may obtain considerable economic gains, especially in the short term. Argentina is, to some extent, peculiar because the country is engaged in an endeavour to reindustrialise and China may hinder that development strategy. With regard to the smaller countries, those of Central America are most directly jeopardised by Chinese competition on the United States' market. The other countries, such as Ecuador, may benefit from new investments and access to the Chinese market.

In any case, all these countries' economic relations with China tend to reproduce a typical centre–periphery relationship. León-Manríquez[37] suggests it may be worth evaluating how applicable the thinking of Lenin[38] and ECLAC is to explaining relations between China and Latin America. Following Lenin's analysis, besides capturing raw materials, the imperialist powers turned to the 'periphery' in the late 19th century in order to apply their surplus capital, so as to prevent rates of profit from falling. That is not exactly the case with China, which is using its companies' expansion not only to gain markets, but also to secure geopolitical advantages. It is at best

Chart 1 Outlook of economic impacts of China's rise on Latin American subregions

	Macroeconomic effects	Effects on industry by sector	Displacement effects on external markets	Net effect on foreign investments
Argentina, Chile and Peru	**Favourable**: trade surpluses fed by high mining and agricultural commodity prices and Chinese demand (better terms of trade).	**Favourable**: effects limited by small degree of verticalisation in production chains of products exported to China; **Adverse**: mainly in Argentina, where industry is more structured, local producers are at risk of substitution in certain sectors or substantially narrower profit margins with impacts on labour market; The risks extend to the textile and garment industries in all the countries, however.	**Neutral**: No significant competition exists between these countries' and China's export products on international markets – with the possible exception of Argentina's exports in some sectors of the Brazilian market.	**Favourable**: localised investments in the primary and infrastructure sectors; **Adverse**: loss of potential to attract investments in certain niche industrial sectors because of Chinese expansion.
Brazil	**Favourable**: trade surpluses fed by high mining and agricultural commodity prices and Chinese demand (better terms of trade).	**Favourable**: effects limited by small degree of verticalisation in production chains of products exported to China; **Adverse**: by virtue of Brazil's more diversified industrial base, entry by Chinese products – thus far limited to substituting other international suppliers – may open up "holes" in industrial structure.	**Adverse**: Brazilian exports of industrial goods to Latin America and the United States increasingly losing space.	**Favourable**: Brazilian firms have set up joint-ventures with Chinese firms on the Chinese market; meanwhile, increasing Chinese investment in the domestic market goes beyond the primary sector. **Adverse**: global greenfield investments, which Brazil could host, are preferring China for its more dynamic

				market and better service and xsupplier infrastructure; and Brazilian firms operating on other regions, such as Africa, are losing space.
Mexico	**Neutral**: not a significant supplier of commodities to China, except for certain mining products.	**Adverse**: domestic producers displaced by Chinese imports, especially electrical and electronic appliances and textiles/ garments.	**Adverse**: far-reaching displacement of Mexican products on the United States market, because of strong similarities between China's and Mexico's export profiles; **Favourable**: although not offsetting the above, some firms manage to become industrial suppliers to firms based in China (intra-industry or intra-multinational trade).	**Adverse**: multinationals' activities displaced from plants in Mexico to China. **Favourable**: insignificant compared with adverse effects above, although greater Chinese investments are being made in the textile/garment sector in order to access the USA market.
Other small LA countries	**Favourable**: depend on export profile and 'fit' with Chinese imports; **Favourable**: imports of cheaper industrial products not vital to the structure of local industry may improve terms of trade.	**Adverse**: most Central American countries, but also the region's other small countries, tend to suffer from greater pressure of competition in textile/ garment sectors.	**Adverse**: displacement on the US market, especially affecting Central American countries.	**Favourable**: investments in export-related infrastructure sectors; **Adverse**: in countries producing on the *maquiladora* model, especially in the textile/garment sectors, there may be a decline in foreign investments not offset by increased investment by Chinese firms in these sectors.

Produced by author.

a proto-imperialist nation willing to cede even economic advantages in the effort to establish a multi-polar order, in spite of the rhetoric embedded in the concept.

The ECLAC approach, on the other hand – even though it may seem questionable in view of the short-term improvements in terms of trade for Latin American countries – may help understand a pattern of industrial specialisation which does little to bring either structural changes or major productivity increases to Latin American countries.

Contrary to the current view that considers ECLAC's thesis as protectionist, its earlier formulations always insisted upon the need to diversify exports simultaneously with the promotion of industrial development.[39] In the context of present China/Latin American relations – especially if the region simply adapts itself to the inheritance of the 1990s in terms of productive structure and model of international integration depicted in the first section – there is the risk that this new Asian power helps to bury, once and for all, any promise of endogenous Latin American development.

On the other hand, China's ascent coincides with the crisis in a system of inter-state power – as configured at Bretton Woods – which admits a small group of hegemonic nations. In that context of a changing international political order, China can play a constructive role that goes beyond its exclusively economic presence.

Brazil and Mexico are the most problematic cases. China, for different reasons, tends to entail a 'trap effect' for these countries, threatening the foreign market strategies they developed in the 1990s. Also, the centre-periphery model is less readily adaptable to these two cases and their relations with China, as is also the imperialism hypothesis.

As regards Mexico, this has to do with the declining dividends and mounting costs of the North American Free Trade Agreement (NAFTA) option. The *maquiladora* strategy is being called into question, and the new prospects opening up on the Chinese market are not of such a magnitude as to leverage the sectors displaced by Chinese competition with Mexican products, whether from national or multinational firms, on both its domestic market and the US market. In perhaps overly simple terms, China mutes the 'beneficial' impact of United States' imperialism on Mexico, while heightening its adverse effects, and without putting anything in its place.

In Brazil, where economic liberalisation did not bring widespread de-industrialisation, the domestic market has continued to be substantial, and the regional market, especially for industrial products, has grown in importance. There, China's advance may generate a counter-pressure, hindering its industry's efforts to diversify outwards and inwards, in addition to putting off investments by multinationals, which thus far had seen the country as a platform for exporting to the region. Here Chinese expansion may hamper the gestation of a new 'sub-imperialist' power – as some prefer – at the Latin American level, by undermining even its domestic industrial base. What seems more relevant to us is that if, on the contrary, Brazil is weakened, that would make any proposal for regional integration of any magnitude unworkable in Latin America.

Lastly, this analysis should not serve to blame China for the difficulties Latin America's industrial systems are encountering in securing a more dynamic external market role. A considerable portion of the dilemmas posed by China's rise tends to be aggravated by a lack of clarity in Latin American countries' priorities as regards industrial policies, technological innovation and regional integration. Also lacking is any sound, coherent vision of what can be expected of China in its relations with Latin America – which is something we shall move on to in the next section.

China's rise probably reproduces some of the strategies of the traditional imperialist nations in their relations with Latin America. However, these nations have not yet 'left the field' and nor is Chinese strategy firmly consolidated, leaving space for coordinated political action by Latin American countries, especially in the changing context of the international political order.

Chinese foreign policy, Latin America and social movements

Despite hasty analyses by the international – and especially US – media, China cannot be said to have any long-term strategy for establishing itself as a global power. What it seeks in that regard is a minimally stable international environment – international peace and stability, according to its diplomatic rhetoric – in order to preserve its independence, sovereignty and territorial integrity. China's focus on domestic development means that it prefers to pursue a more relaxed foreign policy, which is taking an increasingly pragmatic approach.[40]

A realistic approach predominates in China's international relations, where economic development is regarded as vital in a context of competition

for comprehensive power, because it involves the technological, political and military spheres. The nation state is the fundamental locus of action.[41]

China's leaders regard its presence in the international economy as offering a legitimate and effective mechanism for accomplishing its national development. China sees itself as a vast, rich civilisation which, after a century of humiliation and defeats, is striving to build a multipolar order, to move beyond the unilateral hegemony that predominated in the world with the end of the Cold War.[42]

It is in this light that, in place of the international adventurism of the 1960s, China has taken part – even if selectively – in the major international forums. Its main diplomatic weapons to that end are pragmatism, flexibility and the ability to learn.[43] In summary, this is a diplomacy of caution, tailored to its strategic aims, multidirectional and serving to integrate public and private endeavours.[44] More importantly still, there is no strategy to challenge the United States openly, but rather only to occupy the empty spaces it leaves behind in Asia and Latin America[45] by strengthening Chinese economic interests there. Diplomacy in the form of trips by government representatives and trade delegations is intensifying in these regions.

There exists an ingenuous – or perhaps overly self-interested – view that China is pursuing 'bad imperialism' in Asia and Latin America, under cover of a foreign policy that claims to be amoral, because it prioritises

---

Around 50 per cent of Chinese foreign investments in Mexico are concentrated in companies in the garment sector, with an eye to boosting access to the United States market

---

non-interference in the affairs of these countries. This view, contrived by the developed countries (and which supposes there is such a thing as 'good imperialism'), in addition to building on a dualist interpretation of the facts – Navarro[46] is one representative of this view – does not discuss the opportunities that China's ascension offers these countries, especially in a context where the global structure of political and economic power is shifting.

In Latin America, China seeks supplies of raw materials and food, so as to become less dependent on the United States, and support for its geopolitical concerns connected with building a multipolar order. Investments come as a counterpart to these broader goals. No less important, is the relationship with Taiwan: 13 of the 25 countries that maintain diplomatic relations with Taiwan are in Latin America.[47] Although these interests are quite clearly delimited, and generally not on a par with most Latin American countries' craving to attract foreign investment, especially in infrastructure sectors, there is a strategic geopolitical possibility in the offing: of setting up a Latin America–China–USA triangle, which would be profitable for all three parties.

Tokatlian[48] regards this as possible, because relations between the United States and China are more strategic than either of their relations with Latin

---

China has been an important host for multinationals' greenfield investment projects, while Latin America has lost terrain

---

America, while the United States enjoys considerably more influence in the region than China, which precludes their jockeying for position. China's growing importance could even leverage some of these economies, thus exempting the United States from positioning itself any more decisively in the region, as has been happening since 9/11. Obviously there is room for friction on energy issues and in relation to Cuba and Venezuela, but not to the point of overshadowing disputes between China and the United States in other regions.

In summary, for the moment what can be seen in relations between China and Latin America are diffuse traces of a relationship that is unequal, by virtue of China's needs and the potential of its economy, but which is also, because of Latin American countries' limited export structure, generally lacking in investment. This is neither good nor bad imperialism, but an unequal economic relationship, which may lead to a narrowing of Latin American countries' margin for manoeuvre, unless they are able to formulate development policies of their own and establish localised agreements with China, both bilaterally and in the multilateral field, where some interests may prove to coincide. For the moment, neither is this a strategic partnership, given that Latin American nations negotiate largely within parameters set

by the Chinese, and bilaterally, without linking cooperation measures with regional agreements.

From the point of view of Latin America's social movements, there are three issues that deserve discussing. First, some myths about the Chinese model that are very widespread in Latin America have to be dispelled. The notion that China's competitiveness is due ultimately to low-cost labour stems from a slanted analysis. China is competitive as a result of

---

China sees itself as a vast, rich civilisation which, after a century of humiliation and defeats, is striving to build a multipolar order, to move beyond the unilateral hegemony that predominated in the world with the end of the Cold War

---

a series of factors: scale of production, domestic market potential, rising rate of investment, tax incentives and undervalued currency which attract multinationals and encourage exports, state planning and cheap credit. Low labour costs obviously enhance companies' profitability, but there is no correlation between FDI and labour costs, especially in the technology-intensive sectors where China has pushed out into the international market in recent times.

The other myth depicts a developmentist and interventionist state with the ability to resolve all the contradictions brought about by economic expansion and structural change. During the 1990s, social and regional inequalities widened abruptly in China, where social protection and security systems got weaker. China also proved unable to meet environmental and energy challenges, many of which stem from rapid and somewhat disorderly urbanisation.

The second issue relates to the effect of the invasion by Chinese products, especially on Latin American countries' domestic markets. One view identifies this process with poor-quality or pirated products. Although this does occur and is not negligible, China's recent expansion has been concentrated more and more in technology-intensive goods, squeezing out domestic production partly for lack of trade protection policies, but more importantly because these countries have been ineffectual in developing industrial and technological innovation policies. Once again, there is a need to reinforce regional integration mechanisms so as to build up industrial complementation. Otherwise, the region's tenuous production chains may be disrupted once and for all.

In summary, the Chinese threat is not due to cheap labour, but to Latin American countries' inability to develop national and regional development policies. Obviously, if the present situation continues, the impacts will be felt in terms of level and quality of employment, the weakest link in the total costs incurred by firms operating locally. The textile/garment and electronics sectors are the most likely to be affected. That is why social movements must influence the economic, trade and industrial policies introduced by their own countries.

Finally, Chinese foreign direct investment, seeking high levels of return and very often not enjoying the same macroeconomic conditions as in China, tends to turn a blind eye to social, labour and environmental standards. In that connection, field studies and constant monitoring of Chinese firms operating in the region should be among the concerns of Latin American social movements.

China's ascension cannot serve – as the vague concept of globalisation once did – as a pretext for fatalistically giving up on national development and regional integration policies or on reinforcing the state's role with social oversight. On the contrary, it makes these policies more urgent than ever.

This article was originally written in Portuguese under the title 'China e America Latina: Parceria Estrategica ou Novo Imperialismo?'. It was translated by Peter Lenny MCIL.

Notes

1 Mario Cimoli and Jorge Katz (2002) *Structural Reforms, Technological Gaps and Economic Development: a Latin American Perspective.* Santiago: ECLAC, Productive Development Series.
2 Nicholas Lardy (2006) 'China's Domestic Economy: Continued Growth or Collapse?' in Fred Bergsten, Bates Gill, Nicholas Lardy and Derek Mitchell, *China: the Balance Sheet.* New York: Public Affairs Books.
3 UNCTAD (2003) 'Capital Accumulation, Growth and Structural Change', *Trade and Development Report 2003.* Geneva: UNCTAD.
4 Chang Ha-Joon (2004) *Chutando a Escada: A Estratégia do Desenvolvimento em Perspectiva Histórica.* São Paulo: Editora UNESP.
5 Sanjaya Lall (2001) *New Technologies, Competitiveness and Poverty Reduction.* Manila: Asia and Pacific Forum on Poverty.
6 Ricardo Bielschowsky and Giovanni Stumpo (1995) 'Empresas Transnacionales y Cambios Estructurales en la Industria de Argentina, Brasil, Chile y México', *CEPAL Review* no. 55,

Santiago: ECLAC.

7 Rhys Jenkins and Enrique Dussel Peters (2007) 'The Impact of China on Latin America and the Caribbean', *Institute of Development Studies Working Paper*, 281, Brighton: IDS.

8 Yin Xingmin (2006) 'New Ways to the Trade Development Between China and Latin America', paper at the international forum on Opportunities in the Economic and Trade Partnership between China and Mexico in a Latin American Context, Mexico City, March.

9 ECLAC (2006) *Panorama de la Inserción Internacional de América Latina y el Caribe 2005-2006.* Santiago: ECLAC.

10 Chris Alden and Ana Alves (2007) 'China Tango: The Sino-Latin American Trade Dance', in *Global Geopolitics.* Shanghai: CLSA.

11 Yin Xingmin (2006).

12 Jenkins and Dussel Peters (2007).

13 Eduardo Paladín (2007) 'Impacto de las Relaciones Comerciales Sino-Argentinas', mimeo.

14 Maria Helena Tachinardi (2007) 'Surge uma Nova Cultura Exportadora', in *Conjuntura Econômica.* Rio de Janeiro: FGV.

15 *Isto É Dinheiro* (2007) 'Interview with President Lula', 18 October.

16 Lia Valls Pereira (2006) 'Relações Comerciais Brasil-China: um Parceiro Especial?', in *China por Toda Parte*, vol. 1. São Paulo: Cadernos Adenauer VII.

17 Jenkins and Dussel Peters (2007).

18 FIESP (2007) *Análise do Perfil do Comércio Brasil-China em 2006.* São Paulo: Derex/FIESP.

19 Alexandre Barbosa and Ricardo Camargo Mendes (2006) 'Economic Relation Between Brazil and China: a Difficult Partnership', *FES Briefing Papers*, Berlin: FES, January.

20 Renato Amorim (2005) 'Análise Sumária do Comércio entre Brasil e China', mimeo; Valls Pereira (2006).

21 Barbosa and Mendes (2006).

22 ECLAC (2006).

23 Paladín (2007).

24 Lia Valls Pereira and Diego Silveira Maciel (2006) 'A Concorrência Chinesa e as Perdas Brasileiras', in *Revista Conjuntura Econômica.* Rio de Janeiro: FGV.

25 Carla Verónica Oliva (2005) 'Inversiones en América Latina: La Inserción Regional de China', in Sergio Cesarín and Carlos Moneta, *China y América Latina: Nuevos Enfoques sobre Cooperación y Desarrollo.* Buenos Aires: IDB/INTAL.

26 Instituto Observatório Social (2007) *Produção e Emprego no Complexo Sucro-Alcooleiro.* São Paulo: IOS/OXFAM.

27 Tachinardi (2007).

28 Valor Econômico (2007) 'Lula Pede Empenho de Empresários para Bater China na África', 19 October.

29 José Luis León-Manríquez (2006) 'China-América Latina: Una Relación Económica Diferenciada', *Nueva Sociedad*, no. 203. Buenos Aires: FES, May–June.

30 ECLAC (2006).

31 Oliva (2005).

32 León-Manríquez (2006).

33 Maurício Mesquita Moreira (2006) 'Fear of China: Is There a Future for Manufacturing in Latin America?', *INTAL-ITD, Occasional Paper* 36. Buenos Aires: IDB-INTAL, April.

34 Alden and Alves (2007).

35 Gabriela Correa López and Juan González García (2006) 'La Inversión Extranjera Directa: China como Competidor y Socio Estratégico', *Nueva Sociedad*, no. 203. Buenos Aires: FES, May–June.

36 UNCTAD (2007) *Transnational Corporations, Extractive Industries and Development.* Geneva: UNCTAD.

37 León-Manríquez (2006).

38 V. Lênin (1979) *Imperialismo Fase Superior do Capitalismo*. São Paulo: Global Editora.

39 Ricardo Bielschowsky (1998) 'Cinquenta Años del Pensamiento de la CEPAL: Una Reseña', *Cinquenta Años del Pensamiento de la CEPAL: Textos Seleccionados*, vol. 1. Santiago: CEPAL.

40 Fred Bergsten et al (2006) 'Summary and Overview: Meeting the China Challenge', in Fred Bergsten, Bates Gill, Nicholas Lardy and Derek Mitchell *China: the Balance Sheet*. New York: Public Affairs.

41 Martín Pérez Le-Fort(2006) 'China y América Latina: Estrategias bajo una Hegemonia Transitoria', in *Nueva Sociedad*, 203. Buenos Aires: FES, May–June.

42 Romer Cornejo (2005) 'China, Un Nuevo Actor en el Escenario Latinoamericano', *Nueva Sociedad*, no. 200. Buenos Aires: FES, November–December.

43 Eberhard Sandschneider (2006) 'Como Tratar um Dragão: Sobre o Trato do Ocidente com o Complicado Parceiro Chinês', in *China por Toda Parte*, São Paulo: Cadernos Adenauer VII, vol. 1 April.

44 Sergio Cesarín (2006) 'La Relación Sino-Latinoamericana, entre la Práctica Política y la Investigación Académica', *Nueva Sociedad*, no. 203. Buenos Aires: FES, May–June.

45 Fred Bergsten et al (2006).

46 Peter Navarro (2006) *The Coming China Wars*. New Jersey: FT Press.

47 Cornejo (2005).

48 Juan Gabriel Tokatlian (2007) 'América Latina, China e Estados Unidos: um Triângulo Promissor', *Política Externa*, vol. 16, no. 1. São Paulo, June–August.

THE POSITION OF CIVIL SOCIETY ORGANISATIONS IN CHINA TODAY

FU TAO

Fu Tao argues that the circumstances of civil society in China today are very different from what they were ten years ago. The similar interests of African and Chinese civil society in ensuring the equitable distribution of the benefits and opportunities arising from economic development are a strong foundation for future cooperation.

Building a harmonious world

The speeches at this conference have been excellent, no matter whether they were given by scholars or representatives of NGOs. They helped to enrich our understanding of civil society's thinking on Sino-African relations, promoted understanding between civil society in China and Africa, and began building a base for constructive cooperation in the future.

An important point raised by one delegate was the concept of a 'people-centred approach'. The same delegate also raised questions about the equitable distribution of the benefits of economic growth in China and Africa, the environment and sustainable development. The interest shown by African NGOs and scholars in China's presence in Africa and in China's overseas investment reflects the high expectations African countries have of China because of its status as a fellow country of the South. Sino-African relations are not just about political, economic and trade relations, nor are they simply a question of creating a win–win economic situation for all. They are simultaneously a process of social development, of improving systems. They also touch on the promotion of public participation in policy making in Africa and the equitable distribution of the benefits and opportunities arising from economic development.

This viewpoint is not limited to African civil society; it is also relevant to China. Professor Wen Tiejun brought up the question of China's rich–poor divide and how China should take its environmental and social responsibilities more to heart during the process of economic development. All Chinese economic activity, whether it is domestic or foreign investment, should pay attention to environmental and social equity. Extrapolating from this point, Chinese and African civil society have the same demands.

There is a phrase that is very popular in China right now: building a harmonious society. Without environmental and social equity, there can be no harmonious society. In putting forward this concept and in making large adjustments to social policies, I believe that Chinese leaders show that they understand the importance of this problem. China has also rolled this concept out into the field of international relations, with the aim of building a 'harmonious world'. Of course, action and practice are more important than concepts – and this concept is unattainable without civil society acting to mobilise forces outside the political system.

The growth of Chinese civil society

Returning to the main topic of my presentation – the current state of civil society in China. Ten years ago, people spoke doubtfully about civil society in China. 'Does China have NGOs?' was the question, or 'Does China have real bottom–up NGOs?'. At the time, these questions were apt. However, it is only necessary to compare the situation in which Friends of Nature, an environmental NGO, was set up in 1994 with today's Sino-African meeting, organised by civil society groups, to see that Chinese civil society today has acquired a certain amount of space for action.

When Friends of Nature was founded, the founder and supporters of the organisation came to Beijing, to the suburbs, and held their meeting in a park. Because at the time unofficial public assemblies were extremely sensitive, Liang Congjie, the founder of Friends of Nature, used his birthday as a pretext for holding the meeting. Our meeting today, organised by civil society groups, would have been unimaginable at that time. Representatives at today's meeting are from different countries and different backgrounds, both NGOs and academic organisations. This clearly shows that China's society now benefits from greater space and openness than previously.

Of course, the development of civil society in China has not all been plain sailing; it has had its share of ups and downs. In fact, it is easy to see the continued presence of many obstacles, of limitations, originating in legal policy or public consciousness, or the lack of capacity within the NGOs themselves. However, I believe that China is making progress, though there is, of course, a long way left to go and we look forward to the time when progress will be a little faster.

Before China started the reform process in the 1980s, there was definitely not this kind of space for civil society. At the time, it was very uncommon to see citizens carrying out independent action as individuals, or forming associations and expressing opinions on public matters and taking action independently of government. On the subject of the spirit of volunteering, at that time we studied Lei Feng and similar social campaigns – what could be described as politicised volunteering. However, because these were government organised and top–down, individuals were passive. Such campaigns cannot be considered real citizen action.

The market reforms which sprang up in the 1980s created a resource base for individuals and organisations to survive and exist independently of government. With a reduction in the role of government, civil society was able to gain a degree of control over social resources and their distribution. It was able to organise to carry out volunteering activities for the public good. Another important factor has been the growth of citizen awareness,

In the 1980s it was very uncommon to see citizens carrying out independent action as individuals, or forming associations and expressing opinions on public matters and taking action independently of government

shown by the appearance of a growing number of bottom–up, grassroots organisations from the middle and late 1990s. Similarly, many university students join clubs and societies during their studies, and then move into this field after graduation.

In comparison with the past, individuals have much more choice and freedom, and citizen association and rights consciousness are growing. Social transition has also produced a pluralisation of interests within society. NGOs are more and more active, providing social services, while some are taking on the role of representing the public and environmental interests. NGOs are

*The market reforms which sprang up in
the 1980s created a resource base for individuals
and organisations to survive and exist
independently of government*

most active in the fields of environmental protection, poverty alleviation, HIV/Aids, charitable and educational assistance and legal aid. Among those present today, Professor Wen Tiejun, as well as some international and domestic NGOs, all make use of volunteers. We should strive for more choice and for more space for the development of civil society. A growing number of academics are studying NGOs, while traditional and new online media are showing a greater interest in NGO affairs, and the frequency and depth of their reports is increasing.

Policy restrictions

However, the development of Chinese civil society is still encumbered by a number of policy restrictions. For the most part, the legal environment and government policy are restrictive of NGO activity. Registration is a large problem, with some scholars estimating that 10 per cent of NGOs are registered, while 90 per cent remain unregistered. Tax breaks for charitable giving also remains uncommon, and is judged on a case-by-case basis. Government-organised NGOs (GONGOs), and not grassroots NGOs, are the beneficiaries of preferential government policies in fundraising and organising activities. While NGOs are officially encouraged to develop social service provision, in actual practice the government remains extremely wary of NGO advocacy efforts, and the overall policy environment remains restrictive.

The Chinese government has realised the ability of NGOs to mobilise social resources, and encourages NGOs to engage in charitable activities, at the same time directly intervening and encouraging the inclusion of public interest activities in the government agenda. For example, the Ministry of Civil Affairs has tried all number of methods, including fine-sounding publicity activities, to propagate the idea of charity, to encourage public giving, aid to vulnerable groups and the provision of social services, as well as trying to lead or encourage charitable and volunteering activities. Another example is that of government inviting public bidding for the provision of social services. Faced with the low effectiveness of its poverty alleviation activities, government has started studying and using the creativity of NGOs, by providing funding for NGOs to carry out participatory poverty alleviation activities in rural areas. Similarly, in the case of provision of social services, such as those to the elderly, government may provide subsidies to the organisations providing these services.

Despite an avowed commitment to 'small government, big society', government remains strong and influential. Dictated by the need to survive and develop, the majority of NGOs seek to cooperate with government and to engage in public education and social service activities. A study carried out by China Development Brief, found that the majority of NGOs do not engage in challenging or oppositional advocacy. The survey also found, however, that more and more organisations are linking up policy advocacy and social service provision.

The plurality of NGOs

At the same time, NGOs have also become 'pluralised'. Within the NGO field, a debate has arisen as to whether NGOs act as a 'supplement' to government. That is to say, are NGOs a supplement to government, or a partner to government? When cooperating with government, how can NGOs preserve independent values? Is the value of NGOs in making up for the shortcomings of government, or in preserving independence and in influencing government, including exerting pressure on government when necessary?

The small number of challenging organisations that exist do their utmost to increase their legality when working to exert pressure on government. They use existing policies and laws and try to get support from government departments or sympathetic officials. The role played by the media and academics is also important as their involvement has given NGOs a greater voice and an increased capacity to raise their demands. At some levels of government, there is a relatively effective interaction between government agencies and NGOs, for example in public participation in the formulation of environmental policy. NGOs also try to make use of the National People's Congress (NPC) and the Chinese People's Political Consultative Conference (CPPCC), and similar channels within the system to make their views heard.

However, the number of representatives in the NPC and the CPPCC able to act as spokespersons for NGOs and vulnerable groups is limited. A small number of NGO activists have tried to use democratic methods and self-nomination through the electoral process to gain positions on the NPC, but these people have faced restrictions and their influence has been small.

Overall, China still lacks formal channels for the participation of NGOs and the public in the policy-making process. Government trust in NGOs is still limited, and there is a need for a more open attitude, for a recognition of different voices and for systemic guarantees to be put in place to effect these changes.

Some NGOs engage in advocacy by making issues public, by building public pressure through public debate and opinion and in this way influence policy. Some public debates involving NGOs, academics and the media are very lively. While there remains a degree of media control, the liberalisation of public space brought about by the internet is having an effect on public

Faced with the low effectiveness of its poverty alleviation activities, government has started studying and using the creativity of NGOs

opinion. It is also having an effect on traditional media, which are still the subject of relatively strict official control. Although China still does not have free media, the forces of marketisation are starting to force the media into some degree of independence. There is sometimes space for flexibility in reporting, despite the government's periodic tightening of strict controls on the media.

NGOs also try to build networks. The majority of this is concerned with circulating the results of research and meetings, though some NGOs try to carry out joined-up action around specific issues. Of course, for the most part, networking is seen as being quite sensitive, though obviously how sensitive depends on the issue the NGO is working on.

Normally, GONGOs have the trust of government; they are clearly influenced by government, and oriented towards government interests. However, in some fields, GONGOs have transformed. They have become more directed towards the interests of society and realise the importance of

> *At some levels of government, there is a relatively effective interaction between government agencies and NGOs, for example in public participation in the formulation of environmental policy*

meeting the requirements of society and the non-governmental sector. Such organisations can become supportive of grassroots NGOs and can act as a bridge, facilitating communication between grassroots organisations and government. Of course, there are also GONGOs which vacillate between a government line and greater engagement with civil society, and there are those organisations that have returned to their original government-oriented role.

Weaknesses in capacity

A number of NGOs have appeared that are dedicated to capacity building activities, while in some cases, more mature and robust organisations may start to provide support to other grassroots NGOs. Even though growth in China's domestic NGOs has been very fast in recent years, a number of weak points and problems remain:

- Organisations need to increase their degree of professionalism and to be more sensitive to social questions.
- A lot of organisations have only weak links with their constituencies and are not very participatory, so they cannot effectively represent these groups to the public or to government.
- The domestic NGOs are not able to mobilise enough resources, and this has an impact on their sustainability (this, of course, is related to the limiting policy environment).
- Many NGOs suffer from ineffective management systems, a lack of evaluation and oversight mechanisms, poor organisational management, and insufficient financial transparency; they are in urgent need of building public confidence.
- There are not as yet any Chinese NGOs whose field of vision has an international dimension, who are capable of thinking about the role that

they play at the international level, and who can start to pay attention to transnational questions, such as the role of environmental and social responsibility in overseas aid. Domestic NGOs have not yet matured into international organisations able to operate in a transational context, able to rely on their own value judgements and effectively define their fields of operation. As a result they cannot yet carry out advocacy independently of government concerns. Citizens' participation in, and evaluation of, foreign affairs and foreign aid is basically non-existent in China. There exist certain government-organised 'civil activities', such as the international relief activities of the Red Cross, but these are wholly top–down activities.

China is a complicated country, which the progress of social transition is making increasingly pluralised. In terms of relations between NGOs and government, there are differences between the space available for NGO activity at different levels of government, between different areas and in dealing with different government bodies. Overall, Chinese NGOs are weak, as is their ability to influence policy. We should not set our expectations of China's civil society too high, or be blindly optimistic, but neither should we be overly pessimistic. Social space in China has already opened up significantly, and civil society has become an imprescriptable part of China's transitional society. Returning to the theme of today's meeting, and Sino-African exchange, this should not just be an exchange at the level of governments or businesses. Chinese and African civil society also need to strengthen links, to come together to face problems of development in order to make Chinese and African economic development fairer and more environmentally sustainable.

NO HARMONIOUS GLOBAL SOCIETY
WITHOUT CIVIL SOCIETY

PETER BOSSHARD

China's growing cooperation with Africa, Asia and Latin America has boosted infrastructure investment and economic growth in many developing countries. However, as within China itself, the concerns of economic growth, social equity and environmental protection all need to be integrated within this cooperation. Peter Bosshard argues that civil society groups can play a critical role in promoting a balanced development approach.

As part of its 'going out' strategy, China is rapidly expanding its economic cooperation with Africa, Asia and Latin America. China offers technical expertise, investment goods and affordable consumer products, and imports large quantities of oil, mineral and agricultural products from its developing country trading partners. In 2006, other developing countries accounted for more than 60 per cent of China's foreign trade.

China Exim Bank, the export-financing agency of the Chinese government, underpins China's expanding trade and investment relations with Africa, Asia and Latin America. The agency approved loans to the tune of RMB 208 billion ($27.2 billion) in 2006, particularly for infrastructure projects and other investment goods. It is expected to become the world's largest export credit agency by the end of the decade.

South–South cooperation has many benefits. As a developing country, China can offer products and technical advice that are well suited to the needs of other developing countries. China's growing demand for agricultural and mineral products is boosting the prices of commodities on the world market, and the growth rates in exporting countries. More investment in infrastructure sectors is urgently needed. Unlike the World Bank and the International Monetary Fund, China does not try to influence the economic policies of its partner governments. Funding from China helps borrowing governments to become more independent of the policy interference of Western-dominated financial institutions.

Economic growth is essential but not sufficient for reducing poverty. The costs and benefits of development must be equitably shared among different social sectors, and the environment – the basis of the economic livelihood of many poor people – must be protected. By espousing the concept of a 'harmonious society', the Chinese government has endorsed the need for a balanced economic, social and environmental development.

Investment in ecologically sensitive sectors

China's investments in Africa, Southeast Asia and other parts of the world is focused on sectors such as electrical power, oil and gas, mining, timber, and agriculture. While these sectors are critical for economic development, they are also particularly sensitive environmentally and socially.

China is currently involved in several hydropower projects, for example the building of the Kamchay Dam in Cambodia, the Merowe Dam in Sudan, the Tekeze Dam in Ethiopia, and the Yeywa Dam in Burma. Hydropower

Unlike the World Bank and the International Monetary Fund, China does not try to influence the economic policies of its partner governments. Funding from China helps borrowing governments to become more independent of the policy interference of Western-dominated financial institutions

provides approximately 20 per cent of the world's electricity. However, as the Millennium Ecosystem Assessment has found, dams and other river development schemes have also ensured that freshwater is the ecosystem that is most threatened by species extinction. Furthermore, the World Commission on Dams found that the communities affected by dams often do not share in the projects' benefits.

China has insufficient domestic oil resources to sustain its economic development, and invests heavily in oil exploration in Angola, Congo, Sudan, and other countries. Yet historically, the benefits of oil exploration have often been diverted into private pockets. When the benefits were not shared equitably within society, oil exploration has fuelled social unrest and even civil wars in many countries.

Forests are ecologically important repositories of biodiversity, and large forest areas have been protected as national parks or under other designations. China has become the largest importer of timber from tropical countries (while re-exporting 70 per cent of this timber to other countries in the form of processed goods). It imports large amounts of timber from countries which grapple with problems of illegal logging, such as Cambodia, Gabon, Indonesia, Papua New Guinea and Russia.

In sectors such as hydropower, timber, oil and gas, it is important to carefully integrate the interests of economic growth, environmental protection and social equity in an overall development strategy. The Merowe Dam on the Nile in Northern Sudan, which is built by Chinese companies and partly financed by China Exim Bank, is a prominent example of this. The dam will more than double power generation in a country where access to electricity is still very poor. Yet the project's environmental assessment was not approved by the competent environmental authority. Its reservoir will inundate close to 200km of the Nile Valley, Sudan's only fertile stretch of land. And the dam will displace approximately 70,000 people from the Nile Valley to arid locations in the Nubian Desert.

Harmonious society on a global scale

On a national level, the Chinese government has made strong efforts to balance the need for economic growth with the protection of nature and an equitable distribution of the fruits of development. The law on environmental impact assessment has been repeatedly strengthened in recent years. The government is promoting the use of renewable energy and energy efficiency measures. The authorities have also strenuously cracked down on corruption in resettlement programmes for projects such as the Three Gorges Dam.

The Chinese government has recognised that a harmonious society is as much needed on the international level as at home. It is currently creating and strengthening the tools that will help to make global development more harmonious. In his opening speech at the Beijing summit of the Forum on China–Africa Cooperation (FOCAC) in November 2006, President Hu Jintao said that China would strengthen cooperation with Africa to 'promote balanced and harmonious global development'. The action plan that was adopted at the summit announced that 'China will give high priority to African concerns of environmental protection and sustainable development'.[1]

The National Development and Reform Commission, the Ministry of Commerce and Chinese business associations are promoting the concept of corporate social responsibility as a tool through which the private sector

---

On a national level, the Chinese government has made strong efforts to balance the need for economic growth with the protection of nature and an equitable distribution of the fruits of development

---

can contribute to a harmonious society. Companies that treat workers, local communities and the environment with respect can often fetch higher prices for their products on the markets at a time when brand reputation plays an increasingly important role. Corporate social responsibility is a win–win approach, which can benefit all stakeholders.

In August 2006, the Ministry of Commerce issued suggestions for strengthening the safety and protection of workers in Chinese enterprises and organisations overseas. The suggestions urged Chinese foreign investors to hire local workers, respect local customs and adhere to international safety standards in order to protect China's national interests.[2] The ministry has also requested advice from the OECD on how to regulate the global activities of China's transnational corporations.

In January 2007, Cheng Siwei, vice-chairman of the standing committee of the People's Congress, called on Chinese companies to be more conscious of their social responsibility, including in their international investments. In an article in *China Economy Weekly*, Cheng Siwei said that 'irresponsible practices' had prevented Chinese companies from expanding their business overseas, and warned: 'Even in developing countries, foreign companies that turn a blind eye to their social responsibilities will be kicked out of the market.'[3]

China Exim Bank, the largest financier of Chinese projects overseas, has

also expressed a commitment to promoting a harmonious global society. In China Exim Bank's annual report for 2005, President Li Ruogu said that his institution would contribute 'to the strong support for sustainable economic and social development and the harmonious coexistence of human and nature'. 'We will spare no efforts … to contribute to establishing a harmonious society in our own country and a harmonious world at large,' Li Ruogu concluded.[4]

In line with its environmental commitment, China Exim Bank adopted an environmental policy in November 2004. Compared with the environmental policies of other export credit agencies, the China Exim policy espouses strict principles. It states categorically that 'projects that are harmful to environment or do not gain endorsement or approval from environmental administration will not be funded' (unofficial English translation).[5] If 'unacceptable negative environmental impacts result during project implementation', project sponsors need to take immediate preventive or remedial action or China Exim Bank will discontinue funding. While these principles are very welcome, the policy does not elaborate them in any detail.

The [Chinese ministry's] suggestions urged Chinese foreign investors to hire local workers, respect local customs and adhere to international safety standards in order to protect China's national interests

---

Responding to a question regarding China Exim Bank's Merowe Dam in Sudan, Yu Jiang, spokesperson of China's Foreign Ministry, stressed in May 2007 that 'China attaches great importance to the local people's livelihood, takes the possible environment effect seriously and applies strict environment evaluation and standards'. 'China has always requested its enterprises to abide by the local laws and regulations while doing business in Africa', Yu Jiang added.[6]

The role of civil society

Civil society organisations and the media have much to contribute to the promotion of a harmonious society. Many non-governmental organisations have strong technical expertise on ecological issues, and can provide an early warning system for environmental problems. Chinese NGOs have helped the State Forestry Administration to uncover and address the illegal logging practices of Asia Pulp & Paper in Yunnan and Hainan provinces. They also helped the State Environmental Protection Administration to ensure the implementation of China's environmental impact assessment law in large infrastructure projects. The regulations on government disclosure of

As Chinese companies and financiers engage in environmentally and socially vulnerable sectors, they have an interest in working with civil society groups

information, which the State Council approved in January 2007, recognise the important role of civil society and will further strengthen it.

On the international level, non-governmental organisations have played a key role in raising public awareness of problems such as the loss of biodiversity, water and air pollution, and climate change. International civil society networks combine technical expertise with grassroots contacts in every part of the world. They have helped bring about national regulations and international treaties to regulate or stop the dumping of toxic waste, the destruction of the ozone hole, and the trade in endangered species. They have also played a critical role in ending apartheid, banning landmines, and cancelling the debt burden of the poorest countries.

China's economic cooperation with Africa, Asia and Latin America will continue to expand. As Chinese companies and financiers engage in environmentally and socially vulnerable sectors, they have an interest in working with civil society groups that can help identify and resolve social and environmental problems before they create tensions, affect the health of a project, and tarnish the reputation of the actors involved.

In the case of the Merowe Dam, a civil society group have commissioned the only in-depth technical review of the project's likely environmental impacts, and are interested in discussing potential mitigation measures with the project sponsors. The affected communities are not opposed to the dam, but are proposing resettlement sites along the reservoir, which would give them a better chance of sustaining their livelihoods as farmers. The communities are eager to discuss their proposals with the companies and financiers involved in the project, including from China. Integrating such voices into project planning and implementation will allow a better balance to be struck between economic, social and environmental concerns.

Gabon in Central Africa is a major source of China's oil imports. In September 2006, the country's national park service ordered Sinopec to halt oil exploration in Laongo National Park. Conservation groups had pointed out that oil exploration threatened rare plants and animals and the environmental impact study had not been approved by Gabon's environment ministry. In the same year, a consortium of Chinese investors signed an agreement to exploit the huge iron ore deposits of Belinga in Gabon. The project will bring $3 billion in investment, but will also have potentially serious impacts on the country's protected forests. It is in the interest of the host government, the investors and the affected communities to integrate the expertise of environmental organisations early in the process, so that they can avoid repeating Sinopec's experience in Gabon.

Governments, the private sector and civil society play different roles. Experiences with forestry, hydropower and oil projects around the world show that they should all work together to achieve sustainable development and a harmonious global society.

Notes

1 The quotes from Hu Jintao's opening speech and the forum's action plan are from FOCAC's official English website. FOCAC also has a Chinese website.

2 The ministry's statement is available in Chinese at <http://hzs.mofcom.gov.cn/aarticle/bk/200608/20060803022750.html>.

3 Cheng Siwei's quotes are from www.chinaview.cn (2007) 'Companies lacking social responsibility criticised', 29 January.

4 China Exim's 2005 annual report is available at <www.eximbank.gov.cn/annual/2005.pdf>. Li Ruogu's message is on pp. 4f. in English, and pp. 3f. in Chinese.

5 China Exim Bank's environmental policy is available at <http://pacificenvironment.org/downloads/Chexim%20environmental%20policy%20Chinese%20and%20English.pdf>. The quote is from the concluding chapter (pp. 3f?).

6 Yu Jiang's statement is available at <www1.fmprc.gov.cn/eng/xwfw/s2510/t322007.htm>. The statement was delivered in English.

INDEX

 CHINA'S NEW ROLE IN AFRICA AND THE SOUTH

LaVergne, TN USA
10 December 2009
166632LV00008B/45/P